DISCARD

PALGRAVE Studies in Oral History

Series Editors: Linda Shopes and Bruce M. Stave

The Order Has Been Carried Out: History, Memory, and Meaning of a Nazi Massacre in Rome, by Alessandro Portelli (2003)

Sticking to the Union: An Oral History of the Life and Times of Julia Ruuttila, by Sandy Polishuk (2003)

To Wear the Dust of War: From Bialystok to Shanghai to the Promised Land, an Oral History, by Samuel Iwry, edited by L. J. H. Kelley (2004)

Education as My Agenda: Gertrude Williams, Race, and the Baltimore Public Schools, by Jo Ann Robinson (2005)

Remembering: Oral History Performance, edited by Della Pollock (2005)

Postmemories of Terror: A New Generation Copes with the Legacy of the "Dirty War," by Susana Kaiser (2005)

Growing Up in The People's Republic: Conversations between Two Daughters of China's Revolution, by Ye Weili and Ma Xiaodong (2005)

Life and Death in the Delta: African American Narratives of Violence, Resilience, and Social Change, by Kim Lacy Rogers (2006)

Creating Choice: A Community Responds to the Need for Abortion and Birth Control, 1961–1973, by David P. Cline (2006)

Voices from This Long Brown Land: Oral Recollections of Owens Valley Lives and Manzanar Pasts, by Jane Wehrey (2006)

Radicals, Rhetoric, and the War: The University of Nevada in the Wake of Kent State, by Brad E. Lucas (2006)

The Unquiet Nisei: An Oral History of the Life of Sue Kunitomi Embrey, by Diana Meyers Bahr (2007)

Sisters in the Brotherhoods: Working Women Organizing for Equality in New York City, by Jane LaTour (2008)

Iraq's Last Jews: Stories of Daily Life, Upheaval, and Escape from Modern Babylon, edited by Tamar Morad, Dennis Shasha, and Robert Shasha (2008)

Soldiers and Citizens: An Oral History of Operation Iraqi Freedom from the Battlefield to the Pentagon, by Carl Mirra (2008)

Overcoming Katrina: African American Voices from the Crescent City and Beyond, by D'Ann R. Penner and Keith C. Ferdinand (2009)

Bringing Desegregation Home: Memories of the Struggle toward School Integration in Rural North Carolina, by Kate Willink (2009)

Living with Jim Crow

African American Women and Memories of the Segregated South

Anne Valk and Leslie Brown

First published in 2010 by
PALGRAVE MACMILLAN®
in the United States—a division of St. Martin's Press LLC,
175 Fifth Avenue, New York, NY 10010.

Where this book is distributed in the UK, Europe and the rest of the world,
this is by Palgrave Macmillan, a division of Macmillan Publishers Limited,
registered in England, company number 785998, of Houndmills,
Basingstoke, Hampshire RG21 6XS.

Palgrave Macmillan is the global academic imprint of the above companies
and has companies and representatives throughout the world.

Palgrave® and Macmillan® are registered trademarks in the United States,
the United Kingdom, Europe and other countries.

ISBN: 978–0–230–61962–3 (hard cover)
ISBN: 978–0–230–62152–7 (paper back)

Library of Congress Cataloging-in-Publication Data

Living with Jim Crow : African American women and memories of the
segregated South / Anne Valk and Leslie Brown.
    p. cm.—(Palgrave studies in oral history)
    ISBN 978–0–230–61962–3 (hardback)—
    ISBN 978–0–230–62152–7 (pbk.)
    1. African American women—Southern States—Interviews. 2. African
Americans—Segregation—Southern States—History—20th century—
Anecdotes. 3. African Americans—Southern States—Social conditions—
20th century—Anecdotes. 4. Racism—Southern States—History—20th
century—Anecdotes. 5. Sexism—Southern States—History—20th
century—Anecdotes. 6. Southern States—Race relations—Anecdotes.
7. Southern States—Biography—Anecdotes. 8. Southern States—Social
conditions—20th century—Anecdotes. 9. Interviews—Southern States.
10. Oral history. I. Valk, Anne M., 1964– II. Brown, Leslie, 1954–

E185.61.L597 2010
305.896'073075—dc22   2009050940

A catalogue record of the book is available from the British Library.

Design by Newgen Imaging Systems (P) Ltd., Chennai, India.

First edition: July 2010

10 9 8 7 6 5 4 3 2 1

Printed in the United States of America.

Transferred to Digital Printing in 2010

Contents

List of Figures

Map

Photos Following Page 112

- Children and teachers at the West End School, Durham, North Carolina, 1906. Courtesy of the Durham Historic Photographic Archives, North Carolina Collection, Durham County Library.
- Vermelle Diamond Ely, crowned queen of the Queen City Classic, 1948, Charlotte, North Carolina. Ely is pictured with the principals of West Charlotte and Second Ward High Schools, the rival teams that played an annual football game in Charlotte. Courtesy of the Robinson-Spangler Carolina Room, Charlotte and Mecklenburg County Library.
- Midwives Association, New Iberia, Louisiana, 1920s. Members include (*left to right*) Mary Pratt, Mary Guant, Mrs. Prezeal Simon, Virginia Compton, Mrs. Laninia, Mary Traham, Mary Anthony (unidentified), and Patsy Moss. Courtesy of the Iberia Parish Library and the *Behind the Veil* Collection, Duke University Special Collections Library.
- Penn School students selling vegetables at the Farmer's Fair, 1939, St. Helena Island, South Carolina. Courtesy of Lula Holmes, Ernestine Atkins, and Louise Nesbit, and the *Behind the Veil* Collection, Duke University Special Collections Library.
- Margaret Rogers interviewed by Kara Miles, Wilmington, North Carolina, 1993. Courtesy of the *Behind the Veil* Collection, Duke University Special Collections Library.
- Susan Kelker Russell playing checkers with Florida A&M College president, John Robert Edward Lee, Tallahassee, Florida, circa 1930. Courtesy of Sue K. Russell and the *Behind the Veil* Collection, Duke University Special Collections Library.

Series Editors' Foreword

African American history and women's history have flourished in recent decades; indeed they are a defining feature of the current generation of scholarship. And oral history has been essential to both enterprises. Of course, both African Americans and women—and African American women—appear in the written record if we look carefully, a record that is occasionally quite extensive for the more literate, leisured, or prominent among them. But more often when they appear, it is on the whole as a result of their participation in public life or as a result of less than felicitous encounters with the state. Frequently, lived experience is subsumed within a larger context.

Oral history, however, restores to the record the individual voice, especially the *agency* of the less privileged, those who have been disinclined or unable to chronicle their own lives, and who have lived largely outside of public view. Oral history affords insight into not only the texture of everyday life but also moments of change and transformation—as well as the meanings people give to their lives. Such is the case with Anne Valk's and Leslie Brown's masterful *Living with Jim Crow: African American Women and Memories of the Segregated South*, a collection of carefully edited interviews with forty-seven African American women who were born into the Jim Crow South and lived through the enormous changes in race relations characterizing the last half of the twentieth century. These interviews are part of Duke University's *Behind the Veil* Project, which interviewed hundreds of southern blacks about their lives during the period of segregation. Valk and Brown served as research coordinators for *Behind the Veil*, and theirs is the first book developing out of the project to focus exclusively on women's experiences.

The women narrators included here speak of their upbringing, their families and homes, their lifetime of labor, their churches, organizations, and neighborhoods. They speak of the humiliations and injustices of Jim Crow, but also of their determination to build meaningful lives, their embrace of all that life offers, and their acts of resistance—both small and large. As women, they speak of the gendered dimension of their lives, even as they also reflect differences in age, class, and region.

The narrators included here are all survivors—literally, in that they have lived to a relatively old age despite well-known racial disparities in health, health care, and life span. But they also have survived with their spirit intact—they know they have an important story to tell and came forward to tell it, to a stranger, for the record. Not surprisingly then, these interviews—though often shot through with stories of hardship—convey a tempered optimism; recorded during the later years of the narrators' lives, they reflect the coherence of a life well lived and the satisfaction of having participated in sweeping social changes.

Were it not for oral history, the stories included here simply would have died with the narrators, and our collective store of knowledge about the lives of southern black women "behind the veil" would be much diminished. We are enormously pleased to include *Living with Jim Crow* in Palgrave Macmillan's *Studies in Oral History* series. It joins three previously published works on the subject of southern African American life: Kate Willink's *Bringing Desegregation Home: Memories of the Struggle toward School Integration in Rural North Carolina* (2009); D'Ann R. Penner's and Keith C. Ferdinand's *Overcoming Katrina: African American Voices from the Crescent City and Beyond* (2009); and Kim Lacy Rogers's award-winning *Life and Death in the Delta: African American Narratives of Violence, Resilience, and Social Change* (2006). Volumes in the series are deeply grounded in interviews and present those interviews in ways that aid readers to appreciate more fully their historical significance and cultural meaning. The series aims to bring oral history out of the archives and into the hands of students, educators, scholars, and the reading public. The series also includes work that approaches oral history more theoretically, as a point of departure for an exploration of broad questions of cultural production and representation.

Linda Shopes
Carlisle, Pennsylvania

Bruce M. Stave
University of Connecticut

Acknowledgments

The initial idea for this book dates back to the 1990s when we were completing our work for *Behind the Veil: Documenting African American Life in the Jim Crow South*. As graduate students at Duke University, we spent several years (1990–1995) working at the Center for Documentary Studies, coordinating the research phase of this large oral history project. That work was intellectually formative and personally meaningful in many ways. It took us into the South for extended periods, a region where both of our families had roots, albeit on different sides of the color line. As we traveled the South together, one of us African American and one of us white, we confronted the legacies of Jim Crow and contemplated the extent of cultural and political change in the region. We marveled at the physical beauty of many places, especially the South Carolina Sea Islands and the farmland of the Mississippi Delta, but we flinched at the economic and racial disparities evident throughout our journeys.

We also reflected on the necessity of this project to collect first-person information about black life during segregation. We discovered that in local communities across the region, the foundation for this preservation effort had begun with groups that collected and celebrated African American communities and institutions from the Jim Crow era, especially alumni associations of black schools and church congregations. On our travels, we sampled the relatively new museums and cultural organizations that sought to tell the stories—indeed, to build a heritage industry around—the tragedies and triumphs of the southern past. Going to museums and historic sites in Charlotte, Jackson, Memphis, and Birmingham, we saw an emerging interpretation of African American history and southern history with the civil rights movement at the center, albeit an interpretation perhaps fueled as much by contemporary economic interests than any collective search for historical truth or reconciliation. In Greenwood, Mississippi, Helena, Arkansas, and other places, however, African American history, indeed the black presence at all, remained mostly outside the bounds of historical coverage. Observing these historical forces at work and conversing with people responsible for new interpretations of southern history, we found important motivations for the project of recovering untold stories.

Since our years at Duke, we have both completed dissertations and books and moved into the world of academe. But the power of the stories we heard through the *Behind the Veil* Project, and the lasting memories of the people we met through the project, remained strong and compelling. Whenever we had the chance, we returned to these interviews and relished the opportunity to work more closely with them. The draw of these narratives has not diminished over the years. As we finish this manuscript in 2009, the first year of Barack Obama's presidency, we are reminded of the importance of understanding social and political change—and the usually complicated effects of that change—from African Americans' perspectives. These interviews are all the more important as the Obama agenda for health care and other domestic policies takes shape.

We first presented the idea for this collection at a workshop at the 2006 annual meeting of the Oral History Association. Ably led by Deborah Gershenowitz (then of Palgrave, now at NYU Press) and Linda Shopes, the session provided useful feedback that helped shape this book. We're grateful for the enthusiasm that Shopes, Gershenowitz, and other participants in the workshop demonstrated by their encouragement for this book. That support typifies the community of oral historians in the United States, a group to which we feel privileged to belong.

Two mentors and professors from Duke University deserve particular recognition. Ray Gavins and Nancy Hewitt (now at Rutgers University) provided valuable tutelage and friendship that has sustained us over the past years. As teachers, mentors, and scholars they have profoundly inspired us. We would also like to thank our students at Williams College, Washington University in St. Louis, Brown University, and Southern Illinois University Edwardsville who asked questions and voiced perspectives that reminded us why publications like this are necessary. Sometimes these provocations motivated us to get this book into print.

Other friends and colleagues have provided equally important advice and counsel. Thanks are due in particular to Kathy T. Corbett, extraordinary editor and generous friend, who read the manuscript and recommended important changes. Aliza Schiff similarly offered insightful comments and reactions that helped us think about the interviews and our interpretation. Leslie's colleagues in the history department at Williams College read several early chapters as part of a department colloquium and offered thoughtful suggestions that especially helped us produce the book for a broad audience. Annie's colleagues at the John Nicholas Brown Center, especially Chelsea Shriver, provided encouragement and good advice. Max Krochman at the Center for Documentary Studies and Rod Clare of Elon College helped with last-minute research in Durham, and we thank them for their assistance. The staff at Duke's Special Collections Library, especially Linda McCurdy and Janie Morris, were characteristically helpful and responsive to our questions, immeasurably smoothing our research process. As always, we appreciate Alex Byrd's friendship and brilliance; his decision to meet us in North Carolina for a research trip added extra joy to the last stages of our writing.

As series editors, Linda Shopes and Bruce Stave were patient and wise. Their constant interest in the project helped us envision the book and push it through to completion. Chris Chappell was a model of efficiency and professionalism and Sam Hasey tolerated our many questions as the manuscript neared completion. We thank them all for putting up with us.

Finally, but certainly not least, we are grateful to the many people who made the *Behind the Veil* Project a reality. Bill Chafe, Bob Korstad, Ray Gavins, and Iris Tillman Hill envisioned and led the project with foresight, intelligence, and sensitivity. Our gratitude also goes to the interviewers and the narrators who willingly shared their memories and their time. Over the five years that we coordinated the *Behind the Veil* Project, we were fortunate to meet and befriend the talented and energetic coterie of graduate students who served the project at its grassroots by conducting interviews. They did amazing work, often under strenuous conditions, creating a collection of materials that is as rich in content as it is awesome in size. Once again, we thank these interviewers for their investment in this project. This book and the *Behind the Veil* Project would not have been possible without them. That is doubly true for the individuals who agreed to be interviewed and who shared their time and memories for the sake of creating a fuller historical narrative. We are humbled by the work these women did for decades to support their families, sustain their communities, and push for a more just world. We owe them our boundless appreciation; they have our admiration.

We Did Well With What We Had: Remembering Black Life Behind the Veil

In a 1995 interview, sixty-nine-year-old Olivia Cherry assessed African American life in Hampton, Virginia, during the Jim Crow era.[1] "Things were good, but they could have been much better," Cherry recalled. "We were second-class citizens. I mean, that's the way they classified us and that's the way they treated us. But we still had a very happy life and made the best of the situation....It's true that we were segregated and we had used [school] supplies and all of that, but we did well with what we had."[2] Conveying a profound sense of pride on the one hand and resentment on the other, Cherry's comments speak to the complexities of life on the black side of the color line. "What we had," Cherry detailed in her interview, necessarily was provided by and nurtured in black communities: the strength, skills, faith, and fight to confront the status quo of racial inequality, instilled by a network of multi-generational kith and kin and institutional bases comprised of schools, churches, and organizations. Collectively these elements reinforced black humanity in the face of persistent assault. For historically, making "the best of the situation" and having "a very happy life" compelled African Americans to define success and triumph on their own terms, to recognize the limits of "what we had," and yet to "do well," despite the harsh and forceful system of racism under which they lived.

This book presents narratives excerpted from a set of oral history interviews conducted with African Americans who, like Olivia Cherry, came of age in the Jim Crow South, a region and time distinct for harshly codified racial disparities. Born between 1900 and 1947, they were interviewed in the 1990s as a part of a project called *Behind the Veil: Documenting African American Life in the Jim Crow South*.[3] As the Federal Writers Project had done in the

1930s when it interviewed former slaves,[4] *Behind the Veil* researchers—mostly graduate students—conducted open-ended, life history interviews. Ultimately, interviews were conducted in ten states (Alabama, Florida, Georgia, Kentucky, Louisiana, Mississippi, North Carolina, South Carolina, Tennessee, and Virginia). Now housed at Duke University's Special Collections Library and in libraries and archives in communities where interviews took place, the *Behind the Veil* Collection includes more than 1,200 interviews (recorded on cassette tape) with elderly African American southerners.[5] We, the editors of this collection, served as Research Coordinators for the Project and conducted some of the interviews.

In the tradition of documentary, *Living with Jim Crow* renders memories, observations and reflections to document African American women's lives at a particular time. Although the racist system is an ever-present theme, the stories are not just about Jim Crow or race relations. This book does not compare the lives of black women to those of black men, white women, or white men, or attempt to weigh the oppressions endured or the opportunities enjoyed by each group. Instead, these interviews communicate what African American women did and thought about their lives and their roles, the expectations placed upon them, and the aspirations they had for themselves. They speak of lives as children, adults, workers, community members, and activists. In this way, these narratives tell about how African Americans learned "what a woman ought to be and to do," and about their aspirations to be and do just that—and more.[6]

As scholars have written, African American women have their own story— their own history—one that gives race and gendered meanings to oppression and discrimination as well as to freedom and citizenship.[7] What they did, they did for themselves, their families, communities, and the race. In this way, these stories articulate a strong womanist consciousness, one that does not separate race from gender, and that sees the freedom and rights of one inextricably linked to freedom and rights of the other.[8] Although they used the term feminist only occasionally, these interviewees offer a feminist understanding of their worlds. Often, they fended for themselves and their children. They demanded access to women-specific needs for health care, including reproductive rights. And they used their connections with other women as a source of strength and a foundation for collective action, joining together to register to vote, demand fair payment for their work, or to protest segregation.

The interviews collected here also describe the inner workings of black southern life that were often invisible except "behind the veil," as the scholar W. E. B. Du Bois termed the phrase.[9] Shaped by the particular circumstances of the narrators, the context of their lives, and the passage of time, individual interviews must be approached as meaningful expressions of the experiences of singular women. Hardship, tragedy, sadness, loss—as well as humor, joy, accomplishment, and aspiration—coexist, often within a single interview. The memories and commentaries shared by women reveal the personal reservoirs of strength from which they drew, even as they credit family and community for their own survival. Our narrators describe lessons learned, children reared, and elders honored; tricks played, payback scored, and ruses deployed; barriers crossed and obstacles hurdled by sheer determination. Absolutely aware of the effects of racism—undereducation and underemployment that led to poverty; disfranchisement that ensured electoral powerlessness; the quotidian meanness intended to humiliate and degrade black people—African Americans marshalled their energies and resources in their own interests. The struggle was unrelenting. But, the proscriptions of Jim Crow did not eviscerate aspirations. For, as these interviews assert, despite the harsh daily realities of Jim Crow, African Americans did not live their lives with white people at the center. Birth, death, courtship, marriage, learning, worship, and fun typically occurred without the presence or appraisal of whites.[10]

Examining black life in the Jim Crow South through the eyes of women illuminates differences among African Americans, between communities, and around ideas. Thus, these interviews reveal a variety of experiences, based on place of residence, educational opportunities, and year of birth, as well as a diversity of struggles that cut across these differences. Read in the aggregate, however, the interviews also represent a collective past. They echo dissonance as well as harmony; discord as well as unity.[11] The interviews in *Living with Jim Crow* provide an evidentiary base that supports and reiterates much of the theoretical and historical scholarship focused on African American women. For instance, our narrators tell of work done on behalf of families, institutions, and communities. All of these women worked outside the home for pay and did so as necessary contributions to family sustenance; most labored as farmers or household workers, and many as both. Even among the teachers, social workers, and entrepreneurs speaking here, training in farm work and domestic work was a part of childhood. Still, they did not define themselves by their employment. These interviews detail how African American women prioritized their families and their communities. Their discussions explore how African Americans collected those resources—tangible and intangible—necessary for survival and progress. While detailing possibilities and impossibilities, they convey hopes as well as constraints.

It is our task here as editors to mediate between our narrators and our readers. But it is also our task as historians of Afro-America, of the South, of the United States, and of women to bring analytical perspectives to our informants' words. For instance, we are aware that sexism and gender ideology shaped opportunities and expectations that narrators encountered, despite the fact that few dwelt on this topic explicitly in their interviews. Few discuss how their lives might have differed in another social or political context. Importantly, though, our narrators were aware that the construction of gender was racialized, with their sex attached to them as completely as their skin, and that the expectations and realities for African American women differed in vital ways from white women and black men. As narrators recall, even white women with relatively little wealth hired black women as household laborers, thereby establishing a racial hierarchy through women's work, and maintaining a form of white privilege. Still, the silence about sexism stands in contrast to the narrators' discussions of race and racism, a phenomenon that speaks volumes about the relative salience of these forces in their lives.

Stories about work and relationships shared by our narrators give us insight into the ironic workings of gender: in some ways, generation, education, and occupation mattered little; black women's work was black women's work, done by neither white women nor men of either race. Notwithstanding all that was demanded, a profound sexual division of labor existed in most families, even those headed by women, and within black community institutions including churches. This division of labor designated certain jobs as the provenance of girls or women and others to boys or men. Training in household and farm work prepared girls for women's responsibilities to their families—as children and as adults—including employment. Yet women could and did—and often were forced to—do any task that needed to be done, including the heavy work of plowing, a task usually assigned to men. Gender socialization was so ingrained that few narrators questioned the division between the sexes, even in retrospect.[12]

Finally, and perhaps surprisingly, more than a trace of nostalgia appears in some of our narrators' stories. Many seem to wish for another place and time, when a firm hierarchy imposed order. Really, they do not long for the Jim Crow era and its ubiquitous signs of humiliations, but they do yearn for the benefits of community, its alertness, its vigilance, its collective concern—positive and negative—with its residents. "These were all our children," Olivia Cherry observed, remarking on the ways people in the community supervised neighborhood youngsters. Many shared stories of discipline, often physical punishment that any adult could deliver when children stepped out of line. Our narrators did not necessarily approve of whippings, least of all the ones they received. Nor did they necessarily appreciate being under constant scrutiny. But as they understood the role of corporeal punishment, it reinforced the ultimate power of authority, warned of worse things that could happen to a child who lacked self-control around white people, and coerced respect for adults who received little outside the black community. More critically, discipline conveyed children's responsibility for appropriate behavior in public as a reflection on their people, meaning their families, and by extension, their communities and the race. Still, it was in the black community that children found adults who expressed directly a sense of caring and attentiveness. For in addition to the collective supervision of adults, children also received positive feedback for their accomplishments. Our narrators' embrace of strong discipline proffers their expressions of racial affinity, represents a sense of belonging, and details an imperative for the black community to nurture, support, and protect its own.

Looking back from the mid-1990s when these interviews were collected and recalling events and communities many decades in the past, the narrators whose stories we present remind us of the necessity to distinguish between history and memory and to consider the sources from which each derives. History, a compilation of *facts*, or even better, a description of the relationships among facts, records segregation in terms of laws and practices that combined to force black Americans into a subordinate status, depriving them of political rights, confining their occupational choices, and consigning them to neighborhoods and public spaces marked "Colored Only." Memory draws on history, but is informed by individual experience and perspective. This distinction between living memory and recorded history can be seen, for example, in accounts about segregation customs that were never recorded in written laws. Granted, Jim Crow could vary from location to location, and it was shifty. Each state, county, and town enacted its own statutes, and since racism and racist practices do not require law, segregation conventions varied widely within the region and could change at any time.[13]

Narrators' memories of Jim Crow reveal this variety and highlight practices for which little historical documentation exists. For example, Theresa Jan Cameron Lyons says in her interview (Chapter 1) that African Americans could not buy Coca-Cola, only Pepsi-Cola. A similar point is made in other interviews, specific references and inferences to race and access to Pepsi or Coke, and there is a well-known photograph from the 1930s of a Coke machine with a sign that read: "Whites Only." Yet, some interviewees recall drinking Coke or serving Coke in black-owned cafes.[14] In another instance, Ruthe Lee Jackson (Chapter 4), insisted that when she was a girl in Mississippi, "a colored woman couldn't drive a car.... It was against the law." This memory sounds preposterous and almost impossible to verify with written evidence. Yet living memory provides some substantiation. Another interview in the *Behind the Veil* Collection claims that black women were forbidden from driving in the 1930s and 1940s, and a third recalls a black woman being stopped in Virginia by a police officer because she was driving a nice car.[15] Considered within the peculiar constraints of African American women's lives, this collective memory points out segregation's idiosyncratic nature, and the prohibition on driving seems all the more plausible when Jim Crow can be seen as habitual racial and gender profiling.

In addition to pointing out the difference between living memory and recorded history, the preceding examples highlight the challenges of corroboration. As personal accounts, many of the stories in this book cannot be verified by other primary or secondary sources. In fact, the inability to access an internal history of African Americans—as opposed to race relations—in this era was the reason that the *Behind the Veil* Project was conceived. Public or written records rarely reflect everyday life from black perspectives, especially in the early twentieth century. Archives other than those at the historically black colleges and universities rarely collected African American manuscripts. Black newspapers are rich with material about black public life and editorial comment on the plight of black people, when available, but southern mainstream newspapers excised stories about black resistance and white violence. Others maintained a policy to not cover local black news at all.[16] Given the dearth of traditional sources of historical evidence, it was all the more important to gather and assemble interviews that captured the memories of elderly blacks. They have not forgotten this past and wanted very much for their stories to be passed on.

Most of our narrators remember their lives with pride, including—indeed because of—their accomplishments at shouldering tremendous burdens of work and responsibility. The harshness of narrators' lives comes through in these stories, but closely held secrets and deeply personal topics are not the emphases of these interviews. Depression, alcoholism, domestic abuse, and other well-known affects of poverty—exacerbated by racism—can be detected in discussions of these women's lives, but such conditions carried limited weight in the interviews. This is not to say that such questions would or would not have been appropriate in the interviews, or to ignore that such conditions existed. Still, as graduate students the *Behind the Veil* interviewers did follow a cross-generational (and sometimes cross-gender and cross-racial) etiquette—as well as a research agenda—that prioritized other topics among the interview questions.

Finally, the value of these stories as historical sources must be understood as a function of their initial form, the oral history interview. Along with accentuating experiences and issues of significance to narrators, interviews are shaped by the participation of an interviewer who asks questions and records answers. The agenda and interests of an interviewer may influence how stories were remembered and information passed on. Told orally, interviews also involve performance, the telling of stories and the recalling of memories to a listening audience whose responses inevitably shape the account. Words, gestures, tone, speed and pacing, and numerous other verbal and nonverbal forms of expression combine to convey meaning in the interview, but they are not recorded on tape or transcribed onto paper. As one oral historian puts it, "the unique and precious element which oral sources force upon the historian and which no other sources possess in equal measure is the speaker's subjectivity.... Oral sources tell us not just what people did, but what they wanted to do, what they believed they were doing, and what they now think they did."[17]

African American Women Tell about Their Lives in the Jim Crow South

The narrators in *Living with Jim Crow* came of age between two landmark court cases, *Plessy v. Ferguson* (1896), which established the legal foundation for racial segregation and *Brown v. Board of Education* (1954) that overturned the principle of "separate but equal." Their histories reach back even further. They inherited the memories of slavery and dreams of freedom from elders who populated the multigenerational homes and communities where they lived. Their interviews certainly detail Jim Crow as an American apartheid, a system of racial abuses and insults, and they tell stories of struggle against racism.

The book's oldest narrator, Dora Dennis of Arkansas, whose interview appears in Chapter 1, was born in 1900. The youngest, Shirley Sherrod of Georgia, from Chapter 5 was born in 1947. Dennis and Sherrod nonetheless shared many realities. Their interviews both recalled the unremitting struggle to make a living as farmers in the Jim Crow South, the experience of attending segregated schools, and the pervasive violence that threatened to roll back any success. Balancing the economic and racial oppression in their stories, Sherrod and Dennis similarly reflect on the importance of family and community cooperation. They acknowledge the distinctive role played by women who cared for families, managed homes, and stood up to protect the welfare of loved ones.

But separated by more than a generation and their families' different economic status, their interviews reveal the disparate paths black women's lives could follow. Born in the Mississippi Delta and raised without a father, Dennis and her family eked out a living as sharecroppers. The family moved frequently in search of a better situation, ending up in Arkansas around the time the United States entered World War I. For many African Americans war-era migrations led to improved circumstances. With this move, however, Dennis' education ended and she entered the labor force full-time, working in white families' homes. Shirley Sherrod was born in rural southwest Georgia, and when her father was murdered by local whites, her family struggled as well, although they farmed land owned by kin for generations. A generation after Dora Dennis came of age Sherrod attended college, actively participated in the civil rights movement in Albany, Georgia, and with options and choices that Dennis never could have anticipated, embarked on a lifelong career of activism devoted to black landownership.

The differences in Dennis and Sherrod's accounts remind us that the segregated South was neither static nor homogeneous, nor was the black community. Their stories reveal the limits of change in Jim Crow over time *and* shifting opportunities made possible or denied by access to education and economic resources. At the same time, the similarities in their stories accentuate the distinctive characteristics of black women's lives under Jim Crow. Black women played critically important roles in families and communities. Whether living in small towns, large cities, or rural enclaves, women were not just members, but makers of churches, clubs, and voluntary associations. Taking their cues from their fathers and mothers and respected elders, they viewed themselves as accountable to others. These themes, reiterated throughout the interviews reveal how Jim Crow produced and exacerbated the precarious circumstances with which many of our narrators lived as children and as adults. Many more stories tell of insecurity. Dora Dennis moved around a lot, sharecropping with other families. She recalls a white landlord who locked her mother out of their house, forced her to pick other families' cotton, and still refused to settle up with her. Another Arkansan, Cleaster Mitchell (Chapter 1) describes how a landowner threw her family out of their home on Christmas Day because her mother refused to work for him on short notice. In these stories and others, mothers are heroes. Interviewees tell of feeling safeguarded by mothers who protected their children.

But economic insecurity was not the only horrific expression of Jim Crow. Dorcas Carter of New Bern, North Carolina, (Chapter 4) illustrates how a major fire changed life not only for her family, but also for the most affluent of her city's black residents. Violence and terror, like the burning of black neighborhoods, random beatings, murders, bombings, and harassment appear often in these interviews. As women describe Jim Crow, it operated effectively to keep most African American southerners aware of "their place," even if they dared to challenge it. The problem of learning about Jim Crow for young people was that so many racial restrictions were unwritten, following a skewed logic of power relations based on race. Thus the presence of sexual violence is also a prevalent theme in these interviews. Cleaster Mitchell recalled, "I learned very early about abuse from white men [when working in people's houses]. It was terrible at one time, and there wasn't anybody to tell." Accusing African American women of hypersexuality, whites believed that black women were licentious, incapable of fidelity, *and* available for and willing to engage in sexual liaisons.[18] Black women had no means to accuse white men of rape, and no recourse. Thus, within the context of Jim Crow, African American mores were inevitably affected by the past. Slavery had provided white men license to sexually access virtually every African American woman or girl, a circumstance that, as some narrators recall, resulted in separate black and white branches of families with a rainbow of complexions. White males did not easily yield this alleged right when slavery ended, and these interviews tell how white men continued to seek sexual access to African American women, with or without consent, throughout the period about which our interviewees speak.

For the Jim Crow generation, then, girls and women learned a distinct set of expectations about their public and private actions, especially regarding how they should comport themselves around boys and men, other women, and their elders. Given the weightiness of the subject, there is little humor in the ways that our interviewees talk about these expectations, both imposed and embraced. Respectability was not just about manner and morals, although this discourse was always present. Rather, respectability was a way for black women to reclaim themselves, for it required taking ownership and control of one's body and repelling unwanted advances. Forged out of a sense of self-preservation, respectability intended to build a sense of self-esteem and self-determination, self-respect in a setting that granted African American women and men very little. Elders instructed that whites viewed one bad black person as representative of all, and conversely, the positive characteristics of one as an anomaly. In this way, young women learned early that the burden of the race—its image, its progress—rested on their shoulders. As Margaret Rogers (Chapter 2) details, respectability could be used as a criticism of others. Her mother, who had run away at age twelve and had a child out of wedlock, "talked about people having children and not being married, people having sex. . . . The girls were called dirty and no good and they usually would say, 'Well, you know, the apple doesn't fall far from the tree. The mama is no good therefore the daughter can't be no good.' You know, if one person in the family did something, then everybody in the whole family was blamed for it. And so my parents picked who I could talk to." Nonetheless, white-on-black rape and sexual assault were frequent, and such offences typically were ignored by police who, like many other white southerners, considered black people so sexually immoral that consent to sexual intimacy went unquestioned. At issue in these stories is control, or better yet, autonomy, and the tension between what Jim Crow demanded black women be and do and what they wanted for themselves.[19]

Women's stories about work, harassment, economic struggle, and limited education demonstrate that Jim Crow was more than the practice of racial segregation; it was an applied ideology of white supremacy that did not just keep African Americans in a fixed subordinate position in society, it tried to push them further down, if not to eliminate them altogether. Braced by violence, discrimination was built into the legal, political, cultural, economic, social, and educational scaffolding that reinforced white power and denied African Americans the means to improve their lives, hence the term American apartheid.[20] Our narrators speak of resistance and protest that occurred throughout the Jim Crow period and, for some, continued to the time they were interviewed. Inasmuch as these stories provide evidence of the early twentieth-century roots of the civil rights movement, they also prove that Emancipation continued into the late-twentieth-century. Our interviewees inherited the memories of slavery and hopes of freedom directly from freed people, their great-grandparents or their grandparents, and from their parents. Freedom promised autonomy and that promise mattered. And in this vein, as historical actors, these narrators shouldered the cause of racial destiny.[21]

Methodology

The *Behind the Veil* Project, the source of the interviews included in this book, was motivated by the realization that the memories of American apartheid were about to pass with the generations who experienced it. The urgency of the work is evidenced in the contemporary classroom. Generations born after the 1970s know some facts of segregation, but little more about Jim Crow. They are shocked by its severity, its illogic, and its elaborateness. Thus, the *Behind the Veil* Project set out to reclaim a history of individuals, families, institutions, and communities that endured decades of legal discrimination and survived to take part in the mass movements that changed the South's political, economic, and social worlds.

Perhaps more importantly, the oral histories in *Living with Jim Crow* demonstrate the valuable link between the past, present, and future. Collected in the mid-1990s, the interviews tell of the past while also sharing elderly women's observations about the broader culture. Undoubtedly, contemporary issues shaped the topics our interviewees discuss. Most significantly, memories and commentaries reflect on the demise during the Reagan-Bush years of a public social safety net, which some of these women had been part of creating; a major overhaul of welfare under the Clinton administration; the election of Nelson Mandela as South Africa's first black president; the trial of O. J. Simpson for the murder of his ex-wife; and major floods that swept through southwest Georgia in 1994. Our informants also told their stories through the lens of the mid-twentieth century's upheavals, and most describe the importance of changes in legal civil rights after the 1950s. Although differing in their broader historical implications, such events inevitably shaped the conversations between narrators and interviewers and helped shape the interviews themselves.

We chose the excerpts included in this book using several criteria. Most importantly, we decided to exclusively use interviews with women.[22] Notwithstanding the excellent and voluminous scholarship published since the 1990s by African American women's historians, studies of the Jim Crow era reveal a dearth of information about everyday life; there is still much more to understand about the gendered aspects of living with Jim Crow. To get at this information, we sought to represent the diversity of experiences of southern black women, including differences attributable to location. Our interviewees hail from rural, small town, and urban areas; from the upper and lower South; from the Delta and the Sea Islands, and other locations in between. We also wanted the collection to present interviewees' range in generation, education level, financial means, and occupation. We wanted to illuminate the lives of domestic servants and sharecroppers, the two occupations most common for African American women during this period. In addition, the collection includes educators, social workers, hairdressers, and businesswomen, most of who had retired by the time of the interview. Finally, we selected interviews that contained sufficient depth and detail to make them interesting.

The original interviews are long, often two or more hours, and varied in their coverage. Because few oral histories translate smoothly from recording to publishable text we worked carefully to prepare the materials for this book. The act of transcription—moving from the recorded interview and the oral narrative into a written account of that interview—inevitably transforms the original meaning of a narrator's stories. Translating the spoken word into written form requires a series of decisions and determinations that affect the written account. Where to add punctuation? Can punctuation capture the subtext of an interview? How can we convey nuance or emotional content, such as laughs, sighs, cries, or long pauses that embellish and give additional weight to interviewees' words? Oral historians hope that the process of transcription can illuminate the many layers of meaning contained in people's words, remaining faithful to a speaker's intent while necessarily elucidating the content.

Editing for publication imposes still more levels of interpretation and decision making upon oral historians.[23] Our process was guided by the goal of transmitting the power and meaning of the interview. Narratives were changed in several ways. First, we omitted the interviewer's questions in order to emphasize the narrator over the interviewer, although occasionally, a question appears in brackets to provide context for the speaker's recollections. Second, we edited interviews to enhance readers' comprehension. Typically, we omitted repetition and conventions that would be distracting to readers, including stops and starts, "uh's," "um's," and similar phrases. Sometimes we reordered sections or sentences. Words or phrases added by the editors appear in brackets, and only to clarify a narrator's reference. It is our intent to smooth the way for readers; in each case, however, we worked faithfully to retain and convey the narrator's message. The names of interviewers and interviewees appear in Appendix A, and a short example showing how we edited an interview is provided in Appendix B.

The aspects of the interviews that remain unchanged also deserve note. In particular, we elected to retain outdated or unpopular descriptors for African Americans. When interviewees used terms such as *colored*, *Negro*, and *nigger*, we kept the original words. Sometimes these terms are used in specific ways to convey a distinct meaning. In other places, these words express individual preference for or ease with certain vocabulary. We noted that our narrators used the so-called "*n-word*" infrequently. As elders, not all of our informants were comfortable using the terms African American or black, recalling an era when references to Africa or blackness were insults. Similarly, where narrators referred to white southerners as *crackers* we left that terminology unchanged. The mention of Jewish families is also worth noting: narrators' stories often differentiate Jews from other groups of whites, thus hinting at their distinct place in the South's social order. (Indeed, as our interviews detail, Jim Crow relegated Jews to the same neighborhoods where African Americans lived.) Our usages are in line with the current conventions of publishing, but this complexity reminds us of the fluidity of language and that customs regarding vocabulary, like those related to race and ethnicity more generally, are historically and culturally specific.

History and the Jim Crow Era

We would be remiss as scholars if we did not address the history of Jim Crow. This is a difficult task, evidenced by historians' debates about its origins. The phrase "Jim Crow" dates to the 1840s when a white performer, imitating a ragged slave, made popular a song and dance routine, "Jump Jim Crow." Used by African Americans in the nineteenth-century, the phrase references not just the practice of racial segregation, but also the insult of the act and the inferior facilities to which they were relegated. The "jim crow car," where African Americans had to sit on a train, for instance, was the one directly behind the locomotive. It attracted soot and cinders from the engine, carried all passengers' baggage, and served as the smoking car. Used in this sense, Jim Crow references the systemic application of racism applied as white supremacy and black inferiority. As a period in U. S. history, Jim Crow can be bookended by two Supreme Court decisions, *Plessy v. Ferguson* (1896), which authorized racial segregation, and *Brown v. Board of Education* (1954), which ostensibly ended it.[24] This chronology is incomplete, however. Ideologies of white supremacy and practices of racial separation were evident before the establishment of the United States, and in varying forms appeared in most places across U. S. territory. Within the South, the states of the former Confederacy, white officials instituted a convoluted structure of laws, customs, and practices that kept Jim Crow in place after Emancipation. That is, Jim Crow as a practice existed before 1896 and continues into the twenty-first century. The *Plessy* decision sanctioned practices already in place, and the work of *Brown* remains incomplete.[25]

Within a generation after the Civil War, state constitutions across the region had disenfranchised the vast majority of African American residents. Legislatures mandated "colored" and "white" facilities, and even outlawed black political organizations, including the National Association for the Advancement of Colored People (NAACP). Laws proscribed how black people could use public accommodations (transportation, water fountains, theaters, restrooms, and restaurants) as well as where they could live, and where they could attend school, what kind of school they could attend, and for how long. Biased employment and pay practices determined the kinds of occupational and professional opportunities available to black people and how—or if—they would be compensated for their labor. The power of contract remained in the hands of landlords who negotiated and settled as they pleased. Black and white teachers' pay was grossly inequitable. By law the salaries for the weakest and least educated of white teachers ranged higher than the salary of the strongest, best-educated black teachers.

African Americans could not count on the criminal justice system to recognize or protect their rights. Keeping black people out of positions of power, the legal system itself denied African Americans the right to sit on juries or defend themselves in court, and custom prevented African American lawyers from speaking in court. Local policy rejected outright the idea of black policemen or firemen, sheriffs, or deputies, while election laws prevented voting. Activism might be legal but risky. So too was economic stability. Amassing enough wealth or property as to incur the attention of whites could lead to lynching, assault, and arson, as Dorcas Carter implies (Chapter 4) in a story about how whites destroyed the black community of New Bern, North Carolina, because they feared and resented the affluence the black professional class had built.

By the early 1990s when the interviews in this book occurred, the legal structures that supported segregation had been largely outlawed, overturned by the Supreme Court and state and national legislation including the 1964 Civil Rights Act and the 1965 Voting Rights Act. In the aftermath of these changes, historians began to examine black community life in the segregated South, driven partly by an interest in locating the roots of post–World War II political activism in the Jim Crow era.[26] Studies of southern states like Mississippi and Alabama, for example, identified a deep tradition of local organizing that unfolded outside electoral politics and often tied to churches. Tracking backward for clues to the foundations of later mass movements, such scholars illuminated a long history of black resistance. The participation of women and military veterans carried throughout the twentieth century and became a resource for mobilization in the 1950s and later. Of particular relevance to this book is the deep tradition of women organizers operating within their own distinct tradition and connected to women's clubs, churches, labor associations, and other institutions. Other historical scholarship has focused on work and organizing among specific groups, including teachers and other black professional classes and those employed in industrial trades. Still others, inspired by a growing field of "whiteness studies," have looked to the segregation era to understand how racial difference was constructed through law, education, and popular culture.[27] Together, the case studies of communities and specific groups of African American southerners have filled important gaps in Americans' comprehension of this era. They have also generated important conversations among historians about the nature of politics, racial identity formation, and the necessity of understanding class and gender differences among African American populations.

Despite historians' interpretations and disagreements about the Jim Crow era—indeed, because of them—students, teachers, and researchers need more direct access to the voices and the stories of individuals who lived in the segregated South. As a presentation of the multifaceted experiences of women from across the region and across generations, *Living with Jim Crow* illuminates many topics deserving of fuller examination, not only civil rights and freedom, but also the translation of those ideals into concrete aspects of black survival. The book also opens conversations about other historical subjects: race, gender, and health care; race, gender, and ideals of beauty; women and the black church; community life in rural areas; gender and migration; and more. By bringing these stories to readers, this book intends to open new avenues of exploration, comparison, and understanding.

Living with Jim Crow's interviewees share this mission to collect the stories of African American southerners and expand narratives of America's past. As one of the narrators explained, "I often laugh about the rewriting of history, and you never know, now, what you should do when you know that history is being rewritten, the history that you have experienced yourself. Knowing the little bit that I know about history generally, I know that much has been written that wasn't accurate. I recognize that. That's the way history is done it seems. So, how can you say that pure truth is here and a mixture is there? So, maybe if enough samplings are gotten, you can weave through...to some things that might be factual."[28] It is our hope that, through providing "enough samplings" this book might help our readers find out "some things that might be factual."

Interview Sites

1	Hampton, VA	13	Tallahassee, FL
2	Norfolk and Portsmouth, VA	14	Tuskegee, AL
3	Virgina Beach, VA	15	Birmingham and Bessemer, AL
4	Wilmington, NC	16	Memphis, TN
5	New Bern and James City, NC	17	Indianola, MS
6	Tillery, NC	18	Itta Bena, MS
7	Durham, NC	19	Greenwood, MS
8	Charlotte, NC	20	Yazoo City, MS
9	Sumter, SC	21	Cotton Plant, AR
10	St. Helena, SC	22	Brinkley, AR
11	Albany, GA	23	Forrest City, AR
12	Cairo, GA	24	New Orleans, LA

Map 1 Location of Interviews. Map illustration by Amy L. Kendall, 2009.

CHAPTER 1

The Foundation Was There: Growing up a Girl in the Jim Crow South

"At twelve," Cleaster Mitchell told an interviewer, "I knew how to take care of myself. I could work for anybody at twelve, because I was taught." Speaking with pride and without self-pity, Mitchell explained that for black girls in the Jim Crow South childhood was training for self-reliance and preparation for adult womanhood. They learned to work and to care for the young, the old, the sick, and their future husbands. But black survival in the Jim Crow South required more, and so their second lessons were about mutuality and the necessarily close bonds of family and community. It had been—and still was—the responsibility of freedom's first generation—"our foreparents," Mitchell called them—to assure that freedom survived. In passing freedom dreams on to Mitchell's generation, parents and grandparents also passed on information about freedom realities and a third set of lessons about racism: to expect and endure discrimination and yet aspire and achieve a better life than they had. A balancing act made all the more difficult by the shifting rules and practices of American apartheid, growing up a girl in the Jim Crow South required a keen sense for one's surroundings.

Closely protected—often severely so—by elders who demanded obedience, girls remember childhoods spent within the tight bonds of family. Many grew up in extended networks of kith and kin, often with multiple generations sharing a home and contributing to a combined livelihood. Mothers, fathers, aunts, uncles, siblings, and neighbors played a central role in shaping children's understanding of the world. Forced to manage within a system of racial hatred, girls' self-esteem was buoyed by messages from parents and other elders that contrasted with the depictions of African Americans in popular culture. Against a barrage of negative images and the not-so-distant past in slavery, adults worked to imbue black children with self-respect, confidence, perseverance, and accountability. Adults also linked community responsibility and faith in American democracy with critiques of African American exclusion from civic and social life, demanding that the children not only press on but do more. Narrators' memories of family interactions sometimes stress harsh discipline but mostly express gratitude for the sacrifices made on their behalf.[1]

In addition to mentioning important people, the interviews vividly describe the spaces and places where narrators spent time as children. Without playgrounds in their neighborhoods and few manufactured toys at home, girls became inventive, using porches, yards, and streets or rural farms for exploration, fun, and time with other children, black and white. Schools provided some of the most important and positive encounters in our narrators' interviews, albeit they also commented on the poor condition of the educational facilities they attended. Infamously, black children in rural areas were forced to walk several miles to school, even as the local white children rode the bus and traveled shorter distances. Those from rural areas and farming families, especially sharecropping families, remember how little schooling they could attain. Black students' educational access was limited, not only by absence of nearby schools, but also by white landlords who dictated the length of the school year and determined which children could go. Generally, girls who lived in cities had greater opportunities to attend school and access to a wider array of cultural and recreational activities than their rural counterparts. Even so, few finished high school. Fewer still could move on to college or beyond. While some narrators remarked on favoritism practiced by teachers, often on the basis of skin color or parents' occupations, nearly all of these interviews also talk about the importance of teachers as a source of inspiration.

Arranged chronologically, according to the year of each narrator's birth, the interviews in this chapter demonstrate that childhood memories of women born in the first years of the twentieth century differ little from those told by women born in the 1930s. Mostly, African American girls experienced childhood as a period of work, play, and school, even if, of the three, work figured most prominently. Looking back, African American women recalled learning to farm or to do household chores, as contributions both to the family's daily survival and as wage work. They assisted (and sometimes substituted for) mothers, older sisters, and other female relatives, transferring skills acquired through chores into paid jobs in private households and on farms. Domestic burdens fell especially heavily on oldest daughters who were enlisted in caring for family elders or younger siblings, and doing food preparation, laundry, and cleaning in order to free other family members for wage work. That weight passed quickly to the next oldest, with girls moving into the job market as early as age nine.

In contrast to the relative constancy over time, certain experiences of childhood differed according to location (urban or rural) and family resources (both financial and social capital). Girls in sharecropping families recall incidents when landowners' demands superseded parents' desires, especially by yanking children from school to put them to work. In contrast, those whose families did not rely on their youngsters' earnings spent longer years in school and more time at recreation. Vermelle Ely in Charlotte and Marie Fort in Memphis, for example, recall playing games and attending movies and social events (organized by the segregated YWCA, school, or church). These activities were not uncommon entertainments. Some of the interviews illuminate the presence of a rich community life of dances, parties, and competitions. Even with the burdens of domestic and farm chores and the often short span of years that girls enjoyed as children, all of the women remember the importance of the good times they shared with their families and neighbors.

Although their memories are sometimes nostalgic for the ethos of caring, interviewees also express a keen awareness of the difficult labor performed by the adults around them and the harsh world they had to confront. Not all of the stories of childhood are positive, and not all adults were caring. As windows into the internal dynamics of black communities, these interviews also present glimpses of conflict, animosity, and danger. Finally, these narratives tell about how black girls coming up under Jim Crow learned the emotional and economic importance of black women, who in black communities modeled group support, mutual aid, and generosity.

Dora Dennis was born in Mississippi in 1900, and moved with her family to the Arkansas Delta at age sixteen. Her father deserted the family when she was a child, so Dennis' mother raised her children (six daughters and one son) by working as a share-cropper, day laborer, and laundress. The family supported each other financially and shared responsibility for raising children; still, they barely made ends meet. When her family could no longer make a living from farming, Dennis began working in white homes. Her interview describes the difficult situations that families without men faced in the rural South, especially women's economic vulnerability and their reliance on others in the community.

Well, I was born in Mississippi. I was about sixteen years old when we moved to Arkansas, to Forrest City. I really don't know the year now. But I didn't get to go to school very much after we moved to Arkansas. We were out in the country and it was a long way to the school. And then we moved from plantation to plantation. On the farm, we lived by the month, blacks did. They'd let us have our groceries [from the commissary] by the month. And just according to what kind of white people you were farming with, when winter came, if you didn't scuff around and cut wood and do little odd work, you just had a hard time. At that time it was very difficult with blacks and whites. The white was over the black, you know. Black people had to kind of scuff around and do the best they could, in a way of speaking.[2]

That's why we came to Arkansas, because they told my mama that she could do better in Arkansas. But when I was coming up a child, my mama had to work very hard to keep us going, because my father deserted us and I can hardly remember him. But I had one. He turned out to be a preacher, Reverend Strong.

There were six of us girls, and my brother just disappeared, and Mama raised six of us girls. [Black families shared with each other during hard times.] Just like if this family killed hogs this week, they would give Mama some of their meat. When Mama killed hogs, she'd give them some of her meat. Mama had good friends. That's what pulled her through. She had a lot of good friends. She had a lot of good white friends, too. She would get up Monday mornings, her and another lady that had a wagon and mules, and they would go to town, and when they'd come back, you couldn't see them hardly for the bundles of clothes. They washed and ironed for white people. There weren't laundromats and electric irons and things like that. She had her own tubs [and] pots to boil the white clothes in. You didn't boil the colored clothes. You just boiled the white sheets and things that didn't have color, just plain white, because they'd fade them. They had what they called smoothing irons that heated with wood, set them up in the fireplace and heat them. You can't imagine somebody ironing fourteen and fifteen shirts with them kind of irons. That's what my mother did.

[We also] made our living by farming. They sharecropped, Mama and my sisters. Mama started to wash and iron so we could eat, so she could feed us. Because every two weeks Mama would go to the commissary and get our weekly ration, and sometimes it would last and sometimes it didn't. But Mama always raised a garden. She had a garden, and she always had somebody that she could go to and get help from them. Just like somebody she washed and ironed for, she could go to them and get a little help, you know, when [the groceries didn't last].

Some of the boss men were pretty tough and some of them weren't. You want to know how tough Mississippi was? Mama moved on this man's place. He would wait right good until the crops got finished, the labor, and then he would more or less run you off the place. He didn't run Mama off the place, but he ran off the man that she was sharecropping with. Mama was going to move, but he wouldn't let her move, he went and nailed the house up where we were staying. He made her pick out the other man's crops. Well, she picked that out, and he still wouldn't settle with her, wouldn't settle with her, wouldn't open up the house and let her get our things out of the house. He wouldn't open it up and let Mama get her things after she picked out all of her cotton and all the other man's cotton. Somebody told her where she could get help, and she went there and told this lawyer what she had done and what she hadn't done and how this man, everybody in Inverness was scared of him. And so he sent two of his deputies to Inverness, and they went there and kept the doors open and they had wagons there to get everything Mama had at one time. So it wasn't too long before we left Mississippi.

My mama used to tell us how she had come up. It would just make tears come in my eyes. My mama's mama died when she was a little girl and left a young baby. [Mama] had two older sisters and her father was there, but at that time they was scared of what you call haunts, and they was scared to stay in the house where their mama died. [The sisters]'d go to other folks' house, and they left [my] Mama and that baby there, and Mama had to care for that little baby the best she could. It was very sad. It would hurt me to hear her talk about how she and that little baby had to eat, until somebody came along and took them [in] and finished raising that little boy and her. She really didn't even get to go to school as much as I did. But the six of us sisters, we never had trouble. We worked hard for our living and treated people right, went to church when we had something to wear.

When we moved to Arkansas, we also worked hard. Another family, a black man leaving Mississippi, rented McDonald's farm, and he brought my family along to sharecrop with him. He chartered a car box and brought all our things in it. We moved up in the hills on Mr. McDonald's place. We made crops, Mama cleared money, and we lived well—raised hogs, raised corn, made meal, and weren't far from a church. [But] we never did have friends like [we had in Mississippi]. Of course, Mama had been there all her life. Here we got acquainted with [new] people at church and from what little time I went to school. But it seems like Mama was more satisfied when she got out of Mississippi, when she got here in Arkansas.

Marie Fort was born in Memphis, Tennessee, in 1904, the youngest of fifteen children. Her parents insisted that she learn how to achieve within a Jim Crow society, emphasizing the importance of education and the necessity of outperforming her peers. Parental messages about self-respect and pride countered the racist messages of the larger society and inspired Fort to resist injustice. Unlike Dora Dennis, Fort's parents held steady employment and accumulated property, thereby relieving their daughters of much of the labor expected in poorer or rural families. Because they did not need her wages, Fort's parents could prioritize her education and try to shield her from demeaning labor. Compared to other interviews in the chapter, Fort's experiences show some of the greater opportunities for education and economic stability provided to girls in black middle-class families in southern cities.

I was born Saturday, July 30, 10:30 A.M. in 1904. And they said it was a very hot day. I know my mother thought so. I was born on this spot here. The house that I was born in burned down. I had this one built in 1980. And I'm still at home. This used to be a wonderful neighborhood. My mother was from Alabama and my father from Georgia. My mother married him when she was fifteen and he was thirty. In those days girls married fifteen and sixteen, way back then. They married in Alabama and they came here. She had all us fifteen children and I happened to be the last one.

When my mother first came here with a friend of hers, Mrs. Jackson, they had to come under a fence through Lee Woods. And getting under that fence she fell and her hand hit on six bits.[3] She picked it up and a man was up here on the corner selling this property. And she gave the man six bits on this place. And she had a market garden up and picked up potatoes and every time she made some money she put it on this place. She finally bought this place up here at 738, 739, 740, and 746 Speed Street. Then my sister bought down at 782. They bought property all along here. And I can say I grew up not wanting for anything [despite] the kind of labor they did.

I was crazy about my father. He got a job at Memphis Street Railway Company greasing street cars tracks. But first my father taught school. My father had been a professor. You know, if you were teaching in a bush arbor I think they called you a professor back then. He wasn't a highly educated man. He taught us and we were not allowed to sit down outside without a book. Thank God for that. I was distraught over that because other kids would be running up and down the street playing and having such a good time and my mother would say "you're black, get a book." And ooh, I would hate for her to call me black. I didn't want to be black for anything in the world. I thought it was a disgrace to be black because the teachers would [insult you by calling] you black, other children would laugh at you if you were black, and it gave me a bad feeling. But my mama said, "You are a black girl. You've got to do ten times more than the other black girl, twenty times more than the brown girl, seventy-five times more than the yellow girl, and a hundred times more than the white girl to make it and you'd better make it. Go in there and get a book."

But you had to tell my daddy what you read, what you got out of the story. And we had to do that all of our lives. My daddy would say read everything, good or bad. Find out what the other person is thinking or talking about. Read it. And so we would have to read it. When I'd go around a person I'd ask every kind of question. All of [my siblings] amounted to something. I had one brother who was a doctor and one a lawyer. My sister was over the beauticians in the city. And they had an undertaker shop. My people had the first filling station [around here] for black people. And it was because of their diligence in telling us to get a book, read a book, find out something, learn about it. And I'm glad we did.

I went to Klondike School first.[4] And from there I think I was eleven when I went to Grant School. From there I went to St. Anthony's School and then to LeMoyne.[5] And thank God for each school I attended. I was happy at every school but Klondike School because we had a teacher there who was almost white, Mrs. Wilson. I was in the second grade and I was sitting with a girl [who was very light skinned]. Mrs. Wilson said to me, "Get up out of that seat before you get that child black!" I'll never forget it as long as I live. But it gave me a start and made me want to be on my own. She told me I was so black wax was running out of my ears. Imagine a teacher saying that to a child!

I'm telling you, it made black children feel that they were not human for people to say those things. But my daddy took me right down here on Jackson [Avenue]. Blackberry vines used to grow all down there. He pulled a green berry and put it in my mouth and it was bitter. A short while later he carried me back. He put a white one in my mouth, and I didn't know blackberries weren't supposed to be white. But finally we went down there one day, and he got one that was almost black. It was so red it was black and it was sweet. I didn't know why he was doing this. When he got through he said, "Now, you're my blackberry and you're sweet as you can be. Remember that. This is a good berry. Everybody wants one." Well, that gave me a good start. Everything they did it seemed they were pushing me on. But the blackberries were the greatest thing, and what my mother told me about what I'd better do in life. And so we didn't do too bad. Every one of us did something.

We were not allowed to wash anybody's clothes or scrub anybody's kitchens. Mama said, "Your kitchen is better than her kitchen." We were not allowed to eat at anybody's house. We couldn't even take a drink of water from anybody. When I was four a lady named Angie lived across there where my park is. Angie would have me play for her to sing and I'd jazz the music up and, oh, Angie would sing and dance. And one night she asked my mother to let us go with her on Beale,[6] her little grandchildren and me. Well, we went down there and we were singing, and I was just dancing. And it happened my mother was visiting Mrs. Coleman who had a market space down there. She came out on the street and saw me dancing and passing that tambourine. She didn't wait for Angie. She grabbed me right in here and brought me out of there.

Jim Crow was a terrible thing. It was a man making people work to build up a country and saying, "Don't you touch what you've built." And that's what I thought about it. If you walked down the street, a long time ago when I was a kid, a white person could be grown up and would push you off the sidewalk in the mud. And when they pushed me in the mud I'd make sure they got some mud on their leg pants or something. My mother told me, "One day you're going to fight the wrong person one day but don't take anything." Now what did she mean? Well, I didn't take anything. If they pushed me, I pushed back. I didn't care who it was. We'd be coming from church—we're Catholic—we'd be coming from Little Flower Church, grown white men would be in the streets throwing rocks at us. And everybody else would be running, and I'd be throwing rocks. And I never got hit. But I just never took anything. You know, I always figured myself to be human. But I began to enjoy being black when I was about twelve. Because I began to fight back. But the thing of it is, I do not hate white people. I don't. I have as many white friends I guess as I've got black.

In this neighborhood all the children played together, white, Jews, Italians, everybody. We all played together. We learned the Jewish songs. We learned to count in Jewish, in German. And we knew what they knew and they knew what we knew. The Engleberts on the corner, on the second corner, had a big store and they lived upstairs. The Wolfes lived right down here and they had a store and they lived upstairs on Jackson Avenue. And the Goldclans lived back here on Olympic, upstairs. But all the children were very good friends. You know we had no division. And the parents, all the parents were friends with my mama. The lady across the street was Irish but she married a brown-skinned man. We ate together. A lot of times they'd come and spend the night. And I don't know, we got along great until some of the Jews got grown up. A lady that used to stay down here, Mrs. Wolfe, who asked me to come down and help the children with their lessons, told [me] to call her daughter "Miss." And I came home. And Julie [Wolfe] came on behind me crying, "Don't be mad at Mama, don't be mad at Mama. Come on show me my lesson." And she was a little short Jewish woman that I had loved as a mother, and that's what she did. But Mrs. Goldclan was so nice. She never did that. She would come many a day and ask Mama to let me come down there and help in the store. Mama would get my hair curled and I would go down there and Mrs. Goldclan would say, "That's my daughter too." And you know children had a way of saying things that would hurt. This Matthews boy told me that a piece of chalk would make a white mark on my face. That's another thing that made me want to change and I was mad at Mama. I said, "Why did you make me black and you didn't make all the others that black?"

And she said, "I buy stuff and you won't use it."[7]

I said, "I don't want to." Now you can't get me to put any kind of [lightening] cream on my face. I don't want that. I want to be black and let the world know it. Today I'd rather not put anything on my face but soap and water. And I'm glad of that. I'm glad to be me.

Ila J. Blue was born in 1914 in rural Hoke County, North Carolina, the youngest of twelve siblings raised in a family of landowners. With the encouragement of her family, especially the practical support provided by an older brother, Blue received an excellent education. Her interview details the centrality of school in her life and her experiences as a student. She also documents the difficulties that farm families experienced throughout the Depression and during an infestation of the boll weevil. Finally, Blue's life history reveals the importance of family and community in creating opportunities for individual achievement and conveys a set of underlying values that guided such support.

I was born in a little town in the county, Hoke County, county seat of Raeford, in North Carolina. I was the twelfth, number twelve, of children; seven girls and five boys. My papa was disappointed; he wanted six girls and six boys. [My family lived on] a large farm, and Raeford was just one of the small places like Red

Springs and Aberdeen and what have you. Just a hub of them, and all country. All country, country, country. Primarily cotton and grain, like corn and wheat and rye, and watermelon.

We had everything on the farm. My favorite [work on the farm as a child] was plowing. But we hoed cotton, we picked cotton, we plowed. But the family was always very close together. The sisters and brothers married off, and, of course, we survived because, as I say, we did things besides just the farm. Mama raised chickens and sold eggs to the sanitarium that was about two miles away from us, between Raeford and Aberdeen. Selling eggs and milk and butter to the sanitarium was a bonus to the family for money. Especially you had money in the fall. That's when you sold your cotton. We had so many watermelons that people passing by the road would just buy watermelon. We weren't trying to sell them; we fed them to the hogs.

[Education was] very important in our family, because there were twelve children, as I said, but one died; that left eleven. The top third went to college, and the last third went to college, but the middle got caught in the Depression. They didn't go any further than high school. The boll weevil ate the cotton crop, and so they couldn't go. We were lucky, because the other sisters and brothers who didn't go to college, and those who did go, and those who were at home and some who were married, helped us [younger ones] go to school.

School was three miles away. The schools that the blacks had early, and the state made them do it, were constructed by the Presbyterian Church and there was another group, the Rosenwald Fund. The grade school that I attended, one through seven, was a Rosenwald school. The state was not building schools [for blacks] then; the counties were supposed to do it. They didn't do it.[8] The school that I attended was nice. In the center was a large auditorium and a stage, and that stage opened onto closets, big long closets. They were four rooms, two on that end of the stage, two on that end of the stage. You had eight grades then, but the first one was primer instead of first year. You had a primer, one, two, three, four, five, six, seven, and it still gave you the eight years.

When I was five, Mama and my oldest sisters started teaching me the primer. You had to buy your own books. She went to town, bought the primer. Mama said six miles a day, three one way and three back, was too much for me to walk, so they taught me at home. So when I went to school, I [already] knew the primer, because they had taught me at home. So I told a little story. I told my mama that the teacher said you could buy the first grade book, because I was ready for the first grade. So Mama went to town and bought it. So the next day I went in the teacher's room and handed in my book. I promoted myself, you know. So that's how I went through school with my sister.

The Rosenwald school was large. It went through seventh grade, so I would imagine [a class had] anywhere from thirty or forty students. There was a store there, a store down the road. There was a church near and a Masonic lodge there, and it was thickly populated with farmers. It was rural, and the farmers had a lot of children. My parents had twelve. The classes were reasonably large. When I came along, the schools had problems. The children would have to stay out of school for picking cotton and hoeing cotton and things like that. So they yanked a month out of the school year, when the crops were laid by. So when we went to school, I think it was August, nothing was going on, no plowing and hoeing. The crops were already made. So they had school one month. Then we'd go back to school [in the fall] after you had gathered the crop.[9]

[If we] had to stay out of school, I would just swear I was never going again. I said, "If I can't go today, I'm not ever going." I had to stay home to help with the hog killing and the digging sweet potatoes. I'd say, "If I can't go today, I'm not going tomorrow. I'm not going tomorrow." And nobody would say a word; they went on about their business, because I'd be up early the next morning to go to school. I was a school nut. I was just a school nut. I thoroughly enjoyed going to school.

When we finished what we called graded school, there was no high school for blacks to attend in the whole county. So we went to a boarding school, what was then called Mary Potter High School in Oxford, North Carolina.[10] There were three of us [sisters]. The third one had gone to school for one year. She had gone to Livingstone College.[11] Livingstone had a high school at that time, but since my sister and I came along, [our parents] sent us all to Mary Potter. That was better than sending her to Salisbury and two of us to Oxford, North Carolina. So we went there. Then we graduated from Mary Potter by the skin of our teeth. One thing about Mary Potter, everybody worked. Everybody had a job and had to help. Wait tables, wash dishes, sweep the halls, and things of that kind. My brother, he would always send us some spending cash. That meant everybody at home didn't have a dime, because they were sending their money to us.

My [family owned land because] Mama's daddy gave it to them. I'll tell you how. My two grandfathers were slaves, but both of them had no problem with growing up or anything. In the first place, my paternal grandfather was the old master's son, and that was one thing. So he was special. But my maternal grandfather, he was much younger than my paternal grandfather. When [the Civil War] was over, when the northerners rushed through there and swept it out, and the people were saying, "Burn up Georgia," he was in his teens. He was lucky. This is what he told my mama. He said that sometimes you had a very cruel overseer on the farm who was going to beat the boys for nothing. But the boys could outrun him. He says that he'd run to the missus, and she would put a hand on that boy, and she'd keep him around the house and say, "He's going to help me in the day, two or three, 'til all this wear out." Then she'd let him go back to the field. But he said he had run many a day. But, see, he was lucky. He told Mama that he was sixteen or seventeen when the war was over. The

Yankees came through and just swept anything they wanted to, because they had won. Said that [his white owners] called him and said, "Dave, I want you to keep the horses." It's a place we call Lumber River; it's not a river, but there's water and a bridge there and everything. You wouldn't see the horses. It's sand all around. [They] said, "I want you to keep them down here," and the white men brought their best horses, because the Yankees were riding through, just taking them, and gave them to Dave. Said, "Dave, you keep them quiet now." He had a gang of horses, all the best that these people had, because the Yankees would ride through and just take them. He could hear them coming, hear the Yankees coming, because they were making a lot of noise. They had won and they were taking things. He said he just waited down there with the horses. He heard them hit the bridge, a long bridge over Lumber River. He took off his white shirt, and he stopped them right there. He said, "Come over here and get all these horses."

They went down there, and every man took one, and he rode off with them. He gave all the horses away. Then he jumped bareback, didn't even have a saddle, like a wild man, rode on off with them. He knew he had to go or they would have killed him. He stayed off for years and finally went to New York. He stayed off 'til he was grown. He came back, and I guess all the masters were dead when he came back. When he came back, he had some money, but he worked. He was working on this farm. He bought several, several acres. He had three children, two girls and a boy, but the boy died, so he divided it between his two daughters: my mama half of it and my aunt half of it. But, see, he was always enterprising.

[My family] didn't have any money, but we ate. See, we had so many in the family we could take care of our farm maybe Monday, Tuesday, Wednesday, and Thursday. Friday, we would go work for somebody else, those who had tobacco. I remember I would string tobacco, and two of my sisters would hand tobacco to me. We'd go home and thought we had a potful of money when we'd go back home. Of course, my brother sometimes would sell things, like go up the highway and sell watermelon, cantaloupe, things like that. Everybody had his own little pocketbook. Nobody would touch that money. No. You went out and made that little money. That's your money; you can have it. As I say, Mama was a pure genius. Mama insisted that if you wanted to keep something, like money, you put it on the mantle piece or in the wardrobe. If you touched anybody else's, my mama would whip you. Mama would be in bad shape now if you can't whip, because Mama was the kind would tell you, "This hurts me worse than it hurts you."

Mama was an oddity in the world, because Mama thought that the Bible meant you're supposed to give that 10 percent, or whatever it is, give that to the Lord. But we'd have a lot of jokes behind Mama's back, you know. Mama used to tell us, if you've got a nickel, you're supposed to give two cents to the church. You give two to the church and you save two, and you can spend that one, you know. But we were going to school then, and we'd say, "We know two cents out of a nickel is more than 10 percent."

We ate, but we didn't have any money, that was our problem. We didn't need, necessarily, a lot of money, especially [as] children, because our parents bought and kept us in good clothes, and we had hand-me-downs from the sisters and brothers, but, I finally got to the place that they couldn't hand me down, because my feet were larger than the two immediately ahead of me. The one next to me, her foot was always smaller than mine. I believe I came out of the womb with some big feet, for a girl.

Anyway, we didn't have any problem, because we didn't know you could live life the way it's living now. I just thought it was great. I enjoyed growing up. I just thought it was great. Brother would ride us on his back, everybody running around, everybody playing. But Mama would have been a good sergeant in the Army.

Corinne Browne, born in 1917, lived most of her life on St. Helena Island, off the coast of South Carolina, and home to several generations of her extended family. Browne was raised from infancy by her grandparents, following her mother's migration to New York during World War I. Her grandfather, a former slave and a veteran of the Spanish American War, used his pension to buy land, giving the family some financial stability and resources that many others lacked. After her grandparents died, Browne attended the Penn School.[12] Here she recalls academic and dormitory life, including the school's strict rules for girls' behavior and suggests that the rigidity was not necessarily a benefit in terms of preparing youth for the future.

I was reared by my grandmother and [grand]father on my mother's side, Dennis L. Freeman and Margaret L. Freeman. I doubt if I was quite a year old when my father died and they took me. My mother couldn't attend [my father's] funeral because I was just born and she was still in bed when he died. I'm the youngest of seven. My brothers and sisters were reared by other people because my mother went north to New York to find work. One [sibling] was raised in Beaufort. Some of the others stayed at the birthplace until they were old enough to work. A couple of [my brothers] later came to my grandfather's where I was. They would come until they were old enough to go north to my mother and then they left.

My grandmother, she passed in 1924. And then I lived on with my grandfather until he died in 1934. My uncles both lived very near. So their children were always there, Julius, Charles, Mary, Pearl, Minnie. We lived on waterfront down near the end of the island. One porch faced the water and the other porch faced the street. And then we had a back porch off from the kitchen. There were four bedrooms, two upstairs and two downstairs. We had a big dining room and a living room with a fireplace. There was also a fireplace in the dining room.

Then we had the big kitchen with a cookstove. [My grandfather] mostly [ate his meals in the dining room]; I'd fix his meal and take it in there to him. I ate mostly in the kitchen because I always had kids around me, so we'd sit in the kitchen. After my grandmother died in 1924 then I was sort of housekeeper for him. I did a little cooking. Not too much laundrying because I had two aunts that lived nearby who helped me with the laundry for him and I did my own. I had a garden and stuff like that, but it wasn't much. [We grew] beans and peas, onions, beets, carrots [and] corn.

[My grandfather was] a farmer and he was in the Spanish American War. So most of the time I knew him he was retired from that. He was sort of an outdoor person because he liked to fish and hunt and he would take a group of men over on Hunting Island. They would stay over there two or three days and hunt and camp out there. I remember preparing some of the deer meat. But most of it was given away.

I was born in 1917 so it would have been between 1917 and 1918 that my mother went north. I looked forward to boxes coming down for Christmas time. I remember when I was baptized she sent me this little velvet outfit, black and red. I always remember that outfit. Yes, she took care of me. She'd send boxes and stuff for all the holidays and everything, dolls and little tea sets and stuff, regular Christmas gifts. We would go to the Prayer House on Christmas Eve, and they would sing and shout there. By daybreak we would come back, and I saw this big track in the yard and I just knew it was Santa Claus. Everybody on that particular plantation would go from house to house and sing and shout, sing Christmas songs and stuff. They would have something to drink and cake and cookies and stuff. That's how they would celebrate Christmas. I think the last Christmas I had, my grandmother bought this doll, and hid it under her bed, and I knew she had been shopping and so I went seeking. I crawled on the porch and went in the bedroom and peeked at this doll, and every minute I would go and peek at this doll. But she caught me and she said, "Well that's the last time for your Christmas." After my grandmother died then my grandfather didn't play Santa. It was just what my mother sent from New York for me for Christmas.

I went to a little one-room, Land's End School. They were all segregated at that time but it was a little one-room school. There was one room and a little stove sitting up there and long seats in the back. I went up to the fifth grade there because for one thing I had to keep house for my grandfather. Anderson Simmons, the teacher, he was very good. After the fifth grade, he gave me a little class [to teach] to help out with the reading. The books were brought from the white school and they were used. [School went until 3:00 and when I got home] I had to feed the pigs and stuff like that. Bring in the eggs and get the firewood ready for the next morning. Several times I remember milking the cow. My grandfather would get my cousin from next door to do most of it, but I milked the cows. After chores I'd get supper, then do homework.

When I came to Penn, I had to walk seven miles because we lived quite a ways from it. I walked with two other kids. They had what they called a chariot. This was an old bus. The bus would run maybe my direction in the morning but we would have to walk back in the evening. So I did that for awhile. Then my grandfather thought he wouldn't let me do that because I would get home so late [in the] evenings. So I had an uncle that lived across the way and he had a car and would pick me up. So he would drive that seven miles and pick me up, or in the morning when I had to walk, he would drive me to school. That went on for a while until my grandfather decided to buy a car. That was a big thing because many people didn't have a car. My grandfather bought a little coupe with a rumble seat. He bought that and then later the next year he bought another one. You could get them for about $500 then. We always laugh about that. He could get them for about $500, and he paid cash for it because he was a pensioner,[13] so he could afford a little more than the average person. So he got the little car and then I learned how to drive and I'd drive myself and some of the kids who used to go to school and I'd pick them up. They taught me how to drive. That's the way that was. Me and a cousin of mine and one other girl were the only three girls on the whole island, I imagine even in Beaufort, that were driving at that time.

[I was at Penn School] from seventh to twelfth grade. One thing I regret is I don't think I got the background that I should have gotten, you know, by not going to Penn earlier. It was an entirely different situation [compared to Land's End School] and another thing, with no one else in the house to sort of model for me or help or anything, I think I lacked quite a bit. And the [academic] foundation that they got at Penn, I think it was far better. [The teachers at Penn] were all from Hampton Institute,[14] so they were qualified. The first teacher I went to was Mrs. Keith. She taught grade seven. Mr. Lewis taught math and science and biology. Mrs. Flynn, she did the sewing. We made everything from hats to rugs. Mrs. Price taught home economics where we baked and cooked and canned, learned how to make beds, learned how to set the table. It was so good.

Seven of us [graduated together]. When you'd get to the eighth grade it was a great big class, but by the time they'd get to the twelfth grade [most students had] stopped and gone to work and all of that. [Tuition at Penn School cost] six dollars a year, I think. Some could work it out, [getting paid] 10 cents an hour to milk the cows and harvest the crops and all that sort of stuff. They would help work on the [new] buildings and work in the different shops, the blacksmith shop and the shoe shop. The girls worked in the boarding department. We had to do the cleaning and all the cooking and stuff and the baking and everything. We did all the cooking. [Students boarded so] they could get that training and that experience of living with other children and being with others [who] were going through the training. At night you had to have chapel. You had to go to church on Sundays and all that, you know.

[There were a lot of rules in the dormitories.] We had a matron named Miss Mason. You talk about strict, boy! You better be in that room at certain times and the lights out and no talking. You were not allowed to be roaming around unless a parent came and took you. No, you had to be in there. They were very strict, very. At one time the girls would have to play on one side of the playground and the boys would play on the other side. We weren't allowed to dance. They'd have a little social, and the boys would come in and we'd play a little cards or something like that. [And] at one time they didn't accept students from even Savannah because they said the city life would be a bad influence. Other places, that was out of the question you know, other city places. They didn't encourage that. [Once you graduated,] you didn't know what to do. You were just almost at a loss. It was just like they said way back then, they had to tie the chicken's feet to keep them from straying and then when they loosened their feet they'd still think their feet were tied.

Cleaster Mitchell was born in 1922 near Blackton, Arkansas. Growing up in a rural farming family, Mitchell learned a range of tasks and grew accustomed to hard work. Mitchell's parents carefully taught her about racism and talked explicitly about the family's history under slavery, encouraging her to maintain a sense of pride and an awareness of the realities of living under Jim Crow. Here she describes the frustrations and degradations of sharecropping, especially for children.

I was born in 1922 at a little place called Coal, about two miles from Blackton, Arkansas. Coal was never on the map. There was just a little house there. Because the train took on water and coal there, they called it Coal. I grew up around Blackton and I knew all of the merchants and everything and I lived on various farms. We were farm workers, sharecroppers. My father used to fire a sawmill at Blackton. He was the timber man. He made railroad ties. That's how we learned to make ties, me and my sister, because my father used to take us with him. I learned how to saw, cut timber, to plow, to pick cotton. My whole life as a youth was simply working on the farm or working in a home or something like that.

My grandparents on the Smith side had a great big farm out at Blackton. They owned land. My great-grandparents, they were slaves and were born to half-white people. In pictures of my great-grandparents, they looked white as anybody. You couldn't tell the difference. My parents discussed this with us: they told us how come we had light and dark people in our family. It came through things that went on during slavery. There wasn't anything you could do about it, really. That was the time. But they would tell us about this history, what they came up through, how they worked and what it was like for them, and it made it a little easier for us.

People quite often wonder how black people lived through this time. It was because of how we were taught. We were taught not to hate. If something came up that was displeasing or you knew was wrong, they would say, "Well, don't worry about it. The Lord will fix it. Vengeance is God's." They meant you couldn't pursue it. We didn't know, but my parents knew you couldn't pursue whatever it was, because you could get in a lot of trouble then.

You would have to know the South to know what I am saying. If we went to a grocery store and a white lady came in, anybody white, [the clerks would] just push your stuff back and say, "Come on, Miss So-and-so," And you maybe walked ten miles to get this dime's worth of something that your parents sent you for. But that was like the law of the day; you just got back. There wasn't anything you could do about it. But it did not bother us like it would today, because we were raised to expect this. On some real narrow roads, just wide enough for a wagon, people who came by in cars had no respect for you. They would just drive. A lot of times you got in a ditch. A lot of time the dust just covered you. That's why a lot of colored people walked with their heads tied up or wearing an old dress or something over their clothes. Then they would take [the old clothes] off when they got ready to go to church or to town.

It's really something that a person would have to experience themselves to really see how this went, because there were no laws actually governing anything. You didn't have any place to go. We only had five months schooling, and out of the five months we probably went three, because if there was work, the plantation owner would just come by and say, "You have to keep the kids out. They've got to work." There wasn't a law to make them let you go to school then, so your parents did what the owners told them.[15] They would come tell your parents, "You go down and get the kids. I've got something for them to do." Just whatever they wanted done, your parents would do it. Now, the plantation owner would come down to the school and say to my oldest sister, "Mary, the lady said for you all to come on. I've got some beans for you to chop." That was it. You went.

We didn't grieve over it, it really wasn't as bad to us as it seems; we didn't know anything else. It was a problem to our parents, but we didn't know it. Our parents grieved and worried and prayed for better conditions, but we didn't think very much of it. When things just really got out of hand, my parents would sit down and tell [us], "Now, this is wrong. But the situation is that your father can't do anything about this and I can't do anything about it. This is just the way of life." A lot of things they would tell you to keep you from getting to the point that you became hateful and mean and thought about doing cruel things.

We worked and we never cleared a dime. But you expect something when you work all the year. There were five children and my mother and my father. The owner would give a $10 month furnish, as they call it.[16] They gave you an order to a store, and then you went to spend this $10 worth of credit. They settled off the way they wanted it. And if you made fifty bales of cotton, you didn't get out of debt; and if you made ten, you didn't get out of debt. That's just the way it was.

There wasn't anything you could do, because you didn't sell your own cotton, so you had no way of knowing exactly how much cotton sold for, how much a pound. They would go sell it for 20 cents, and then come back and say, "Well, we didn't get but 7 cents, Mary. That's all we got." And you had no recourse, no way you could dispute his word. Now, you could say, "Well, I heard in Clarendon they were getting 20 cents."

"Well, I don't know about that, Mary. I didn't get 20."

That's the end of it.

It sounds terrible when I talk about it, but that's exactly what happened. I experienced all of these different things, how they settled off.[17] And you could work by the day, and if he didn't want to pay you off, he would just come out and say, "Don't come up here. I'm not paying nobody off today." You were getting 50 cents a day for ten to twelve and sometimes fourteen hours. If he decided not to pay you off for that 50 cents a day, he'd get in his car and go somewhere.

But you know today that wouldn't work with too many people, don't you?

But then it worked. You'd go home and you would cry. You'd be mad. You'd be expecting to go to town, and you thought you could do a lot with it; that was a lot of money to us. As children we would plan to get some candy, some chewing gum, we'd get a cold pop, we would get ice cream, and those were the nice little treats that your parents would give you to at least make you feel good about yourself for working for 50 cents a day. All of these things were very important to us. But then when you didn't get it, you'd go home and cry and they had a little remedy. They'd say, "Oh, don't worry about it. I'm going to bake you all some teacakes and I'm going to make some homemade ice cream." See, [parents] would go all out of their way to do something a little special. That is to keep you from being so down and so mentally depressed. The South was a tough place to live if you didn't grow up here. I've had good experiences here and I've had terrible experiences here.

My mother worked for lots of people in Blackton. She cooked from 1925 up until 1936. On Christmas Day, 1936, she was cooking our Christmas dinner, and Mr. Roberts came about 10:30 and said to my mother, "Mary, I come after you to go up there to serve for Mrs. Roberts."

My mother said, "Well, I can't go today, Mr. Roberts, because I am preparing my children's Christmas dinner, and I always fix them a Christmas dinner. If I had known, I would have tried to make some kind of arrangements to have gotten started early and maybe I could have served for dinner for you all." He was so mad. About an hour later, he came back out and called my mother to the car. My mother lived in his house.

"I want my house," he said. "I want you to get out of my house, and I want you out of here tomorrow."

She just told him, "Yes, sir." After she got through with Christmas dinner, she went down to see Mr. Bennett. He had an old vacant house where the horses and things were stored. That's where we moved, all because she refused, and didn't go because she was cooking our Christmas dinner. That's what you had to contend with. You did what they said or else you suffered the consequence. There was always a repercussion. It was always something.

Now, if your child said something, they would go to your mother and take the spite out on her. "Mary, I can't use you no more because I was talking to your little old gal (that's what they called you, your little gal), and she stood up there and looked at me. She didn't say anything, but she stood there and looked at me and rolled her eyes." You see the repercussion? After my father died in '35, then my mother just had to depend on these people for a living. She would work, wash, iron, cook, do everything.

This is why they taught you what to say, how to say it, and sometimes not to say anything, don't show any emotion at all, because even just your expression could cause you a lot of trouble. You couldn't react to anything. It was bad. I've cried many a day. They would accuse you of something, and if you tried to say "I didn't do it," they would say "you're lying, you did do it." I wanted to say, "I'm going to tell my mother," but you couldn't say that. Yeah, I cried a lot of times.

Black people are a strong nation of people, because a lot of people don't really see how they survived under these conditions. But in 1930 during the Depression, you did not see black people committing suicide, and they learned how to feed themselves. We didn't go that hungry. My parents knew how to pick certain weeds and things to eat, like they call them wild greens. They grew in the field, in the yard, everywhere, and we knew all of the ones you could eat. We would get them and cook them, cook them just like regular greens, and they were very good. It was a way that we stayed healthy. We didn't have doctors where you could just walk in their office and they'd wait on you. Most of the babies were delivered by midwives, and if you got sick or got cut or something, you didn't see a doctor. Your parents had to doctor on you. If you broke your ribs, they knew how to bandage you up and everything. If you had pneumonia, they knew what to do. They would make a mustard plaster and plaster you up, and they would take cornmeal and heat it and make a plaster for pleurisy. Now, if you got cut real bad, they would just run and get sugar and just pack it full of sugar and bandage it up, and that stopped the bleeding. They made their own medicines, cough syrups, everything. They doctored on you for the average thing that happened to you, because there were no doctors, really, or they were so far away, if you got cut or something you'd probably bleed to death.

Everybody shared with each other what they had. Some people raised a lot of potatoes, and they would share with people who didn't have a lot of potatoes. And maybe this person raised corn, had lots of corn, and they would give you corn. And you took it to a gristmill, and you made your own cornmeal. If people had lots of cows and you had lots of children, they would [loan] you a cow to milk. They wouldn't give you the cow. They'd let you have a cow to milk so you could have milk and stuff for your kids. That's one way you survived, and it made you very close. That's how come everybody, in a sense, thought they were kin to everybody. If a person was a certain age, we had to call them "Auntie" and "Uncle." You couldn't just walk up and say, "Hey, Brown" or "Hey, such and such." You always had to give them that respect.

All the communities where we lived were black. Whites could move to our community, but we could not move to their community. And I know we had several white families move in our community, but they were in the same shape we were—extremely poor. At that time, if you were extremely poor, regardless of what color you were, then you were treated like you were black. So [one white family] had to live in a little shotgun house like we did, and my mother fed them. Their children would come to our house and eat. The wife, she really wasn't nothing but a kid, but she had two children, and my mother worried because [the white woman] didn't know how to take care of the children. So my mother showed her how to care for her kids and sew for them and make things. My mother would teach her how to cook and stuff just like she did my sisters. And maybe the little children wouldn't have survived if my mother didn't help her, because if they were sick, my mother would doctor them. They were down there with us about two years. But if they pulled up a little bit, they had to get out from down there.

It was tough when I came along, and I imagine it was worse when my foreparents came along. One thing my parents taught me was honesty. They always impressed this in me, "Don't you take anything." They'd tell you, "Don't talk back." They would tell you to do a good job and all these things. But the catch was, I had been going to work with my mother from the time I was four or five. I had grown up in this. It's not like waiting and saying, "You're fifteen now. You can go do some work." I've been self-supporting ever since I was twelve years old. I've been earning my own living. I know how to work. At twelve, I knew how to take care of myself. I could work for anybody at twelve, because I was taught. You were just trained like that and understood at an early age what you do and what you don't do.

Juanita Clarke, born in 1923, grew up in Birmingham, but some of her early memories center around her grandparents' farms in Greene County, Alabama. After her parents separated, Clarke spent her childhood moving between her grandmother's farm in Alabama, her father's home in Chicago, and then finally lived with her mother in Birmingham. A child during the Depression, Clarke recalls her family's struggles to make ends meet and describes the individuals who were important in shaping her life. Her memories of her family also reveal the gendered nature of work on the farm and in the city.

I was born in Forkland, Alabama, in 1923. My first memories were of Birmingham when I was about four, but I spent much time in Forkland after that.

My mother's father lived on twenty acres of land: it must have been my grandmother's land. Next to it were two other tracts of twenty acres, and two of my grandmother's sisters lived on those with their children and husbands and family. I got to know both of those [women] very well, but my grandmother was dead by the time I went to visit down there. My grandfather was pastor of the church in the community, a Methodist church, and he had a small farm there. He had married again. My grandmother, she must have been a slave or right out of slavery. I just imagine that the master must have given [the land]. I don't know how they got the twenty acres, but each one of the daughters had twenty acres right there together.

I spent some time with my paternal grandmother over in Sumter County when I was about five. My mother sent us there for several years. My grandmother had a big farm, about 300-and-some acres, with a lot of cows and horses, and she ran the farm by herself. We had a good time running all around. There was one horse that we could ride, and there was one cow that we could milk who wouldn't kick us. We were from the city, so we had a good time those few years running around the farm, and those were some of my fondest memories. That was in Sumter County, about three miles from Demopolis, Alabama. When I was living there, there were three of us. My brother was the youngest, I was the middle, and my sister was the oldest. She had most of the responsibilities. She helped my grandmother do everything. My brother and I mostly played. They had a hard time keeping up with us, because we were always running through the pastures and that kind of thing. I don't remember any special responsibilities, except maybe sweeping the yard. We used brushes to sweep the yard to keep it clean. We could help pick cotton, but we didn't have to, but we would go out there and pick it some.

When my grandmother wasn't feeling well after a while, my father came and got my brother and me and took us to Chicago, but left my sister there to help Grandma, because she was a big help to Grandma, but we weren't. And she had big crops. I remember when she got the sugar cane, and when she would process that, she had some men to come. They put the sugar cane in big bunches and they had a tub up under it, and they had ropes and horses to go around. The man would drive the horses around so the ropes would squeeze the sugar cane. Juice would fall down into the pan underneath, and that's the way they harvested, made the syrup from that. She would have hog killing days, when the men would come and help her kill the hogs, and they would skin them and all. She had some stepsons, her husband's children who lived out in a couple houses out on the fringes of the property, and they would come in and help some. I think most of her help really was hired help. They may have been neighbors. They helped with the cotton picking and all that.

She let us have a little garden so that we did plant seeds and all. She was very patient with us. She taught us a great deal. She had lots of African sayings and all. When we were sick, we would have to go to bed and she'd take a flannel cloth and put it in camphor or something, and put it over our chests. We never had a doctor. She was the doctor. She had little roots and different things for you to take if you had a fever. She would make different kinds of little poultices to put on your chest and to put on injuries. She had little drinks that she would make from roots and different things that we would drink. It was only later that I connected it with African culture, but I'm sure that that's what it was, plus she had little sayings for everything. She said, "See a penny, pick it up. All the day you'll have good luck." Right now I still say that. She also had a parlor where she had all kinds of books and little interesting whatnots. We weren't supposed to go in there, but anytime we found the door open, naturally we would go in and we'd just sit in there and read the books and look through all her things, until she would come and put us out because she didn't want us in there too much. She kept it locked. It was the parlor and it was for company, and she had all her important things in there.

There was a church just a few miles from the house, and it was on the property. My grandfather had been a minister when he ran the farm. We all had to go to the church every Sunday, and we started school there. It was just one big room, and we learned to read while we were there. We also read all of Grandma's books. That was the basis, I think, for most of my knowledge, reading all of those little Bible stories and all that she had in there. She just had so many treasures in there like that. So we really did get an education in those few years. I doubt if I would have been very smart had I not had that experience, because we learned so many things. We didn't know anything at all about a farm or anything like that, but we saw the whole process.

The thing of it is, though, when Grandma would harvest her crops and take them to market, she was never satisfied with the prices she got. Although she worked very hard and she had the harvest, I think she went deeper into debt or something. She talked about the mortgage. And eventually it became too much for her, and I think that's when she had my father come get the two of us and she kept my sister with her. After we were up [in Chicago] for a short time, we heard that she was on the way up there with my sister, but she didn't make it very far. She became ill. She stopped in York, Alabama, and she died there, and then my parents went and got my sister. So she had a pretty tough time trying to run [the farm] by herself, as I look back.

My mother and father were separated. My first memories were with my sister, my brother, and my mother in Birmingham. I don't know whether my mother became ill or what, but she sent us to stay with Grandma. My father was still in Chicago. Finally, my mother sent the two of us to Chicago. My father had a sister there who helped out at first, and then later on we just stayed with him. That was the time of the Depression, and he was doing all right when we first got there, but after we were there a little while, he had trouble finding work.

He showed us the corner where he stayed. He stood there waiting for work.[18] But actually my brother and I always ate well. We didn't realize that we were that bad off. So he took very good care of us. Eventually, he developed tuberculosis and he died there. He never did go back to the South.

My mother came to get us and took us back to Birmingham. In Birmingham, we moved a lot. I remember that little house we had, a shack, an old wooden house that went straight back, on 12th Street between 7th and 8th Avenue in Birmingham. We lived in there, and we went to Lincoln Elementary School. I was in the fourth grade. Sometimes Mama would have trouble paying the rent, but the man would let her by a lot. So people were nice. But we didn't stay there very long.

But when we left there, we moved to a big house up on Avenue D and 27th Street on the south side. That was a great big house, and we went to Lane Elementary School. That was down on 18th Street and about 4th Avenue South. That was a pretty long walk. But in the house, there was a sewing machine up in the attic, and I used to go up there and fool with the sewing machine. I'd get some oil and oil it, and I finally learned how to peddle it, and I'd just go up there and stay for hours and hours playing with that sewing machine. When I got to the fifth grade in school, my sewing teacher asked, "Who can operate a sewing machine?" I raised my hand up, and I was the only one with my hand up. So sewing has been very important to me throughout my life. As a matter of fact, I majored in home economics in college because I wanted to be a sewing teacher, because I found that sewing machine up there.

Lane was a small black elementary school, with eight grades. The principal was kind of stern, and he was a strong disciplinarian. It's very embarrassing, but he did paddle me one time. He had a big belt, and I've forgotten what I did, but it was very embarrassing. You had to go in there and lean down while he gave me about five licks. They didn't really hurt, but it was very embarrassing and I didn't tell anybody about it. So that's the way the schools were, actually. I spent a lot of time in sewing class, and whenever I could be out of another class, I was in there, too. I would walk over to my sewing teacher's house in North Birmingham, and that's all the way on the other side of town. But during the summer I would walk over there and stay over there as long as I wanted to and became a member of their family, more or less. She's still a good friend of mine, and I was basically a member of their family. That was my second home over there. She would give me some of her dresses made out of nice material, and I'd cut them down and make dresses for myself and stuff like that. Her sister was a seamstress, too. I'd go over there and help her sister, and I guess I learned more about dressmaking by going over there helping her sister do handwork and stuff.

I started at Parker[19] around 1936. The school was well run, and everybody was very proud of it. We wore a uniform, a blue uniform. Girls had to wear little dresses and all. Conduct was exemplary or whatever. There was a big band, a big marching band. The teachers there were revered by everybody and everybody in Birmingham knew them by name, and Dr. Parker[20] and all of the teachers were some of the most important people in Birmingham. Everybody in Birmingham knew who worked at Parker and if you taught at Parker High School, you were very, very special to the black community and looked up to as just the tops.

My mother was not working outside of the house much then. She had been a teacher back in Forkland years ago. To teach then, you only had to finish the ninth grade or something like that. She had attended Barber Memorial School,[21] but she had a teaching certificate, too. But there was some kind of welfare program where she supervised a playground, and that helped her get through. We would go to the playground every day, and it gave her enough money to pay the rent and to provide food. Our diet all the way through school was basically peas, beets, or greens or something like that and cornbread, and very seldom much meat or anything like that. Actually, we ate once a day, and that was dinner. I don't understand now how we were able to get up in the morning, go to school, and walk all the way to Parker and walk back, and eat dinner and that was all. We didn't have any lunch money or anything, and still we did all right.

Dolores Aaron was born in New Orleans in 1924, where she grew up, attended college, and eventually became a teacher in the city's public school system. Her mother operated a boarding house and sold insurance and her father was an undertaker; their separation meant that the family experienced precarious finances during her childhood but, as Aaron describes, her mother was both enterprising and protective. As a child, Aaron lived in integrated communities, forming friendships with white children and interacting with black and white adults in the city's streets and businesses. Her interview sheds light on the complicated race relations of New Orleans, particularly with regard to race, gender, and the use of public space.

I was born in 1924 on a cold Monday morning. Mama says ice was hanging from the tree, it was just that cold and yet she said, "you [were] so warm." When I was about four years old we moved to a portion of Tremé Street and we lived in that neighborhood[22] for quite a number of years. There was a fighting ring where all of the major fights were held over on St. Louis Street and I suppose it was cheating, but we could sit in our back window and we could see the ring, so we didn't have to buy a seat to go in and see the fights at the arena. And of course we lived near churches, Grace Methodist Church where I was christened. I went to Wicker school. And then somebody got the bright idea in the administration that all the children that lived on a certain side of the town had to go to Craig School, and going to Joseph A. Craig School, which is truly in the heart of the Tremé, was truly a turning point in my life. And when I say the turning point in my life it's because that's when I really was able to feel that there was nothing better than your teachers. We had the most caring teachers in that building.

[The principal] was rough on discipline and the teachers were highly disciplined too, so that caused us to have good teachers. And so when I moved on to sixth grade and on up to high school, the foundation was there. There were poems and plays and we did plays about slavery and we did dances. Every evening you were either in a play in school to help to bring up your cultural side, or you were in a play at church. We were always practicing for something.

In Tremė, there were lots of restaurants and nightclubs that you knew better than to even peep into. As young children we understood that these were places for adults. In later years this street became a strip for nightclubs and music, but everybody had such a high regard for children when they went to school that we had no problems. The people who hung on the corners were very respectful of the children. Children in that day always had a feeling that they were going to be somebody because we just had people to look up to and all. Parents put emphasis on education. I don't remember being friendly with any child whose parent didn't talk to me about school and how important it was to finish school. Church and school is all I heard, as a child.

During my young years it was very common to have white folk living next door to you, who would speak to you, be very polite with you, walk to school with you, and continue on to their school. The schools were segregated but the Longeaus, who lived up the street from here, walked me to school. Their mother had a grocery store [that] was right next to us. We [listened to] the radio together at night, we could sit outside, [and] if there were black kids on the block whose parents didn't have a radio, then all of us congregated on the Longeaus' steps and we would sit and actually listen to the radio. And somebody in the group would say "that's Alexander's Ragtime Band" and the man on the radio would say, "That's right," just as if he heard you.

When it was time to go to school we'd walk to school together, we would stop on Bienville Street [where my school was] and the Longeaus would walk to Cleveland Street. When we came home we [competed] with those children who were in the same grade. We used to brag on what we knew because that's what we did. We used to compare lessons [and] we compared books and that's how we knew that they got new books.

That competitive spirit came from our parents, and also our Sunday school teachers. Our Sunday school teachers were always preparing us to do a better job and always using white people as the standard. Please, white folk have always been the standard, and this was not necessarily always the best thing to do, but that's what black people did. I believe that many middle-class black folk were sort of condescending. [They] just made us feel like if we can just do what they do, then we're okay. But we're not to expect them to accept us. But at least be able to do much of what they can do.

I suppose I was eleven or twelve years old when we moved to the French Quarter. I lived at 926 Toulouse, that's the heart of the French Quarter. Most of the residents of the French Quarter were white and they were not mingling with black people anyway, so [we] never had problems and it really didn't bother us, it didn't bother us at all. In the French Quarter we didn't visit anyone, because people didn't visit, people who were right next door to you had polite, short conversation. Mama rented a fourteen-room house and then she sublet the rooms. If you wanted one room, you could have one room, if you wanted a furnished room, you could have a furnished room, and that is how my mother managed to send us to school. By that time my mother and father were separated, and my father was sending us small amounts of money and sometimes nothing. He was in Mississippi, back home. My mother paid $28 a month for a fourteen-room house, and she rented it to the extent she probably tripled what she was paying. It was very comfortable. We used the largest rooms and we were able to maintain it so well that people wanted to live there. There were two swimming pools in the back yard, and there was a patio. My mother bought a piano for us to busy ourselves with because when we lived in the French Quarter we didn't go outside, but we certainly did have a lot of fun inside.

My mother was a good looking woman, a very pretty woman, Creole type. Her mother was French, and my grandfather, I understand, was a very, very handsome black man. My grandfather ran into a lot of difficulty because she was a French girl, and he didn't marry her for a while because at that time it was not easy for blacks and whites to marry, but he did eventually marry her. Her family cut her off completely because she married a black man, but I understand that she loved my grandfather. My mother was possibly sometimes mistaken [for white], and it wasn't so popular for her to say that my sister and I were her children. I don't think that's any reflection on me or my mother. We had to survive and we did survive and she ran a very reputable house and the people were very good to her.

The French Quarter closer to Canal Street was like a red light district. My mother saw to it that we walked on Rampart Street because straight up Burgundy Street was the red light district. The ladies were out there hustling and calling men into the doors and that kind of thing. All of these women were white and if they weren't white they were passing for white. But they used to put extra powder on their faces anyway, they tell me, just to be sure they appeared white, I guess because the men wanted to make sure they were white women. Even the lady who lived across the street from us when we lived on Toulouse Street was one of the ladies of the evening. There was a lady who lived immediately next door who was a light-skinned woman passing, but once you found out that this was occurring, you didn't move into it; if you live in a glass house you don't throw stones. You didn't make any accusations. You didn't discuss it with anyone because you were so busy trying to keep your own business quiet. Then why would you talk about the lady next door?

My mother would buy clothes from the Volunteers of America across the street. The man was friendly with my mother, and he would call her when he came in with a very nice batch of good clothing that he had gotten, as he said, from the sedate ladies who were the Jews up on Saint Charles Avenue. So I always looked nice because my mother would take those clothes and she would redo them because she sewed beautifully. We were always highly regarded as very neat, well-dressed little girls, and our shoes were hand-me-downs because my mother would buy shoes and everything from over there, but of course nobody knew it at school. You don't go to school and tell everybody, "I got my clothes from the Volunteers of America."

Mama was an insurance agent for one of the insurance companies in New Orleans and so she used to travel in an old Essex. We would get up early in the morning and we would go to the bakery and we would buy hot bread, and we would have the butter and cheese and we would eat in the car. To us that was a treat, to go early when the bread was coming out of the oven. Those were the kinds of things we did with my mother. If my sister went out with a young man, my mother would drive her and her boyfriend and we would not come home. We would have a late supper in the car, or else we'd go out some place and buy something, and we'd come back and sit right outside the place wherever it was and wait for my sister. It's strange, but that's what my mother did. My mother used to go to the dances with her. I can see my mother at the PTA dance and she would have me by her side.

Vermelle Ely was born in 1933 in Charlotte, North Carolina, and grew up in a large household that included her grandparents, parents, one brother, and, for a time, her great grandmother. Her parents worked as teachers, a profession that Ely selected for herself despite a visual impairment that made it difficult for her to read. In her interview, Ely shares vivid descriptions of the neighborhood in which she lived and of the larger world of black Charlotte. Through Ely's recollections, readers can glimpse the extent of urbanization in the South after World War II when a major road construction project transformed her neighborhood. Many of her memories center on her early teenage years, when she explored the city on foot and by bus, taking advantage of many organized—and informal—recreation opportunities including movies, sporting events, and school activities. At the same time, city life tested families' ability to protect children from harm, exposing them to intracommunity rivalries and possible dangers from outside forces.

I was born right here in Charlotte on January 10, 1933, at the same place that I lived for many, many years. That address then was 616 East Stonewall Street. That's where I was born, at that particular house. I lived in a section called Brooklyn. Another name for it was Second Ward. It was one of Charlotte's black neighborhoods, one of the sections that was geared to businesses and entertainment and that kind of thing. The only black high school was located in that same neighborhood, called Second Ward. I'm not really sure how it really got its name, Brooklyn. Brooklyn consisted of all types of homes, all kinds of people lived there. You had some doctors, some teachers, some people that worked in service. It was just a neighborhood of all kinds of people. You had large homes. You had small homes and some referred to some of the homes as shotgun houses.[23] It was just a neighborhood that consisted of all kinds of homes and all kinds of people.

We had one elementary school, which was called Myers Street. We lived close enough to walk to Myers Street. We walked to school each day. Of course, some of the streets were paved and some of them were not. Stonewall Street was not paved in my early years. Alexander Street, where the school was located, was a paved street. The paved streets were the ones [that led] from downtown, where the buses traveled or [the] trolleys before that. The side streets were dirt streets, little roads, very close together.

The houses were well kept. We didn't have grass and stuff like people do now. Most houses didn't. We had a nice clean dirt yard that we kept just like people keep the grass. We swept the yard nice and clean; then, when we finished, we took the point of the broom and decorated it real pretty. So, people took pride in their homes even though they didn't have grass or flowers.

Our house stood about middle ways down the [street]. We lived in, I guess, maybe ten rooms in that house. [In the 1940s,] they moved the houses back and Stonewall Street became Independence Boulevard.[24] When the boulevard was opened, the house was moved back so far that the fig tree [by the back steps] came up in the front yard. Of course, it was interesting to see them move those houses. They put the house on rollers and people came from all over to see them move. When they moved our house, they didn't get it finished before quitting time one afternoon. My grandmother told the men that were working, she said, "Please let me know when you get here in the morning. I want to be out of here when you decide to move this house." [The next morning] we were still in bed and she was fixing breakfast. When she went to the door to find out if they were ready to start moving the house again, they had moved it so easily that before she could ask the man about it, he said, "How did you enjoy your ride?"

Our house had [a large] backyard. My mother and father were both teaching school but we had chickens and we had pet rabbits. Of course, the chickens were not all pets. They weren't pets, they were for our livelihood. We had a garden where [my parents] planted beans. A lot of people did that. I remember when they got ready to open the boulevard, when they had to move the houses back, we had to do away with the chickens and all.

A lot of people didn't have space to move [their houses] back and had moved them to other sections of town. They put those houses on a truck, a flatbed or whatever you call it, and you could see a house going down the street some days. They even moved a stone church that they turned around. It was a huge thing.

They turned it from facing Stonewall Street to facing the other street. So that was really something to see.

The street was our playground, more or less, because they didn't have places for us to go and play like they do now. It made it nice because we were surrounded with people with a lot of children. We'd play in the street. We'd have softball games or what we called roller bat. You hit the ball and then you roll the ball to hit the bat. We were just surrounded with all kinds of people. We were not separated, like teachers and all lived on one street and somebody else lived on another. We were just all mixed up. You'd have your little petty arguments and fights but they didn't ever amount to anything very much. There would just be childlike things.

[There were bad sections of town.] A part of Brooklyn was considered a bad section of town. There was one corner that I can remember, growing up, that they would call Murder Corner because they had a lot of things to happen that were near the corner of First and McDowell. [But] I don't think any [part of the city was] really bad. I didn't get that impression. We had, as children, and I think adults too, we had like little neighborhood fights and things. The kids from Third Ward would always run you back home if you were over there, especially if you were talking to somebody else's boyfriend or girlfriend. If you [went] to visit them, of course they'd run you back home. But nothing like now. It was just rocks and running. We would just have those kinds of fights.

But there was a part of Second Street that was referred to as "The Block" because they had a lot happening there on the weekends. There were restaurants—they called them cafes during that time. The theater was there and of course there was an entertainment area that was called the Green Willow Garden. It was behind a fence, because that was off-limits to us. But you know, as children, we'd always try to find a peep hole to see what was going on behind the fence. There you had your dancers. They would have, on weekends, gay parties. We'd sit on the sidewalk on Friday and Saturday night and watch them dress up. You knew who they were, of course; they had on men's clothing all week and on Friday and Saturday nights they dressed up in high heels and went to the Green Willow Garden to their parties. Of course, we never got a chance to see except through the fence. Those were the only sections that were just referred to as being bad. Of course, I think Brooklyn just may have gotten the name of being bad anyway, just period.

Some of us were not even allowed to go to Second Street, period, to The Block. McDowell Street was not a good place until later when they opened a theater. We had a theater on Second Street which was called the Lincoln and another theater eventually on McDowell Street. That was after the street got better. The name of the theater there was the Savoy. Of course, we had our own theaters. I have heard older people talk about going to the movies downtown, like the Carolina [Theater]. They had white movies that they would allow blacks to come in and sit upstairs. [But] during my time they stopped blacks from coming to the [white] movies. From what I understand, [black patrons] would throw popcorn and stuff down on the [white] kids. I don't know how bad that was, but I imagine they did. But they had stopped [blacks] from going to the [white] movies.

Of course, the black theaters would have your chapter pictures. They called them serials. You'd go to see them every week and see what happened last week. Hop-Along Cassidy and all the westerns, Johnny Mack Brown, Superman, Captain Midnight. [My brother and I] went to the movie just about every Saturday to see the serials. My brother would pop a grocery bag full of popcorn and go the movie and we'd spend the day, eating popcorn all day. I don't know how they ever made any money, because kids would go and spend the day. Later we were able to catch the bus and come out on this side of town [near Johnson C. Smith University] to see a little better movie sometime. It was a little quieter and little cleaner and that sort of thing. On this side of town, where the ritzy blacks live. There was an old [man], I think he was Jewish, a real nice man, Mr. Nugent. Mr. Nugent would come down here and he had a flashlight and he'd shine it in your face, especially if you were making too much noise. He'd shine the light and he'd come down the aisle and say, "Vermelle, your mama said catch the next bus and come home." He knew everybody by name. He'd come in there and get you and tell you, "It's time for you to go home. Your mama said for you to come home."

On Sundays, we'd catch the bus. Bus fare was like seven cents and we'd go for bus rides on Sunday and go to the soda shops and meet friends to talk. There was a place called Sunset Park which was kind of like a dance hall at night, a club, where they had lots of entertainers to come in like James Brown and some big names. They built a swimming pool there, too. That's where I learned how to swim. But I went with the Boy Scout troop. My girlfriend and I had brothers that were Scouts. Of course, we begged the Scout master to let us go. We had to get up at five o'clock in the morning. Buses didn't start running until six, so we would walk from our house to downtown to the Square and then we'd catch the bus. Sometimes we'd walk all the way because we'd save our money and go to Krispy Kreme for donuts. We took swimming lessons with the Boy Scouts [because] they didn't have any classes for girls during that time. So the two of us did learn how to swim then. I even took a lifesaving course while I was in that class with them. He just let us do the same thing the boys would do. Of course, when time came for the closing, [the teacher] made us get in the closing exercise, too. Of course, we were the laughingstock. We were almost ashamed. All those boys and two girls with the Boy Scout troop in their water clothing. But at least we learned how to swim and we had a good time.

There was a place called the Armory and that's where they used to have all the dances. The bands would come and they'd have the big dances. Of course, we weren't allowed to go. You'd have shoot-outs and stuff where somebody stepped on somebody's foot. I remember somebody getting shot one time. That's why our parents didn't allow us to go. When we got older, of course, you know we tried to slip off and go, when we were old enough to get our own tickets.

Second Ward was the first high school [for African American students in Charlotte] and they opened West Charlotte in later years, in the late '40s, I believe. Then we became great rivals, the kids from this side of town and kids from the other side of town. Of course, they referred to us as the bad kids from Brooklyn. We would always have fights over games, over boys and girls or whatever. In fact, the two high schools were great rivals. They had scheduled games with the other high schools around. But they eventually had to stop Second Ward and West Charlotte from playing because of fights. Usually it was not the students that were doing this, it was other people in the neighborhood, younger men, people that were not even in school. But we got blamed for it. Like I said, Second Ward was always the bad section. Eventually they stopped us from playing for a few years because of fighting.

In the middle '40s, somebody got the bright idea [and] decided to let us play again and we played at Memorial Stadium and called it the Queen City Classic. That was an exciting thing because in 1948 they decided to have a queen for the Queen City Classic and I was the first Miss Queen City Classic. That was in 1948. I don't remember if they fought that year or not. I was kind of away from it if they did. The year before that I was Miss Second Ward, in 1947. [Being selected gave me] a real good feeling because it gave [me] the feeling that the students liked you for who you really were and not for who your parents were; otherwise I would not have been chosen as Miss Homecoming to represent the student body. It was a real good feeling. It was an exciting thing, especially the Queen City Classic, because I got a bouquet from the mayor. There was a dress shop here called Lucille's [where] I got my dress and crown, which I still have. I had a hairdo from one of the white beauty shops that I couldn't do anything with. It was really, really a good feeling to be recognized and to receive all the recognition and support that I got not only from the students but from [my] family and friends and from the community. [But I did feel a certain responsibility] to live up to. [I felt] like other kids were still kind of saying, "this is something I would like to do, I would like to be." You have to do certain things; we had an honors society and you had to be in the honors society. But those were exciting times and times that you look back on that make you proud.

Theresa Cameron Lyons was born in 1934 in rural Durham County, North Carolina. Although she lived only several miles from Durham, one of the South's most renowned black communities, Lyons grew up economically and psychically distant from the symbols of black success. She drew aspirations from her teachers and inspiration from her grandmother. Her interview captures the challenges that

*sharecropping families confronted in the waning years of Jim Crow, and the oppor-
tunities presented by the World War II economy. Finally, Lyons describes the path
that eventually took her from poverty to a position at one of the most important black
businesses of the segregation era.*

My family name is Cameron. My grandfather lived on Stagville Plantation.[25] He
was a slave who became free when he was a teenager. That plantation is where
my extended family was living when I was born—my grandmother, my uncles,
my aunts. My mother had two sisters, and they were all very close. Actually, I am
the product of an unwed mother. We all lived together. At that time families just
all lived together. Even though they were grown, they always lived in the same
house. I can remember my mother's friends; they all lived at home with their
fathers, and when they got married, they still lived there for a long time. That
was just the thing they did. I went to Millgrove School, a segregated school. Back
during the time, we lived all over the area because we were tenant farmers—very
poor, living on the land of the owner, who was, of course, white. We used his
mules, and he paid for the seed and the tobacco and the stuff that we planted. Of
course, as I look back now, I know how they cheated us, because we never had
anything. I went to school with shoes with holes in the bottom, where I had to
put cardboard. We would go sell the tobacco, and I'd be so excited thinking I was
going to get some new clothes, but there was nothing left because after he took
his share, there would be nothing left, but maybe a little bit to buy some flour
and some sugar and stuff like that.

We were just pitiful. But I didn't think at that time we were pitiful, as I look
back now, because everybody else was pitiful. We played and we farmed. And
in the summer I would be so glad for a thunderstorm to come, because then we
could go home and rest. I just can't remember ever when I didn't have to work.
When I was, I guess, maybe three or four, I would have to bring the stove wood in,
wood for the stove. I remember little things that happened, the kind of house we
lived in. It would rain through the roof and we'd have to put the buckets down to
catch the water. Somebody named Wright owned that house; they were wealthy
people. They had a child that was slightly older than I was, and they would always
bring me all the hand-me-down clothes. I thought I was rich because I had coats
with little fur collars. When I would go to school, I was the envy of the other kids
because I had things they didn't have. It made me feel good for them to give me
stuff. I didn't realize they were taking all our money, anyway, and what they were
giving was hand-me-downs. Also, we used to raise pigs for some people that had
a bakery in the city. They would bring all their old baked goods—cakes and pies
and stuff that they couldn't sell in the store—and bring it to us to feed to the hogs.
I mean, it was just like Christmas for us, because we ate it. The hogs didn't get it.

I remember neighbors helping neighbors. I remember borrowing coals for
fire, because we didn't have any matches. My grandmother would give me a little

bucket and she'd say, "Go up to Mrs. Markus' house and tell her I said send me some coal. And you hurry back," so the coals wouldn't go out. We would help the white farmers when they needed help, too. They'd come over and ask my uncles if we could help them. They would help us. They would help us if we had a crop that had come in and we were short of help. If somebody was in jail and we didn't have enough [people] to help us, then the white folks would help us. There was never any money passed. We had corn shuckings and all of them would come then and help shuck the corn. And wood-cuttings—they would all go and help each other cut wood. We would help them and they would help us.

But when I was about ten, my best friend was a white girl. They lived just right across the road from us. We had the best time playing. You know how black people put oil on their hair? I used to oil her hair down. I'd have her slicked down just like a cat. She would wear my clothes and I would wear her clothes. I remember when her family moved away, I was devastated, because that was my very best friend. I knew she was white and she knew I was black, but we just had fun. She'd spend the night with me and I'd spend the night with her. I always thought that they moved away because we were friends. Her parents were never mean to me, but she just loved me so much that she would just insist that I would spend the night, and they would, of course, let me.

But back to the segregation part. When I was a child, we used to come to town on Saturdays. That was our outing. We didn't come every Saturday, but when we got the opportunity to come, that was it. There was one person in the neighborhood who had a car, so everybody would get in his car and he would let us all out at the same place, a little hot dog place on Main Street. It only had window service. You couldn't go in. You'd buy a hot dog at the window. Then they had some benches out there where all the black folks sat. When I was a little girl we would go in this place downtown called Kress' Five & Dime Store. I always wondered why we couldn't sit at the counter to eat, because all the white people were sitting. I used to ask my mother why couldn't we sit down. I was tired. She would be fussing, and she would just tell me, "Shut up." One time we went in department store. They had two water fountains, and one said "Colored" and one said "White," and I couldn't read, but I knew some letters. I thought "C" stood for "cool" and "W" stood for "warm." So I drank out of both of them. I told my mother, I said, "I drank out of both of those fountains, both of them, and one said 'cool' and 'warm,' but they were both warm." I thought she was going to kill me. She grabbed me by the arm.

She said, "Don't you know that's for white? That's for white and colored. You can't drink out of the water fountain for the white people!" She took me out of that store. I thought she was going to kill me.

But now that I look back at it, I was innocent. I remember when they only sold Cokes to white folks. You could only buy Pepsi. If you'd go in a store and ask for Coke, they would reach in there and give you Pepsi. I do remember in the shoe stores that they wouldn't let blacks try on shoes. You'd just have to go in there and they would measure your foot, and you would say, "I want that pair," or that pair or that pair. But you couldn't just sit there and try them on. You could shop [in most stores], but if you walked up first and a white person walked up later, they waited on the white person first. I mean, it was just known that you weren't going to get waited on. No matter how badly I wanted something, I wouldn't buy it. I would leave.

The highlight of the year was going to the county fair. The white folks had the first week and the black folks had the second week. I remember distinctly it would always rain the white folks' week, and the black folks' week, we would always have the beautiful weather. Then they decided to change and let the black folks have the first week and the white folks the second week, and it reversed. It would still rain their week. The fair would always be in the fall when the farmers had some money. They were selling their tobacco, and you'd have some money to go to the fair.

World War II required additional sacrifices. You could not buy panties with rubber [waistbands], you had a tie, because they were using that material for the war. I remember not being able to have margarine that was already yellow; it was white and you had a little package of stuff that you put in it to make it yellow. You had a ration book to use if you had to buy a pair of shoes.[26] And we saved the silver [foil] from cigarette packs because we were told that if you saved silver and just wrapped it in a ball, you could sell it. We had the biggest old ball of silver. We never figured out who we'd sell it to. Also you couldn't buy meat. The principal of the Little River School got beaten up real badly by some white people at a store. Being a principal, he thought he was somebody, and he stopped in there and asked them if they had any meat. It was just something like fatback or a strip of lean or something like that. They beat him real bad, because they said he was out of his place, that they didn't sell meat to niggers.

During two years of the war I lived with my mother in Portsmouth, Virginia, where there was work for women in the Navy shipyard. It was a better job than working in the tobacco factories and it was a long-term job. Most of the jobs at the tobacco factory, the year round jobs, were sewed up, so you could only get a seasonal job where you worked two or three months. By that time she had gotten married, and the man was in the Army. She wanted to be able to make her own money, and that's what she did. When my stepfather came out of the service, he wanted to move back to Durham. They moved back to my grandmother's and then moved out and got a house, went back to farming. Although they farmed, my mother still had another job where she worked domestic work. So she was working and bringing in some money, and my stepfather was one of those, he'd work two or three days and stop, two or three days and stop. Later they stopped farming. He got a job working for the county schools for a little while, and he worked for Duke a little while. He worked for Wright Machinery a little while. But he never worked very long. My mother was the mainstay.

My grandmother was a very strong person. I think any values that I learned I got from her. She was very religious. My mother was young when I was born—she was just eighteen—so she was still dating. So my grandmother was really my mother. I remember when I got old enough to start going out, about fifteen, she would always tell me "You cannot go to the movies unless you go to church." So I would always get up early, walk to church, because I knew that I would want to go to the movies that afternoon. Church would give me hope that I could live from this week to that week. I enjoyed going to church, I did. My grandmother had other rules: you couldn't curse, you couldn't play cards, because that was a sin. You couldn't dance. She didn't like certain kinds of music. My aunts used to play that "Blind Boy" Fuller music[27] on the Victrola, and she said we were going to die and go to hell. I loved it. I used to hear my uncles curse, and I just thought that was cool. But she would always tell me I couldn't curse.

The only reason I would go to Hayti[28] would be to go to the movie theater. There were two theaters there, the Regal Theater and the Booker T. Theater. My grandmother didn't like for me to go down there, because there were a lot of businesses and a lot of men hanging out on the street and all, and she said that it was not a place for a young girl to be. And when I got old enough to get my hair done, I would go to Doris' Beauty Parlor on Pettigrew Street to get it washed and straightened and fixed. It was a beauty parlor [and] barbershop. You'd walk through the barbershop and there was the beauty parlor in the back. I would always make sure that I would catch the bus right away. I never just walked up and down that street, because I knew my grandmother would kill me if she found that I had. She didn't care if I went down there to the hairdresser or to go to the movie, but I had to go specifically for that purpose.

I remember one important person that lived in the community, a deacon in the church. In my family, my uncles didn't go to church. To see this man dress up on Sunday and go to church, although he was in overalls, I always wanted to see my uncles do that. They never did. I had three uncles and they would get drunk on all of this home-made liquor. They made the liquor and sold it to white folks and neighbors. I thought one of them was mean and I hated him, and one of them I liked because he worked in the city and he would always bring me things. The one uncle was a very strict disciplinarian. When my mother was at work during the day, he was very abusive. We used to have a towel on the wall, and he would take that towel down and whip me with it. I wanted to tell my mother, but I was scared that he'd whip me again. He would say, "It's time for you to go get the wood." If you didn't move right then, that was a whipping. I don't know why my grandmother wouldn't stop him, but she never would. One time he whipped [me] bad, and I told my mother and she told him if he ever whipped me again, she was going to kill him. And he didn't. He didn't whip me anymore.

Most of the time one of my uncles would be in jail and the others would live with us. Then when they would go to jail, the white man would make us move because we wouldn't have anybody there to help plow the mules. We would move so often that I don't think I ever went to the same school more than maybe two years at a time. But I was always a very good student. I would just get in the class and I would just catch up. We didn't have electricity; we had a lamp. I would just get up to that lamp, because it gave out very little light. Get up to that lamp and try to read, to catch up with whatever school I was going to. And when I graduated high school, I was valedictorian. Most other children quit, because there was no [law requiring] going to school until you were sixteen.[29] Most of them quit. In fact, the cousin that lived with us quit. She was older than me. She quit in, I think, fifth grade. They wanted to teach you Home Ec so you could learn to sew and to cook and get married, have children. And that's all they wanted. They didn't care whether you went to school or not. [But I kept going to school] because I never wanted to live the kind of life that they were living. I wanted to learn how to count money and to be able to say, "No, not half." They would just take the man's word, whatever he said. I just always thought I could do better than they were doing. When I would go to school I would see the teachers and they had cars and they were dressed nice, I would say, "There is another world."

CHAPTER 2

What Is Expected Of You:
Gender and Sexuality

Thinking back on the lessons she learned from her family about how girls should behave, Mississippi resident Mandie Moore Johnson recalled, "A young girl, she can do right if she wants. She can stand up on her principles if she wants." For African American girls who grew up in the Jim Crow South, learning to "do right" involved embracing the imperatives of respectability. Enacted as good manners and high morals, respectability regulated explicitly the ways that young black women could and could not express sexuality, demanding mindfulness as well as chastity and sobriety, resourcefulness, and common sense. "My grandmother didn't allow me to run out with [other] women's husbands. I learned that on my grandmother's porch," Johnson noted.

This chapter focuses on African American women's memories of gender roles in their communities, including the messages they received—and sometimes resisted—regarding respectability. Multigenerational households passed life lessons from one generation of African American women to the next. Mothers and grandmothers—and in their absence other female kin—taught young girls about their bodies, if not always about sex. Girls were instructed about how to appropriately dress and behave in public by observing the actions of others and by explicit teachings. Girls also learned the consequences of violating expectations. One of our informants remembers that her husband could not stop a beating she suffered at the hands of an uncle who disapproved of her dancing in public. Another recalls that young women who did not conform to community mores were shunned. Others describe standards for women's appearance, including prejudices about skin color that affected how women perceived themselves although they could do little to control this aspect of how they looked.

Lessons about how women were to present themselves in public are remembered here primarily in the context of protective families and neighbors, but black institutions also emphasized these standards. Educators, ministers, political figures, and reformers railed against sin and degradation, and promoted respectability as an aspiration, as a cornerstone of racial advancement, and as a responsibility of girls and women. Schools and colleges enforced gender roles and sexual mores through regulations such as curfews, dress codes, and prohibitions on dating, although as Florence Borders' interview in this chapter reveals, such rules might be bent or ignored. Most schools barred married women from teaching and banned single women teachers from living alone. Churches promoted women's roles as caretakers of the material and spiritual needs of parishioners.

Although most narrators embraced their distinct roles, not all conformed to community standards. As they detail in their interviews, the failure to meet expectations could have severe consequences for women. Unmarried mothers were expected to give their babies away to others to rear. Without social services, fostering children became a community responsibility, taken on by the extended network of kith and kin. Narrators who were raised by grandparents or other family, typically following a mother's death or migration, remember this arrangement with appreciation. Indeed, one informant views that system of child care as a stronger situation than the one that leaves black children "hung in the system," unadopted or abused. But women who dared to keep their "bastard young 'uns" might find themselves ostracized, along with their children, by community members who demanded that their own daughters keep their distance.

Of course, boys and men also received explicit messages about their roles and responsibilities. Men operated socially in a separate sphere that excluded women and children, where they articulated and facilitated boys' development into adult men. Male respectability related to family responsibility. Men and boys could engage in drunkenness and bootlegging without falling into disrepute, as long as they attended to family needs. A man responsible for a young woman's pregnancy was expected to marry the mother of his child, and it was not unusual for the fathers of young brides to demand that grooms respect the women they married. Within African American communities, the harsh penalties for nonconformity were worse for females than for males. Outside, however, white authorities exacted severe punishment against black males accused of social or sexual "crimes," from "eye rape" (when a black man "looked at a white woman too hard") to sexual assault to consensual interracial affairs. Black girls and women's improprieties with white men might result in social death in the black community, but black boys' and men's interracial improprieties resulted in beating, castration, torture, and lynching.[1]

More so than dwelling on the dangers of nonconformity, narrators in this chapter talk about love, romance, marriage, childbearing, child rearing, separation and widowhood, and the joys and terrors of each. They speak of marriage as partnerships, where they paired with husbands to survive the present and prepare for the future, and of how they balanced their own attractions with their parents' expectations. Even as they detail the usual teenage tensions about dating, their recollections suggest that they understood why parents, fathers as well as mothers, were strict. With protection in mind, parents limited their daughters' exploits, not only as a way to preserve the family reputation, but also as a way to prevent their children from making bad choices. Georgia Bays remembers that after she informed her parents of her planned marriage—at age fourteen—her mother was silent for a week, absorbed in prayer and worry about her daughter's decision. When Julia Wells married, her father appealed to her new husband, insisting that he let her finish high school. In these instances, parents worried about the toll that adulthood would take on their young daughters, given the many additional responsibilities they would assume. After marriage, most rural women labored in their own households, performed unpaid farm work beside their husbands in the fields, and did poorly paid domestic labor for white families. Education neither changed nor shifted women's responsibilities. Professional women were still expected to manage their households, take primary responsibility for children, work outside the home, and actively serve their communities through churches and voluntary activities. Each role required ingenuity and enormous energy, traits magnified by the effort to balance employment and family.

Nevertheless, the ability to manage all of the responsibilities of womanhood provoked a sense of fulfillment, even as the interviewees describe the immense and unrelenting burdens they carried. Generally neither women nor men questioned the sexual division of labor. Failure to confront this division could imply subservience on the part of women, but that conclusion would be mistaken. In their interviews, women recount many acts of assertiveness, especially regarding intimate and familial relations. A number of interviewees address instances when they (or other women in their family) stood up to prevent or escape abuse or exploitation or to protect others from harassment. And, of course, marriage was not solely an economic arrangement. For most young women courtship was a source of positive attention that was not derived from their abilities as workers. Marriage also could establish a woman's respectability and could bring a reprieve from close parental supervision. Thus, despite their familiarity with the hardships that women could face as wives and mothers, young black women still held romantic ideals and looked forward to love and intimacy.

Finally, our interviews point to an additional female role often overlooked in historians' analyses of the past, reproductive labor, childbearing and midwifery. Narrators discuss abstinence and abortion as methods women employed to prevent pregnancies or to limit the size of their families. But women also describe large families; some of the narrators gave birth to more than twelve children, not all of whom survived.[2] Women recall their children with love but also remember the challenges of delivering infants and caring for babies in addition to their other tasks. Before the 1940s, most women gave birth at home, and in the earliest years, midwives delivered prenatal care and education as well as babies, an arrangement that began once a pregnancy was determined. At the time, midwives had little formal schooling or training. Rather, each practitioner had her own remedies for discomfort, herb and tonics that stopped a labor begun too early or induced labor when the baby was late. Only occasionally did they depend on doctors for backup in case of problems or emergencies. Practitioners passed on their knowledge and skill from grandmother to mother and, as an informant notes here, to daughter. Over time, as African American women gained access to hospitals, the role of midwife and the practice of midwifery declined. So it is with ambivalence that one informant describes the end of this distinctive relationship among women.

Georgia Bays was born in 1914 in Dentontown, in the hills of Mississippi. Married at age fourteen she gave birth to fourteen children, not all of whom lived to adulthood. Here Bays outlines the lessons she learned about the importance of respectability, hard work, and pragmatism about relationships. While these messages applied to boys as well, she also received preparations specific to girls, including how to avoid being labeled "fast," what marriage entailed, and what to expect during menstruation and childbirth. Her interview also highlights the unquestioned sexual division of labor within her household. She spent years working a "double shift," laboring in the fields alongside her husband, and then working in her own home and in the homes of white landowners.

My mother and my grandmother all raised me, and I'm not bragging, but just facts. My mother, Leila Denton, was just as sweet as peaches. My mother was so sweet, it was pitiful. She endured everything. She was really a nice lady. She worked hard and she didn't have but three children, two girls and one boy, and I was the oldest one. She was a church lady, and she worked in the fields, and her [wage] work was around white people, helping them doing things.

My daddy, he was a nice man. He drank whiskey. He would get drunk, but he never bothered anybody. But back in them days, when my daddy and his company drank, we didn't see them.[3] We would sneak and peep sometimes and see what they were doing, but let me tell you, you didn't let them see you sneaking and you didn't let them see you peeping. I never did hear my daddy cuss, and my mama, either. Nowadays, you can't even hardly push your children. [But] I got whoopings. The Bible says bend the sapling while it's little. Can't bend it when it get grown. And that's mostly what we're trying to do now. When they get grown, we start trying to bend them.

People would get together in those days, parents would come together about these children. All these children belonged to all of us. That's the way you were raised. Everybody raised me. All around my neighborhood and when I went to church, school, I better obey. My mother and my grandmother and my Auntie and other women, other neighbors' children going to school, passing folks' house, they'd stop and tell me how to carry myself. Well, I would listen and I learned to do it, because I was taught that at home and everywhere I'd go they were saying the same thing, so I couldn't get by.

When I had my monthly time,[4] I had a time. I cramped, I cramped. When I first started, my mother carried me to an old doctor, and he told her to give me a little wine cordial. It's kind of like dark vinegar. That's what my mama used to take all the time for when she started. It was good then for women to take. So when they changed life,[5] it wouldn't hurt them. I didn't take too much of that. She gave me a little turpentine. That was the biggest thing I'd take. My mother didn't allow me to take a bath until I got through my monthly period. I didn't think it was tough then, because that's the way we lived and we couldn't go anywhere to better it.

Around boys they'd tell me what to say and how to do. "Sit down. Don't flirt. Don't sit this way." When I sit down, my dress was going to be down, below my knees. "And when you sit down, Georgia, do this way. Put them legs together. You sure better straighten up when you're sitting with boys and men-folks," that's what Mama said. Some of the children's parents were buying them short stockings, cotton, with garters and a little flower on them. But Mama and Daddy wouldn't buy me this. My mother didn't allow me to take any presents, no money from anybody. My first little boyfriend, he bought me a pair of garters for a Christmas present, and you know what my mama did? Made me give them back to him. She said, "Do not ever take money from nobody, no boys, and don't ask folks for money, no menfolks. Don't ever." She told me, "If you take money, that's going to cause something else." My mother didn't allow me to whistle. She said nobody whistled but boys. "Don't ever whistle, Georgia, and don't ever swear." That's what she said. I'd sing and holler, but I couldn't holler too loud because that's too ugly for a girl. She wouldn't let me go to a dance. My baby sister, when she came along, she went to little picnics, but I didn't in my time. I could go to school when they were having a play or something like that, but she wouldn't let me go to these picnics. But I'm glad today that I didn't get to do like I wanted to do.

She made my dresses out of flour sacks. We'd buy flour in these white, big long sacks, and she'd make my dresses out of these old meal sacks and starch and iron them, gathered all way around and with little short sleeves. She'd starch and iron the little dresses and make my panties out of the same thing and my underskirts, and that's what I wore to church. That's the way I dressed. When I'd wonder why I couldn't get what the other girls had, she said, "Georgia, let me tell you something.

We ain't able. Learn to not want things that you see your neighbors' children wear. Don't worry about them, because you don't know how in the world they're getting their clothes." Oh, I'd lay around and cry. I thought it was the worse thing in the world. I couldn't go to town and I couldn't have a pretty dress. I didn't have lipstick, powder, grease to go on my hair but just lard out of the bucket, the hog grease. The things that I didn't have, I just had to wait, do without, and that's why I can do without now. That's why I can say it isn't going to kill you to do without.

I married when I was fourteen and my husband was twenty-two. What do you think about that? Wasn't I fast? I wasn't fast. In that day you could marry when you were ready. When we first met, my brother and I [had gone] to the well. I saw this man that Sunday walking up to his brother's house (that's where the well was), and my brother said, "Ooh, Georgia, who is that?"

I said, "I don't know, Bud, but he sure looks good to me." I said, "Look at that mustache." A black man, tall, slim, hair all fixed back. I said, "Mmm." Here I am, fourteen years old, hadn't stopped wetting in my drawers.[6]

But [after] I first met him, Mama didn't have trouble getting me to go get water. Before he came, she'd tell me, "Georgia, you come out of the field and cook dinner. Go get me some water."

I'd say, "Mama, wait a minute."

"Georgia, come get that water so I can finish your daddy's dinner. He'll be here directly."

Before I knew anything, Mama would [take] a switch just about that long, and come in there [and threaten to hit me], and I'd grab that bucket and go on to the well. But after I saw this man, boy, she didn't have trouble out of me getting water then.

I wasn't but fourteen years old, but I loved my husband since I first saw him. We were married sixty-five years, and I loved him and I stayed with him through thick and thin. It wasn't good all the time, but I stayed there. When I got ready to marry him, I was going to slip off from school. We had a little old country schoolhouse off in a little break somewhere, and the boys would slip out in the woods and send their partners up to the schoolhouse to get the girls to marry them. When it came time for me, my husband sent another boy in there after me. I said, "Uh-uh, I'm not going. Now, if he can't come and get me, I'm not going." [So] my husband asked me. My mama had told me all about running around or getting off too far with boys, so I wouldn't do that.

My husband had a minister to talk to him about married life, and generally men like that would tell menfolks how to do their wives. After we got married, a minister told him how to do me. I was young, and he told him how to do and when to do. He wasn't a church member. Anyway, he obeyed him. He took care of my body. There's a way a man can take care of your body, and I never have seen a rough day in my body. I'm not bragging, but just stating facts. I never have seen a rough day in my body. My back, my stomach never have worried me.

My daddy found out I was going to marry, he said, "Georgia, I want to talk with you before you go." He said, "Do you know how to treat Otis?"

I said, "Yes, sir." I was fast, because I would talk up. I put my little hand on my hip, and I said, "Yes, sir, I know how to treat him."

He said, "You don't know how to treat no husband."

I said, "Yes, I do."

He said, "How?"

I said, "Do Mama know how to treat you? I do like Mama done do you."

You know what he did? He had a handkerchief in his pocket, went back out and got it, and he walked off from me, wiping tears. He said, "Georgia, you don't have to go nowhere. Mama can cook you a little old dinner."

It was long about that Monday and I married that next Sunday. Mama sat at the fireplace that whole week, wouldn't say a word, wouldn't do nothing but get up and cook for us, and get back in that chair by that little old fire, wouldn't say a word to nobody, just get up and cook, get back in that chair. Finally, one morning I said, "Mama, what's the matter with you?"

She said, "Nothing." She never would tell me.

So on Saturday morning she got up, cooked breakfast, and she was stirring up them old cakes, killing them old hens, making stew, potato pies, cakes, and things for my wedding that coming day.

Then my husband came down that Saturday and asked me what I needed to wear. I told him I wanted a pair of black slippers, with the heel just about that high, and a pair of stockings and a dress. It was silk and wine-colored and trimmed in white, and he got me that to marry in.

And so Mama cooked that dinner, and it was years [later], after some of my children left, before I knew what she was worried about and wouldn't talk about. She was praying. She was sad because she knew I was crossing over into another world. After my first child, my aunt came and said, "Now, this is what your mama was worried about, was praying about, you marrying at an early age." But they didn't even try to keep me from marrying. They fixed me up and sent me on. And then one time after my husband and I had several little rounds, I came home. I walked in and Papa said, "What's the matter, Georgia?"

I said, "Otis hit me."

He said, "All right. Go sit down."

The next morning, he talked to me. He said, "Georgia, I ain't going to tell you to stay, I ain't going to tell you to go, but my door's open," and walked out. That's all. Well, I was a little jealous of Otis, because it looked like they cared more about Otis than they did me. They were crazy about that man. They would have nothing to do with our little ups and downs. All he would tell me was, "The door's open. I'm not going to tell you to stay," and wouldn't have nothing else to say.

[After I married we] worked in the fields. We chopped cotton. We lived on a man's place. He had about a ten-acre plot, and that's all we could work then, ten acres.[7] My first baby, I didn't have a nurse. [Otis took] some planks and built four legs to get that little pen up off the ground, and then put a bottom in it. It was just big enough for him to turn around and play. I'd put a sheet or quilt over the top and put it right in the middle of that field, that ten-acre block, so we could be passing him all the time, and we could holler at him and we could step across there and watch after him.

I'd go home at eleven o'clock and cook dinner. [Otis would] come out at twelve, and we'd eat. I'd have my baby's diaper tied up, it was an old sheet. My mama gave me some old sheets and I hemmed them. My first baby had no soap, no Johnson's Baby Powder. Castor oil is what I used on him. We made all his clothes. But Leila Mae, my oldest daughter, she [had it different]. The white folks wouldn't give us Johnson's Baby Powder, Johnson's Baby Oil. I couldn't buy it at the store. They wouldn't sell it to us. But the white folks got it for their babies. [But I got it for] Leila Mae. I had a Sears Roebuck catalog, and my husband gambled and he won some money. I got that catalog and I ordered her some Birdseye diapers and some Johnson's Baby Powder and soap to bathe in.

I had all of my children at home except three. When I first came down here to the Delta, I lived at Drew. Two were born in Drew, and I had a midwife there. When I moved on Mr. Mullins' place, he didn't allow any midwives on his place. He said that if something happened to me, I'd still have to go to the hospital. So he carried me to the hospital when I had the last two. They cost $80. They just put me to sleep, and when I woke up, here was the baby.

The Bible says you go through death six times, and that's right. My first baby, I was two days and a half having him, and the others, a day and a night, all like that. My first baby was a boy. I got sick on a Sunday night with him, and that baby wasn't born until Tuesday. But that midwife I had, she said that was all right, said I'd just have to learn, and that's what I did, had to learn how to bear pains. Stayed sick two days and a night, having hard pains. My mother and my Auntie had to stand and hold my hand. But that midwife knew what she was doing. The midwife would be there telling me how to do, "Georgia, give me that long breath. Now hold it. Hold it. Just hold it." You breathe this way, that's the way you push the baby out. You don't just give up and start crying and going on. See, that'll make you longer. If you hold it long enough, sometimes they give you a snuff bottle and let you blow in that, and that'll make them pains come on.

I had a pretty good time with Leila Mae. They were having services up there at the church, and the minister was coming to eat dinner. I remember my husband and this minister, they were sitting down eating. I was sitting at the table and having pains, and, boy, I wanted them to hurry up and go to that church. So they got through, and my husband told me, he said, "Georgia, I'm going. If you happen to start having pain, you turn this porch light on." That's when we first started having lights. He said, "I'm not going in church. I'm going to be around outdoors, and I'm going to be watching for this light." And sure enough, that night I took sick with Leila Mae and I stepped out there and turned that light on. The midwife didn't stay too far from the church, and he came by and got her. They came on there, walked, didn't have a ride, and Leila Mae was born the next day.

I had a grandfather who'd always come to see me all the time. That was my mama's daddy. He passed there while I was having Leila Mae. Mama went to the window and said, "Papa. Georgia said come see about her."

"Nope. She's going to be all right."

My grandfather didn't come to see me. Leila Mae was a month old before he came. No men would come around [during labor]. Only women in them days, honey. The husband of the house didn't go too far, but he wasn't around in there unless you called him for something. And those days, I didn't go anywhere. When I had a baby, I didn't go anywhere till that baby got a month old. A month old. I didn't go out of the house. If I went out of the house, I'd take a walk around the house and come back in the house. That's the way they trained me. You don't want to be around nobody. And no washing hair. And I couldn't get wet when it was raining. I had to go to the fields, but when it rained, I had the boss man to know I wasn't supposed to get wet, not for six months. That's the way we did. Then I'd go where I want to. I'd go out once a week and go to church. That's the way I was taught. I was a mother of fourteen, but I lost some. Well, it was an enjoyable thing to me. That's the way we all lived, see.

[On one place where we lived, I helped the owner's wife every day.] I cleaned house and cooked. That's all I ever did around white folks, clean house and cook. They didn't pay any money. No money, period. No money, period. Some of us colored people didn't have milk cows, didn't have hogs, like I told you. When we worked around white folks, we worked extra [for] meat and sometimes lard, a little sugar, a little meal, and flour. I'd spend all day just working for them. I'd leave home that morning, come back that evening. I'd get up and go milk the cow or churn for white people early in the morning, before I went to the field. I had to get up early, because I go to the field at six o'clock. So I went and churned and got some milk, an old ham bone, or something like that. Every day. On Saturday and maybe at night I'd do most of my work.[8] If I had to go work for her the next day, I'd do my work at night, because I wasn't going to bed early. No one but the children went to bed early. If she said, "Georgia, I want you to wash for me in the morning. I want you to churn for me in the morning," I'd go. I could say no, but that was what I wanted to do because I needed that. If you wanted an extra piece of money, you get up and go make it. They had it. I didn't. I didn't have a cow, I didn't have butter and eggs and maybe she'd give me something left over or cooked today. I'd put it in a bowl, bring it home, feed my children. At night after I come out of the field, I'd get my greens or my peas or whatever I'm going to [cook] for my children, my family, to get ahead of myself the next day so I can work for this. I pick it and I wash it and I put it on, while I'm running over there scouring up this and scouring up that and doing little things in the house for my children to enjoy. Then when I get up the next morning, all this is done. My dinner's near about done, while I run down to this white woman's house and churn that milk.

Many a morning, I'd get that butter and that gallon of milk and that pound of butter and beat it back home before my husband got up out of the bed. Sometimes I'd get paid off with molasses or they'd give me an egg, two eggs, or things like that, and so my dinner would be nearly done. When I'd get back before my husband got up out of the bed and my baby woke up, my children woke up, well, I'd fix them a little something, maybe some thickened gravy. We called it thickened gravy—take flour and pepper, pour water in it. Sometimes I didn't have nothing but salt and a little old taste of sugar. If I had a little old taste of sugar, I'd take it and brown it in a skillet, put some water in it to make it look like syrup, and feed them. If I didn't have a biscuit, fine. I'd cook that cornbread on top of that stove and give it to them, and they enjoyed it.

Then I'd be ready to go to the field. Dinnertime would come, I'd come out at eleven o'clock, and my vegetables would almost be done. By the time my husband got there at twelve, we were ready to eat. And then when he'd get through eating, we'd get ready and go to the field. Come out at six o'clock, cook a little supper, do what I have to do so I wouldn't be caught on a snap the next day. [After my children were grown] I didn't have to do quite as much. I just stopped work here this past year, and now I have plenty of time. Times got better. I got paid. I could buy my own eggs.

Susie Rolling was born in 1935 and grew up in Yazoo County, in rural Mississippi and left school after having a child at a young age. Her interview recounts the values that parents and other elders passed on to children, sometimes using harsh techniques in their attempts to ensure that young people would act with propriety. Rolling recalls, especially, the community's disapproval when she became pregnant as an unmarried teenager. Still, Rolling's family pitched in to raise her baby and she was able to continue her schooling.

Parents gave us values. They raised us with respect. There was no such thing as acting up in church. The parents didn't have to do anything, because the ushers got you. And talk back? No. You did not talk back. You know how children jump up and say, "No, she's just lying. I didn't do it." If you said that, you'd be swallowing teeth for days back there then. They just didn't allow it.

If you got pregnant at a young age, you got treated like they treat people with AIDS today.[9] You did not have any more friends. If you had a whole truckload of friends, if you got pregnant, the fellows fell off like apples. You didn't go to school, and the schoolchildren did not have anything else to do with you.

They didn't even talk to you. They weren't even allowed to talk to you. The young men had rules too. If he didn't get married or whatever, he wasn't to be seen back there, and your parents would go to that boy's parents' house and tell them to keep him from coming. He wouldn't dare be showing his face back at that house any more. There was no coming back.

I had some very good friends, Dorothy and Dallas and Minnie and Ella and Mary Ruth and Virg. But when I got pregnant, it was a lonely time for me, because I didn't have anybody. I didn't have anybody come. They used to meet up at my house, and there'd be a yard full of us out there. But after I got pregnant, that took care of that.

And I didn't go to school. My aunt was living in Detroit, and she tried her best to get her brother to let me come, because he told me he was going to take the baby anyway. She told him, "You all going to keep the baby anyway. Send her on up here and let me put her in school and she wouldn't have to miss too many months and she could go on and get an education." He said, "It took her nine months to get her education, so now that's what she's going to stick with," and he did not send me.

I remember [one time after] I married my first husband I was on the floor dancing. The next thing I looked, my uncle was coming in the door with a stick. I was married, had moved away from home, and somebody saw me on the [dance] floor [and] told him about it. The next thing I know he was coming up in there with a stick. He drew that stick back and told me if I didn't get off that floor [he'd beat me], and then my husband ran up and tried to say something, and he said, "The same thing I got for her, I got it for you."

Eighteen, nineteen, twenty, twenty-one, twenty-two, I wasn't thinking about doing anything to better myself. I was just running wild. That's the way I grew up, until I took hold of my life. I just asked God to lead the way, because I did not know how to do it, but I knew I wanted more for myself than what I had. I wanted more for myself, and He helped me to get from there to here. So that's about it.

Willie Ann Lucas was born in 1921 in Hughes, Arkansas, and grew up in a farming family. Her father worked as a logger while her mother worked as a school teacher, seamstress, and midwife. Lucas' mother had learned midwifery from her mother; and, in turn, Willie Ann trained as a midwife at her mother's side. She worked in Arkansas as a licensed midwife from 1945, shortly after she married, until 1972. Like her mother, Lucas combined her work as a midwife with paid employment as a teacher. Here Lucas discusses the work of a rural midwife and the way that role changed throughout the twentieth century.

Well, my grandmother was a midwife, my mother was a midwife, and I guess I took it up from my mother. But I had to go to school a year to learn all about it and everything, and after that I had to go out with an experienced midwife, which was my mother, to deliver babies. The first one that I went with her that she delivered, they named their child after me. My first delivery, the lady named it after me.

Yeah, it was a requirement that you go to school a year to learn it, so I did. Of course, that was way back in the '40s when I started. I think I got my license in '45. But back in those days, you delivered a baby for $5, and sometimes you didn't get that. I remember before then, in the late '30s and all, my mother would deliver babies and they would pay her with corn. Corn was 50 cents a bushel. Pigs were a dollar. They would pay her in corn, pigs, and you'd get a half a calf sometimes for $5, and that's the way she got her money most of the time for delivering babies back in the Depression days.

In my mother's days, if [women] got pregnant, they would come and ask you if you would deliver the baby for them at such and such a time [when] they thought they were going to deliver. But in my days, I had to have what they called a blue card. They would issue them to me from the health office, and I would give them to the patients when they came and engaged me to wait on them. They would have to take them to the doctor, and every time they went to the doctor, the doctor would fill out this card with their blood pressure and whatever else on there. And if they had any danger signals, like feet swelling or high blood pressure or something like that, they wouldn't recommend that they have a midwife to deliver. When they went for their last checkup [the doctor] would mark whether they're safe or unsafe for a midwife to deliver, and if anything happened, then he was responsible. He had to come if I called him. That was my backup. He had to come.[10]

But back in my mother's days, the midwife just delivered the baby. When World War II broke out, well, then doctors were scarce and everything else. So, therefore, a midwife was just like a doctor back in those days. She'd wake up twelve o'clock at night and hear this wagon coming down the road, and she'd just get on up out of the bed because there wasn't anywhere else for them to be going but coming after her. They'd come in the wagons. They didn't have any cars. She would come in sometimes when it was raining in the wintertime and her clothes would be frozen stiff on her. She'd be standing up there, and I said, "Oh, I'd never be a midwife." And bless goodness, before I knew it I was one. You had a briefcase to carry. In this briefcase, you carried everything necessary. You had a set of towels and you had masks. You were required to have a mask. If they didn't have anything to put on the child, you had something in your bag that you could dress the baby with. Back in those days, you had what they called a belly band. They don't use them anymore, and that's why you see so many babies have a hernia, because the band kept the navel from protruding. And you had a pan and scissors. You carried your own pan because that's what you had to sterilize your scissors with, and you would put that on and boil your scissors and sterilize them so when you cut the navel cord, umbilical cord they call it, it wouldn't set up an infection or anything. And you had to carry this tape, umbilical tape, that you'd tie the cord with before you cut it. But they didn't require you to use gloves. Because one thing, you didn't do any examining. You didn't give any medicine. You weren't allowed to give medicine.

The most difficult deliveries were breech births. Breech is where they come backwards. Instead of head first, they come folded up and their rear first, and that was the most difficult and the most dangerous. [Sometimes midwives] used quinine, if women were in labor and having them little old piddling pains. They'd give them some quinine; it would cut them off if it wasn't their time.[11] And if it was their time, they would go ahead on and make the labor pains come closer and harder and they would go on and have the baby. Some midwives would give the patients castor oil, but I never did that. That's about all they were allowed to give, you know, is something like that. Of course, when I started, I learned a few more little techniques, things you could do—using a hot towel to keep [the birthing mother] from tearing, things like that. I got my license for a practical nurse, and that helped me out a whole lot, too, with my midwifery.

When I started doing midwife work, we had telephones. And then when they called and asked me if I would wait on them, I would tell them you have to come see me and I have to talk to you and I have to give you a blue card and you will have to take it to the doctor every time you go. After the doctor examines you and everything, fill it out. He would put the date on there and everything when you visited him. So that was the difference, you know. I had to have proof and my mother didn't. [Women] just would come to her house and say, "I'm pregnant, going to have a baby, and I'd like to get you to deliver it for me," and that was it. Some doctors, when World War II was going on, they sent them to my mother. They would send them to her to deliver. I guess they didn't have any money and they weren't going to be paying. And I had some to do me that same way here in Brinkley. They owed the doctor and the doctor said he wasn't going to wait on them because they owed him, they didn't pay. "They didn't pay me; maybe they'll pay you," he said. And then they would call me and ask me if I wanted to wait on them. And I have some that still owe me. At that time, it wasn't but $15.

Most of my deliveries were at home, and the majority were from rural areas. I delivered for both black and white. I delivered quite a few white. But like I say, it was the poor whites that didn't have much money, not rich whites. And the same way with the blacks. The rich blacks could afford to pay. Well, they paid, and so did the whites. But I delivered a lot of white babies.

To me, it was just natural. It wasn't anything. I didn't get afraid, nothing scared me or anything. I could still be doing it, but they got all these health clinics now and they wrote me a letter and they said they wouldn't renew my license because they have enough facilities to take care of the OB patients. And so that's why I'm not doing it today. I would still be doing it. I loved it. It didn't bother me one bit.

Catherine Wilson was born in 1925 and grew up in First Ward, a black community in Charlotte, North Carolina. She recalls a "very good life" at home where she was raised by her parents and surrounded by eight siblings. Her father was a brick mason employed by a building company and her mother was a homemaker. Her siblings had few occupational choices—her oldest sister worked as a maid, making enough money to send the next youngest girl to school; and "then we just passed it right on down to the next one." Thanks to their generosity, Wilson got an education and became a social worker. In her interview, Wilson describes what happened to African American girls who got pregnant before they married. Her recollections echo those of Susie Rolling (page 62), emphasizing the social stigma that unmarried mothers faced, and the ways that family and community nonetheless cared for the children of such mothers. Wilson also describes how adoptions and foster care arrangements overseen by public social service agencies gradually replaced the informal arrangements that had prevailed within African American communities. As a trained social worker, Wilson was thereby responsible for facilitating this transition from informal to formal means of caring for children, a change she considers detrimental to black families.

Black girls [who got pregnant were ostracized more or less.] "That's a bad girl." They went away and had babies. They would have to leave school. Some of them probably did go to school later, many years later, but you didn't get back into the public schools. If you got pregnant in college you got sent home. At Livingstone,[12] a girl whose boyfriend was there got pregnant and this was this young man's senior year just before graduation and she wrote President Trent that she was pregnant and had to drop out of school. He called [the boy] in and said, "Well, you ruined that girl's life and you will not graduate from here. I want you off of this campus." And he had to leave and he did not get to graduate. But you had no home for [pregnant] black girls. They kept their children and somebody in the family would rear those children.

My mother was born in Lancaster, South Carolina, but her mother died when she was about six weeks old, I believe. So she was reared by people who were not really related. But you know during that time blacks took in blacks; you became a part of that family. That was what you called the extended family and it was truly the extended family. People never gave them up for adoption either. The adoption program was not designed for blacks. It was designed for white girls who had babies born out of wedlock so nobody would ever know. The Florence Crittenton Home[13] was about four blocks from our house, in the black neighborhood right there in First Ward. That's where white girls when they got pregnant came. We didn't know what the Florence Crittenton Home was, but we saw pregnant girls because every evening they'd get out and walk and here they were all pregnant and then it dawned on us, this is what this is. They're putting them over here but you see they were shielding them. There were no Crittenton homes for blacks.

I worked at only one place for thirty-seven years and that was at the Mecklenburg County Department of Social Services. I started working there in January of 1949. I was in different programs during that tenure but I enjoyed it. Now we were segregated when I went there. Blacks did not have white clients there. We only did blacks. But whites could do both. As blacks we had to have some form of social work training before we were hired. But whites could come right out of college and some came right out of high school and got jobs doing that.

I was the first black in the county that became the program administrator of the child welfare department. I had seventy-two people in my department. I used to be unsure about integration but it didn't take me long after I got into that department and I was sure about how I felt about it. When I got in there we had [black] children who had been in foster care, hung in the system, and they were telling me that nobody wants them, they don't have any relatives. Until one day I got enough of it. I was working on foster home licensing and relicensing and this child's name popped up and I said to the supervisor, "I had this case a long time ago. What's going on here?"

"Oh, they don't have anybody."

I said, "You mean to tell me that all the family got killed in an airplane or in a car wreck at one time?" So I got the name of trying to be smart. But [African Americans] started giving our babies up for adoption, and a lot of them never got adopted because we didn't want them. Well, I won't say [black people] didn't want them, but the guidelines that they put for adoption for whites were the same for blacks. Now how many blacks would have a bank account of X number of dollars, have education, before you could adopt a child? So consequently [the children] were hung in the system because [black potential parents] couldn't meet the guidelines.

Florence Borders was born in 1924 in New Iberia, a rural Louisiana community, and grew up in New Orleans. Here she discusses her experiences on black college campuses—first as a student at Southern University in Scotlandville, Louisiana, in the 1940s and later as an employee at Bethune-Cookman College from 1947 to 1958. Her recollections emphasize the impact of World War II on women's experiences and how that war transformed gender roles and the regulations that guided life on historically black college campuses. Borders' story emphasizes the support women were expected to give husbands but also the importance of women learning independence, given high mortality rates in black families.

My college years exactly coincided with the years of World War II and the most striking event of my freshman year was the bombing of Pearl Harbor. That changed the whole college experience for all of us who were in college at that time, because once that happened, of course, the men on our campus began voluntarily to leave because they knew that they were going to be in any first draft, once it was put into effect. And they expressed the feeling that they would have a head start if they would just go on and volunteer because some of them had ambitions of going to Officers Candidate School, and they would have those few months ahead of some of the people who would be coming in later. So despite the advice of some of our faculty people who had been veterans of World War I, men left the campus wholesale before even we broke for Christmas which was just a few weeks more. They were being advised to just stay and finish out the semester and with the older wiser heads saying, "The war will end at some point. It will not last forever, and you might as well finish this semester so when you come back, you can begin at that point." Well, they chose not to listen and just every day we would see the young men dragging their trunks across campus to get to a point at which a taxi could assist them in getting the trunks to the station. And many of those young men, we never saw again. A lot of the girls cried. Sometimes because the young men involved were their boyfriends, but [also] because they had then begun to feel that this was a separation. This was a good-bye and our paths might never again cross. And so instead of all the joy that I had expected for my freshman year of college, within a few more weeks the country was at war.

I had [gone to] church that Sunday. And when I came back my roommate's ears were glued to the radio and as I came in bubbling with news of what had happened on the trip, she was saying, "shhhhhh. The Japanese have bombed Pearl Harbor." Well, not many of us had ever heard of Pearl Harbor. We had heard of the Philippines. We had heard of Manila. But Pearl Harbor was just unknown to us by name at that point. But long before we finished that freshman year in college we knew the geography of the Philippines. We knew Corregidor and Bataan,[14] and everything that was connected with the war, and we were steadily praying for the tide to turn, because at first, of course, [the Americans] were definitely the underdogs. And we started learning the map of the Philippines and of the near east, the far east, and everything else, because once the letters started coming from the young men, again there were places that they were mentioning that were unknown to us.

But that changed the way college was for me for my freshman year, although we had nice little activities. We still had our dances and even after football games the dances turned into formals and truck loads of GIs would be invited from the Air Force base which was near us and from Camp Plauche and Camp Leroy Johnson here in New Orleans. It wasn't that we did not have men to dance with, we probably had more men than we would have had if the war had not occurred and the guys had remained on campus. But it was just that they tried to make everything so special because they began to feel that this might be the last special thing some of these young men would experience. So we dressed in long formals for what would have been just a sock hop after a football game and tried to make each thing special. After the war, many of the girls married returning solders who would have been upperclassmen, and who would have gone by the time they would have reached the stage that they were in the normal course of events.

When I went to work at Bethune-Cookman College,[15] I married a returning veteran who was in college continuing his education under the GI Bill,[16] and most of the young women on that faculty married returning veterans who [were coming back to school]. And a lot of the codes for behavior between faculty members and students had to be adjusted because there had once been a no fraternization policy between faculty and students. The first thing these returning GIs felt had to go was some rule telling them that they could or could not date certain people who might be the people of their choice, and they had a strong argument. They had just gone through a whole lot of stuff for the right to choose their mate, and it didn't matter to them if that mate happened to be on the faculty. So nobody really said that rule was abolished, but it was merely ignored. And several of us at Bethune-Cookman College at that time married returned GIs who continued on through their college and graduated, as my husband did. But that was one of the ways that the war had affected us.

By the time I finished library school [at Southern] the war had ended and the veterans were returning to college campuses en mass and staff had to be increased. So I could have had my pick of jobs just about, because librarians were very much in demand, and so I chose to go to Bethune-Cookman College because of Mrs. Bethune.[17] I looked forward to meeting her, working with Mrs. Bethune, and being able to do things with her and help promote programs which she was interested in implementing. And Mrs. Bethune could work four or five secretaries to a frazzle. So everybody who could push a typewriter had to help get out correspondence and things when she had big projects underway. And she sat and talked to us about her dreams for young black women, and one of them was to see more of us enter into politics. Oh, I remember how much she encouraged me. She was really a very family-oriented person despite all of her other outside involvements, as the president of an insurance company even after she had retired from the college as administrator.[18] And she had a number of things to do keeping the National Council of Negro Women going and encouraging the women at Bethune-Cookman to see that there was an active chapter right at her own doorstep. All of this occupied a lot of her time, but she was nevertheless still a very strongly family-oriented person.

And she was very mindful of women. She did not want women to have to give up their professions because they had families. She wanted to see us married, and raise families, and still work at whatever it was we chose to do. And the thing that impressed me when I went to work at Bethune-Cookman

College was the large number of women who headed departments. But then when I thought about Mrs. Bethune having started the whole thing, it wouldn't then seem so strange that she put confidence in women. The Dean of Instruction was a woman. The head of the Education Department was a woman. I mean, women really were in the leading administrative positions after the president and that was true for many of the departments. I was frequently offered the opportunity to work elsewhere at larger salary increments, but I felt if Mrs. Bethune had made the kind of sacrifice she had made to do what she had done, I could give up a few little old luxuries and make whatever contribution I could make to help further her work. And I think that a lot of people that worked there had that kind of mentality. We knew that we could make more money somewhere else, but that wasn't why we were in the profession. And so, you know, we were getting along. We weren't starving and we weren't candidates for welfare.

But I knew that my husband's eventual goal was to attend Meharry,[19] and when he was ready to go, despite Meharry's advice that wives and children stay home, I joined him and took the children. We all left and went to Nashville. I was working at Tennessee State and the women had a little group. Many of the women of the fellows who were enrolled in Meharry worked and they called it the PHT Club—putting hubby through. Putting hubby through. It was really a way of having one income continue. I worked and that maintained us on a daily basis. I wasn't unique in that. Unless you came from a professional family with somebody who could afford to send you to medical school, you usually had wives who worked.

But he died before he completed his degree. He died in '59 and I had the two boys who were nine and ten and the girl who was three. He suffered from a coronary embolism which resulted from his pushing his car up a hill in Nashville. And it happened that my husband was buried on his thirty-third birthday. So it was a really tough period for me, but I often think about how my mother helped me. Because every time I'd sit down and start feeling sorry for myself, she would say to me, "You might as well get up and go on with your life. Your great-grandmother was widowed at twenty-seven with more children than you and much less education and she made it. So you ought to be able to make it, but you aren't going to be able to make it if you're going to sit around pitying yourself." So I said, oh well, I guess I'll go ahead on and get a job near my family at least. So I did.

Margaret Sampson Rogers was born in 1939 Wilmington, North Carolina. Her mother, who had run away and had a baby out of wedlock at a very young age, was determined to protect Margaret from a similar fate. Here Rogers explains the lessons her mother tried to pass on about the people she should associate with and those she should avoid. Rogers' mother expressed many prejudices about skin color, morality, and respectability that her daughter challenged. Rogers describes how her own behavior did and did not conform to her mother's admonitions and how she understood the expectations put on black women under segregation.

Our black people are very prejudiced. They always have been and my mother was one. She was a very fair-skinned lady and she often made the remark that she didn't like black people. The only reason she wore black shoes was they went with her outfit. So she was very particular about with whom I could associate. Because she would say, "well, you don't need to associate with that person because his mother's not married," or "her mother's not married," or "they drink a lot. You don't need to be with these people." She was a very bigoted individual, very bigoted. When I got ready to get married, she told me I had to be careful whom I married because [otherwise] I could have children that looked like ink spots. But this was stuff that went in one ear and out the other. I couldn't see that. I never could see that. But she was very bigoted. People would tell her, "I waved at you when you were driving down the street the other day."

She'd say, "Well, child, I didn't see you. I was just looking straight ahead. I didn't see a soul." Yes, she did. Yes, she did.

My mother was not welcome in neighbors' homes. But my father was welcome in everybody's house. She was very bigoted that way and I didn't like it and that was one of the [issues between us]. I felt that we were having enough problems with the whites. Why do we have to have this problem within the race? The fair-skinned blacks, especially the fair-skinned blacks with long hair, were very much disliked by the darker skinned. They didn't like to associate with them and a lot of them were very nice people. They really were. But it was jealousy. It was perpetuated down through the generations that the lighter, the fairer were the more intelligent, the more talented, and that's why you had a lot of blacks who tried to pass. Because if you were dark you weren't given the same considerations. And somehow it just kept going and then the children would pick it up from the adults, and it just kept going and going even to today. In some cases the teachers played favorites because of color. The teacher played favorites because of occupations. The doctor's children and the lawyer's children were treated differently. The very fair-skinned were treated differently. In a lot of instances, when they had the beauty pageants within the schools and whatever, the fairer skinned girls were usually the first ones considered. It just went on and it wasn't something that any thought was given to. It was just an assumption. This is the way it's going to be.

If you became pregnant that was the end of your education. They didn't want anybody to see you. Folks didn't want to associate with you because [you would be] considered [a] bad girl. See, it was still a double standard. These same people who were talking about what this girl who's pregnant had done, in a lot of instances they were doing the same thing. Having sex wasn't the problem. She got caught. But in a lot of instances she wouldn't have gotten pregnant if somebody had told her how not to. But you couldn't during that time. I couldn't ask my mother anything about sex. Because every question I asked her I got slapped in the mouth. So then you had to find an adult that you could go to to ask who would tell you what was right and what was wrong. I had to ask my librarian at high school. I used to call her my second mom. She had a miscarriage and I was in the tenth grade, but I had no idea what this was. I knew she was pregnant because I had seen [her] abdomen in [her] clothing. But when I went [to the hospital] it wasn't there. So the first thing I wanted to know was well, does it go down immediately, is it like a balloon? Because I had no idea what happened to the abdomen once the baby was born. I really didn't know how the baby came out unless she had an operation. So I asked her and she would sit and talk to me.

My mother ran away from home when she was twelve. She got married and she had a baby when she was thirteen. Once I became twelve I was not allowed outside after dark. I had to be home, in the house, before street lights came on. That included the years I was in college, until my senior year, and I had just had it. I sat on the porch at the people's house across the street and let the street lights come on. I just simply refused to be home before those street lights came on. I was just too old for that. My mother talked about people having children and not being married, people having sex. She never used the word sex, of course, oh, no. If you said that you got slapped in the mouth. The girls were called dirty and no good and they usually would say, "Well, you know, the apple doesn't fall far from the tree. The mama is no good; therefore, the daughter can't be no good." You know, if one person in the family did something then everybody in the whole family was blamed for it. And so my parents picked who I could talk to. When people called on the phone, they had to know who it was and if it was somebody from a family they didn't want you to talk to, I couldn't talk to them. But if I had to talk to them without my mother knowing, that's what I did. I just don't see it. But you fought that Jim Crow stuff on both sides. It wasn't just on the white side. That's what is so sad.

One of my dear friends lived on the street around the corner from me but our back yards connected. But [my mother said] I couldn't go to her house because her mother was not married, and she had a bunch of "bastard young 'uns." So I played with Hattie anyway. Whenever my mother left me home and she went out in the car, then I'd go out in the back yard, hop the fence, and go play with Hattie. And the kids would whistle and let me know when they saw that Buick coming, and then I'd scramble back in the back yard and when she came home I'd be out in the back yard playing.

And then there were people she wanted me to associate with. What she kept bringing up to me was the fact that I was an illegitimate child. I was constantly told this. This was something that black people did, too, which does not help the children. But she was telling me I was going to grow up and have a bunch of "bastard young 'uns" just like my mama. So being as stubborn as I was, I figured out there was one sure way not to have any and so I didn't have sex until I was married. But it was not because I did not want to. Let's clear that fact up. It was that I was so stubborn and determined that the only way to prove to my mother I was not going to [get pregnant] was not to have sex.

I dated a guy in college[20] for about four months before I found out he was white. I didn't know. I would date the service men. They could take me to the movies. They had the money. A jealous classmate found out he was white and told the administration. This was during the 1950s. They called me in and said, "You get rid of him in twenty-four hours or we're expelling you from school." And if I had been expelled and sent home, my mother would have killed me graveyard dead. There was no doubt in my mind, this lady would have killed me. And I did not have the nerve; I could not find it within me to go to this boy and tell him the school says I can't date you anymore because you're white. I thought he was Puerto Rican, really, is what I thought. He was well liked. At homecoming he sat with the president and his wife during the game. He would be on campus after curfew. He was a well-educated person. He was stationed at Fort Bragg.[21] He was in the Army, staff sergeant. So once people found out he was white, I could not come right out and tell him that these people are so prejudiced, they say I can't date you. So I told the guy that I couldn't see him one day, that I had to work. He was on campus anyway. When I saw him, I grabbed a buddy and we walked past and I was all over this guy like white on rice, you know, because I knew it would upset my boyfriend. I kissed him on the jaw, you know. And so my boyfriend got upset and he called me later and was asking me about it. And I said, "Hey, well, you know, that's how the cookie crumbles." It was a mess. But I knew that I could not bring that white man home. I knew I could not let the school expel me for dating this white man because my mom would not have allowed it. She didn't like dark-skinned black people but there was no way in the world I could bring a white man in that house. Not and ever plan to come back in there.

It was expected, and it still is to a certain degree, that a woman has three or four jobs. She works out of the house. She's the maid, cook, and chief bottle washer. She is expected to be there for the husband whenever sex is required, whether she wants it or not. That's the third job. Okay. Then if there are errands, whatever, take care of the kids on top of all the other stuff. So you have a good four or five jobs that you do and it is expected that you do this. Your husband expects that you do this, white or black. [But if you were black,] then you worked for the whites. You did everything that they wanted done. So then that added another job. And if you said, "Well, this is Miss Ann's house, why can't she...?"

"Oh no, white women don't do that."

"Well, why don't white women do that?"

"White women just don't scrub the toilet."

And I want to say, "But you use the toilet. If you use the toilet then you can clean it." So you had the discrimination, the belittlement, I guess, from both sides, and then as a black woman you were made to feel that you really weren't that good because you're going to be asked to do something that a white woman would never think of doing. So it perpetuated itself and in a lot of ways it was just always there and it just depended on how you decided to deal with it. And I just decided to deal with it right out in the open.

Julia Wells was born in 1936 and raised in Sumter County, South Carolina. She characterized her childhood as one of "extreme poverty." After her mother died, Wells was raised by her grandmother. She chose to marry when she was still in high school, a wedding that occurred on the day her husband shipped off to military service. During her husband's absence, Wells worked her way through college, and later returned to teach at the high school from which she had graduated. Here she recalls the tragedies that shaped her life as a child and the lessons that she learned from her grandmother. She also recalls the circumstances of her marriage when she was seventeen and how the lack of access to birth control impeded women's opportunities for employment, thereby constraining families that relied on women's income. Like Margaret Rogers in the previous interview, Wells describes how women's appearance, especially skin color, was treated within her community. Also like Rogers, Wells' interview reveals generational tensions about respectability and how younger women pushed back to create their own cultural mores.

My mother died in childbirth when I was three, having my baby brother. And my mother and father were very young. I was their second child. And they were sharecroppers and when she had the problem birth, the midwife noticed that something was going wrong with the pregnancy. They sent my daddy to town to get a doctor but he didn't get back until the next day with the doctor and she was dead by then. And I've heard the stories over and over of how his mother took me and my sister in her arms and how people got the baby and wrapped him and took him away. For the first six months after she died, my sister and I and the newborn baby lived with my daddy's mom.

My mother's mother was the third wife of an old man who I believe was nearly eighty when we were born, but my mother's mother was a fairly young woman. She could not hear, was hard of hearing. That was a phrase they used. And after we became adults, my sister and I, we came to realize that most people thought she was what they called "off," not really all there mentally. But she is the most significant other in my life and this is where poverty comes in. Out in the country with my daddy's people there were always a lot of people around because there were children and grandchildren and everything. And I think my daddy and my mama sold liquor. And my daddy would take my sister and me around with him from one liquor house to the other. But I can remember one day my mother's mother came out to get us and it was an argument to no end between her and my father's mother. She was saying things like, "your son killed my daughter and I'm not going to let you kill her children. These are my children." But she took us up and took us back home with her. Well, she lived with this husband who was almost eighty then and he had a lot of extended family there. He had children and grandchildren from those second and third marriages, but he was a man of some means. In fact, he owned some of the choicest property in Sumter. We went to live with them over here in the Swan Lake area and he had three little houses and some of the relatives lived in the others.

We weren't there a few months before my grandmother left him. The thing that really made her leave him was he came home one night. On Saturday nights he'd come home singing. He was really a fun person. And she'd made some bread that smelled real good and she sat it on the window sill to cool, and we were going to have that with peaches or milk or something. And when he got home instead of coming in the house he walked around the house and he thought it was a joke, he chewed tobacco and he spit right in the middle of this freshly baked [bread]. After that argument we left. I mean it wasn't any violent and terrible abuse and that's the closest thing I've come to seeing abuse. But she was a woman I think who had a hard life and had strived for perfection a little bit too much. You know, the whole marriage was crummy. Then her only daughter, who she loved so much, somebody married her and, in her mind, killed her.

Now this is why I say she was one of the smartest persons. I learned from her that you don't take abuse from any man. He verbally abused her. We never saw them fight. But she left him and moved down to the woods with my sister and me when I was about five and my sister seven. After my grandmother walked away from this husband who had a decent house, land, and everything up there, my grandmother, my sister and I lived there in a one room house, no toilet. She made a living doing domestic work in the various people's houses. But I was trying to make a point that we were very, very poor, and we were poor because she walked away from him and stayed down in the woods with us.

Grandma Laura,[22] the woman who kind of really shaped our values, she knew everything. She had all the answers to teen pregnancy. She had all the answers to AIDS and everything, you know. And she really was a feminist in a way because after she moved us back there in that hole, she [figured out how to] cut through the tape and get an allotment made out to us from my daddy's military service so she wouldn't have to be up there begging his wife, our stepmama, to support us. And just looking back on that, that was really interesting. And then she would let us sometimes babysit. We were in a neighborhood where there was nothing but whites, people who were from Shaw Air Base mostly.[23] It was an area where people from Shaw rented, but then it was a segregated Army so you're really talking about white people. But she never would let us go babysit alone. Two of us would have to do it, because she didn't want any sexual molestation. She was a smart woman, I'm telling you.

She did domestic work and she did field work. Now I can remember how she cussed this man out when he wanted us to start school late and stay home and pick his cotton. I mean my grandmother had a mouth. She smoked a pipe, by the way. She was a petite woman. Very chocolate and dark. And she could tell us these stories about how "cleanliness is next to godliness. It's no sin to be poor but it is a sin to be nasty." She could tell us how black people always had time to sit on the front porch and the dishes are in the sink dirty. But she was a very cultured woman, now, even with all of this. On summer evenings my grandma and my sister and me, we would walk up to the road and we'd get right on the edge of where the whites had a pavilion and a jukebox and they'd be dancing in their swimming suits, and it was just a grand hangout for hillbilly white people. She'd walk up there with us, spread out our stuff, open our box of cookies and milk, and we'd sit up there and listen to all the big band music on the jukebox until we got tired, and about ten o'clock at night we'd go home. That's the way we were entertained.

Coming up then, during segregation, black girls had to suffer the humiliation of being black and dark-skinned. Even when Wells was dating me he would say, and these were jokes, "I'd rather see a black girl"—that means dark-skinned—"lying in a ditch with her leg broken than to see a red bone[24] with a run in her stockings." That was supposed to be funny. "If you black, get back. If you're brown, stick around. If you're white, you're all right." When I was in high school every year there would be the Irish festival parade in Sumter. That was the white parade. But they would let the black high school have a float. And custom had it that the smartest four girls in twelfth grade would ride on that float. When I got to twelfth grade all the smartest four girls were my color and darker and those people changed the rules and went to ninth grade and got the cream-colored girl and put one gorgeous-looking cream-colored curly-haired girl on the front. Oh, that thing has worried me 'til this day. I went to the blackest teacher we had, and she loved me to death. She gave the dark-skinned children the lead in the senior class play to try to make up for it. Those were things we had to live with. Grandma Laura would tell my sister and me that we had pimples on our skin because we had bad blood in us, and it was that white blood that came from my grandmother, my daddy's family. My daddy was a very nice man as far as I'm concerned. He was the one who made my sister and me feel beautiful when the whole world was telling us we were not. Oh, my God, he'd call us the prettiest children in the world.

I went to Lincoln High School in Sumter. That's where I met Wells. They got school buses the first year I went to Lincoln, so he was a school bus driver when I got there. And they drafted him. He was in twelfth grade when I was in eleventh grade, and they were drafting for the Korean War. When he got drafted, he had the idea to elope. It wasn't my idea. [On the day] he got drafted he took the kids to school on the bus that morning, went home and got his daddy's car, and we went down to the courthouse. And he told me to tell the people I was eighteen, to lie. He got in there and said he was nineteen.

I said, "Well, he told his right age, I'm going to give mine."

And the man said, "Sorry, you've got to get your parent's permission."

I said, "Okay, we can't get married." But Wells was a smart sucker. We walked two blocks down the street, went in the post office, and he wrote my daddy's name on that thing, and we went straight back and the man married us. And as soon as we walked out of the office, here came my daddy walking up the courthouse steps, chewing on a toothpick. Somebody had called him and told him we were up there. But he did not kick up a fuss. He shook his finger in Wells' face and said, "you'd better let her finish high school." Anyway, that summer he was in basic training down in Alabama. Gone to Alabama and I had visions of traveling all around the world with my soldier husband. All I wanted was a house full of children and that's how I wanted to get out of Sumter. But Wells was thinking about what my daddy said, and he sent me back home to finish high school. So he was in Korea when I graduated from high school. And back then birth control pills had not been invented yet. So Gloria was at my graduation, my oldest daughter. He spent something like fifteen months over there. And when he came back [from Korea] it was 1953 and I'll be darned if he wasn't back a month before I was pregnant again.

My sister took care of my children while I lived in a teacher's cottage and taught at Roberts High School during the year [after I graduated from Morris College].[25] The teacher's cottage[26] had three bedrooms. And another girl who had finished Morris College, she had a job down there too and we had a little room together. [Living at] the cottage was my first encounter with lesbians. There were six women who lived in the house now. One was me, one was that other girl, and then there were four other women. I used to come home every weekend because I had a family. But one weekend I didn't come home and I noticed they were having a party. The music was getting louder and there were a lot of people coming; they were all women. Okay, that was fine too. But I was standing there with my coat on [ready] to walk outside because it wasn't my party and all these women were older than me. And somebody came up to me and said, "Wells, come on, let's dance." That still didn't strike me. And then she said, "Take off your coat so I can feel you."

And I kind of looked around and I said, "Oh my God." So I decided to go visit somebody who lived nearby for the whole party.

She said, "That whole house is full [of lesbians]. You mean you didn't know that?" Anyway, that was real interesting. And after that year I came here and I taught at Lincoln where I graduated high school.

By 1964 I was in higher education and I was there simply because of sexism. In South Carolina they had laws on the books that paid male teachers a thousand dollars a year more because they were head of household. They had laws on the books that said if you became pregnant you were supposed to inform your principal before you started showing. And certainly not later than the fifth month, [you had to] resign your position, go home, take care of your baby for a year, and then when the baby was a year old you could come back and compete for a position in the public school system. Now this is no joke. Okay, remember birth control pills had not been invented.[27] So I was twenty when I graduated college. I had two children when I graduated college because Wells came back from over there in 1953 and in 1955 I had the second child. And when the third child was born, I was teaching at Lincoln. The baby came in August but, being very thin and tiny, I managed to make it to the end of the [school] year. And of course I told the principal, but I had to resign. The baby came in August; school started in September. I could not go back to work. At the end of the year I went back and applied for my job and I went back to the public schools and I taught from 1960 to 1964 and got pregnant again. That rule was still in when I got pregnant again. And by this time I was chairman of the English department of the school. And I'll never forget the ten women who were there, most of them had been my teachers. They liked me a lot. One of them offered to pay for an abortion for me so I wouldn't have to leave. And I can tell you there are women who were my friends when they were teenagers, but they're dead today because they wanted those jobs and they'd go to them back alley abortionists to get those abortions and they're dead. One best friend had a sister who was a nurse somewhere up north, and she'd go up there and her sister would give her [an] abortion so she wouldn't have to lose her job. So these are experiences that I've lived through.

CHAPTER 3

You Are All Under Bondage, Which Is True: Working Lives

"I knew I wasn't ever going to be rich. I just wanted a good education so I could get a good job, a better job, paid more than what my mother was making," Rodie Veazy said in her interview. "But I have worked as hard as my mother," she concluded. Here Veazy and other narrators tell about what work meant, what it was like, and how it changed, or didn't, across the generations of women in their families. Work was one of the defining features of black women's lives in the Jim Crow South, and all of our informants were employed in at least one job throughout their lives, while also carrying responsibilities for work in their own homes.

Given the constancy of work, our narrators realized the tensions between economic and educational imperatives. But learning to work was as important in African American children's preparation for adulthood as formal schooling, paving the way for future employment. On farms, girls shouldered responsibility for household chores but like their brothers, they also learned how to plant, hoe and weed, and pick cotton, tie tobacco, or shake peanuts alongside their elders.[1] Girls learned from older women how to perform the domestic chores which transferred to wage work and marriage. Lessons about dealing with difficult white folk blended with lessons about seasoning and healing. By age seven African American girls were prepared to seek paid employment—light cleaning, yard work, delivering papers, gathering coal, or selling farm products—to provide cash for family needs. And by their preteen years many girls had gone to work in private homes for white families.[2]

As children grew older, their work expanded in hours and strenuousness, cutting short the times they had no responsibilities. Young people replaced school and play with employment as they neared their teenage years. Children seldom kept their wages but instead contributed to the family coffers from which adults paid for food, clothes, or school tuition for other siblings. Older siblings sometimes discontinued their own schooling so that younger brothers and sisters could attend school. Even then, most girls who attended school, even private school, worked before and after the school day. They spent summers employed full time in fields, factories, and homes. The requisite and constant demands for their labor denied many young men and women the opportunity to pursue—or even consider—careers or employment based on personal preference or individual interest. Instead, economic privations forced most black folk to take whatever jobs they could find. There is no doubt that prioritizing work over education compromised the ability of many black southerners to prepare themselves for desirable or lucrative positions, should they ever become available. As our narrators explain, they had few choices: "doing better" or "doing well" meant finding enough work to prevent hunger, to buy clothing, to educate children.

Yet each generation sought to improve the circumstances of the next. Mindful of history, our interviewees frame their hopes and measure their experiences relative to the opportunities available to their parents and grandparents. Rather than dwell on their lack of opportunity relative to their white counterparts, narrators quickly remind us that bondage was not so distant for black people, and that the further African Americans moved from slavery, the greater their freedom to leave unsatisfactory jobs. Few of our informants voice complaints about the amount of physical strain entailed in their work. They frequently express pride in their speed, endurance, and resourcefulness. They speak of wages, however, mostly with outrage, as evidence of race and gender exploitation, resenting white employers' capriciousness about black women's pay.

These interviews tell us even more about the ironies of gender—or better, the vicissitudes of Jim Crow—as applied to African American women's lives. For instance, these interviews reveal that professional women did not necessarily confront a lesser financial strain than farmers or domestics. Communities expected educated women to give themselves over to the work of uplift through teaching or nursing, and our narrators speak here of seeking positions that allowed them to make contribution to a larger community's welfare. For teachers, the opportunity to nurture a future generation was poorly remunerated. By law, black teachers were paid less than white teachers, even in the same school system. In addition, except in urban public schools, teaching was not always a steady job. It was seasonal. In rural areas the school year ran only three or four months, and then not in succession. Teachers moved from assignment to assignment, paid at the whim of white officials or by the ability of local families and communities to raise funds. Married women in the professions were expected to leave work, which stopped one income stream while pregnancy added another expense. As the stories of teachers remind us, Jim Crow reinforced race and gender inequalities in income and opportunity, disadvantaging African Americans, and especially women. Under these constraints, poverty abated slowly. Unable to accumulate capital and purchase property, African Americans hoped that through hard work and struggle their children and grandchildren might acquire money, education, or luck that might bring greater financial security.

As to work itself, for most black women farming and domestic labor (including child care, nursing, cooking, and laundering) were the most viable means of earning a living. According to decennial censuses, more than half of African American women worked as domestic servants in 1900, a proportion that increased, rather than decreased as the mid-twentieth century approached.[3] According to these interviews, black women worked two or three jobs, even as the census counted only one. Household labor provided the fallback position for many who could find no other work, including women employed in teaching. As late as 1960, nearly one-third of African American women continued to be employed in domestic work.[4]

The conventions surrounding domestic work played out the South's race/gender order in the place of employment. Not surprisingly, low pay and other forms of exploitation made domestic work the last choice, even though it was the position they were mostly likely to get. Sometimes women were denied wages from domestic work altogether, or might be paid with leftover food or used clothing instead of money. Although some women found "good" situations working for white families, as our narrators tell, household labor also exposed girls and women to insult, abuse, and even molestation by their employers. Employees had to enter white household through the back door, rather than the front. Employers often refused to use women's correct names. Women recall their attempts to assert their dignity in these situations by refusing to answer to names other than their own and insisting on entering homes through the front door; they also left jobs when employers treated them intolerably or when better positions came along.

Tellingly, domestic service was excluded, along with farming, from federal legislation passed in the 1930s that established a minimum wage and Social Security and disability benefits, thereby increasing the chances that African American women would become mired in life-long poverty. This exclusion may explain why one narrator, Cleaster Mitchell, recalls the ritual of applying for a Social Security card, an important moment in her transition out of agricultural and domestic work when she left the rural South.[5]

As Mitchell's story demonstrates, women found a greater range of choices in southern and northern cities. Throughout the twentieth century, increased mechanization, such as the introduction of tractors, brought some changes to farm work, but greater reliance on machines over manual labor did push some black southerners off the farm. When the Depression, droughts, or periods of infestation dried up agricultural work, women flocked to cities to take advantage of wider—albeit still constricted—employment. Industrial jobs, including work in North Carolina's tobacco factories, Virginia's waterfront industries, or Memphis' mattress factories, were physically challenging, often dirty and dangerous, and still segregated. But the pay at these jobs might compare favorably with domestic or farm work.

For those women privileged enough to complete high school or college, options widened to include clerical work and the professions, mainly teaching, social work, and nursing, jobs that were cleaner, more autonomous, and higher status, if not higher paying. Enterprising women might venture into business or trades, with some working as beauticians and others running shops. But even the historically black colleges and universities (HBCUs) blocked women's access to programs in law, religion, or medicine. Frustrated by limited capital our narrators still chafe at how discrimination and segregation limited their customer base in addition to their aspirations.[6]

In general, black women's work opportunities changed little from 1900 through the late 1950s. Some women remember the 1930s, the era of the Depression, as a time when things became especially difficult. As the economy shrank, white families went without domestic help, leaving many black women unemployed. Some remember turning to public relief during this period, while others vividly remember how they pulled together income from odd jobs, doing laundry, selling home-raised produce, and relying on family gardens to help put food on the table. For families that already managed without much cash, these changes were distressing but not devastating.

Our interviewees explicate a shift in black women's employment that began in the 1960s as demand for household labor shrank and desegregation opened new workplaces. Slow and uneven, desegregation brought some black teachers and social workers into previously all-white schools. In these new locations, black women educators assumed the burden of advocating for black people in addition to their regular workload. They describe difficult colleagues and prejudices that made their work challenging but infused them with a renewed sense of mission. The Civil Rights Act of 1964—which outlawed employment discrimination on the basis of race and sex—also brought women into manufacturing jobs and industrial unions which had previously excluded them. The War on Poverty, a federal initiative in the 1960s, also provided funds for Head Start programs and youth jobs programs, making new lines of employment possible.

Whether before or after the so-called desegregation era of the 1960s, work was the place where black women interacted most extensively with white southerners as coworkers, employers, or customers. Thus, work became a venue in which women encountered Jim Crow in new forms. Narrators' memories are colored by their anger at mistreatment by employers and hostile coworkers. Black women recall the abuses and humiliations they faced at work, and clear inequities, such as the greater pay or resources whites in the same position reaped. Even urban professional women confronted animosity. But the nature of the insults varied: from rural women who were outright denied payment after a day spent laboring in the fields, to domestic workers who fought off sexual predations, to teachers incensed by white coworkers' neglect of black students. Insults poisoned women's work experiences and fostered their desire for greater control over their work conditions.

While economic circumstances often meant they could not leave unsatisfactory positions, these interviews describe ways that black women resisted the worst exploitation and asserted dignity in the face of employers' attempts to degrade and take advantage of them. Recalling individual acts of defiance, many describe risking jobs by refusing to perform degrading tasks. Others joined collective efforts to use unions or other groups to bring about improved conditions. Finally, at the same time that women's interviews express their anger, they also demonstrate their enormous pride in their achievements and contributions, skills, abilities, and talents. Thus, in the face of an economic structure intended to exploit black women's labor, our narrators ultimately find satisfaction in their capacity to contribute to their families and communities and in the work they did on behalf of the next generation.

Blanche Davis was born in 1900, in Montgomery County, Alabama, and grew up in the country between the cities of Montgomery and Tuskegee. In 1920 she married and moved to Birmingham. With only a sixth-grade education, Davis's work opportunities were limited but she tried to find the best situations. In her interview, Davis describes her work as a domestic and remembers her strategies for living on a small budget that was strained even further when she married and had children. The family depended on public relief during the Depression, but over time, thanks to Davis' thriftiness and her husband's steady employment with the railroad, family finances improved.

[When I turned 20] I left Montgomery County to visit a brother of mine who lived in Birmingham. After visiting him, I didn't ever go back [to the county] to live. I got married in 1920, and I lived in Walker County for about three years and after that moved here to Birmingham. I separated from that husband in '27, married again in '36. So I've been in Birmingham approximately seventy-some years, just about that long.

The first job I had was right up here on Claremont Street in '23, I believe. I made $5 a week. And from then, different jobs around, around, around. I remember once I wanted a new job. That's when I was about thirty-five years old and working [as a domestic] in Mountain Brook when this happened. After serving lunch for them that day—they had a bridge party—I decided I'd go in there and ask God to give me another job. And I did. I went in the kitchen and

I said, "Now, my grandmother, she had to pray with her head in a bucket, but I'm asking you today for another job." And I got that job, worked on it thirteen years and eight months without any trouble. So I do know the Lord will answer prayers. Finally, I got tired of this housework. I worked at a [steel plant] cleaning an office just about half a block from my house. That's the job I made thirteen years and retired from there at age sixty-three.

At that time, $5 could do more than $20 can do now, in a way. My rent was very cheap. My rent was only $9 a month, that's a room and a kitchen apartment, and we made it pretty good. But it was kind of rough. No clothes much, no money much, but we made it. I know that sounds funny to young people to think that anybody nowadays worked for $5 a week, but that is true. Five dollars, and I had to have breakfast on the table at seven o'clock, seven-thirty every morning except Sunday and stayed in the kitchen until seven at night, $5 a week. [The people I worked for] were very good to me, though. I didn't have any trouble wherever I worked. I give that to them. They just didn't pay any money. But they were very good to me, very good. I tried to treat them like I wanted them to treat me, and so everything went along pretty good when it came to being on the job.

When I first came to Birmingham, you could go anywhere and buy your clothes if you had the money. When I first came to Birmingham there wasn't too much shopping to do. I'd buy material. After I married and had two children, I made most of their clothes. I remember once a woman paid me $1 a week to do washing and ironing. I had two little girls. I'd get a yard and a half of cloth for one this week and a yard and a half the next week out of that dollar, 25 cents a yard [for] material. That was tough. Then we raised chickens and had a milk cow and a garden. With all of these things, we never went hungry. We had plenty to eat, because we had to raise all that kind of stuff. Everybody was the same. Very little money. Oh, yeah, very little.

Things were pretty rough during the Depression. My husband had two children and I had two, [and we got relief].[7] They'd give us a lot of food because they would give so much for each child. So we got along pretty good. But there wasn't any money to be made. My husband was working for the railroad. He wasn't making any money anyway, about $2.40 a day. And I was doing this odds-and-ends work. After I had small children, I couldn't go out on the job, so I was doing washing and ironing at home. I would probably go out one or two days to work and made that $5 and I'd do their washing for $1 a month or go out and do ironing for somebody for $1, and that gave me a little change. We didn't pay much money to the church, because we didn't have it. In those days, people were paying 25 and 30 cents in church.

After we were married, on down the line my husband finally built a home. In fact, he built two houses. He built a home house and a two-family rented house. Then we began to buy nice furniture. He worked for the Louisville National

Railroad about twenty-five, thirty years, or forty. I was blessed to ride the trains anywhere I wanted across the country for railroad passes half-fare. That was one blessing. I would take my children when they were small. We would go to New Orleans, Detroit, Chicago, anywhere we wanted to go, we could ride a railroad pass for half-fare. People would criticize things going on in the South a lot when I would go north. "You all are under bondage," which was true. We had to go in the back door different places. It was just kind of rough, yeah.

Annie Joyner Gavin was born in 1911, in James City, North Carolina. Like Blanche Davis, Gavin made money working in the homes of white families where she took responsibility for child care and thereby freed white women for leisure activities. Rather than a life-long occupation, Gavin sought domestic work during summers when she was in high school. Ironically, then, Gavin relied on domestic work as a way to stay in school, gaining an education that was intended eventually to open other avenues of work to her. Here she recounts her experiences in several homes, where she developed intimate bonds with white families that sometimes compromised her sense of ethics and safety.

When I was growing up most jobs for women were either housework or farms. And you would work in the house and take care of the white babies, and they learned to love you. I worked for a Jewish family in Baltimore when I was still in school and she had two boys. One of her sons was in an accident so he was kind of deformed and dripped at his mouth. But he was a sweet little fellow, and she couldn't keep a maid because of Jo Jo. Jo Jo wanted to stay with the maid all the time and [they had to eat with him]. Some of the maids didn't like that because he dripped at the mouth. But I played games with him. Now you see, I got slick with him. I'd say, "Jo Jo, I'm going to see if you can eat your dinner before I eat mine." And then he'd eat his food out of his plate. So when it dripped, it dripped in his plate not mine. Some of the girls had left because he wanted [to] hang on to their shoulder and stuff like that. But he was a very sweet little boy.

The children learned to love you. When Jo Jo was a baby, I slept in.[8] Both of these were Jewish people, and the husband traveled and she loved to party. So, she was gone about all the time. Sometimes she just did beat him in, and she would have just gotten in when he [came home]. Her husband almost caught her gone one time and I [lied] for her. But, she was out and gone all the time, because she could trust me with the kid, and her baby, Jo Jo. At first when I went to work there, Jo Jo didn't want to lay still for you to diaper him or put his clothes on, and I had heard other maids say, "If you want to spank a white baby, you've got to use a wet cloth," because they wouldn't leave a mark. "Just get a wet wash cloth and spank their little butts," and they'd know how to be still. So, I found that out. I never was harsh with him, but I'd tell Jo Jo to be still if I had other things to do. I'd get that wet cloth and pat his little butt and he looked so funny the first time, but he got used to it. And learned to obey. And loved me to death. When it was time for me to get off and go home, he cried, hollered, wanted to go with me.

As I say I worked for this Jewish family and Jews are much more tolerant.[9] Well, I can't say that's the truth, but they are much more easy to get along with than gentiles. At least they were that time. Because there was a gentile family living below Mrs. Steinberg. And her maid asked me, "Y'all got roaches up there?"

I said, "What do you mean asking me that? No, we don't have roaches. Yes, our place is clean." So she finally told me why she asked me. Her boss lady had asked her, because they considered Jews filthy. I said, "Tell her come up and see."

Another time I worked for a family and she didn't have any children. And her boyfriend was there in the house when her husband came home. I spoke to him loud when he came in, because he'd always go back to his room and change his clothes when he came home in evenings. And this man got out of there, through the hall and downstairs. That man got out of that house. So I didn't ever mention it to her and she never mentioned it to me. But when she came through the dining room, I was setting the table for dinner. She smiled at me. She knew what I had done. So I left, I wasn't going to be there when somebody killed somebody.

Olivia Cherry was born in 1926 in Hampton, Virginia. In 1937, her family moved to Aberdeen Gardens, a racially segregated public housing project in Newport News that was designed, built, and occupied by African American residents as part of the New Deal. Cherry began working for wages as a youngster, helping her family financially while she attended school. As a teenager, she still found her job choices limited. Lacking options, she could choose between enduring harassment or risking unemployment if she protested mistreatment. Here she describes her working conditions and how she responded to some of the worst forms of exploitation.

When I went to high school, I wanted a part-time job, so I could have an allowance. My stepfather had passed when I was fifteen years old, so our income was really low then. We were not poor, we were making ends meet, but I wanted my own money. Basically I did domestic work because that's all I could get.

My name is Olivia, which I feel is a very pretty name. My mother thought that way. That's why she gave it to me. And I had trouble with my name. One white lady said, "Oh, that's what I was going to name my daughter." But her daughter's name was Mary. I mean, how do you jump from Olivia to Mary? I would be upstairs cleaning the bathroom, and she said, "Susie." They loved to call me Susie. "Susie."

So I didn't answer. I was a spunky kid then. I was like thirteen or fourteen, and I didn't answer.

Finally, she came to the steps and said, "Olivia, you hear me calling you?"

I said, "Now I hear you. Now you said, 'Olivia.' That's my name."

When we were living in Aberdeen, there were farms around us—potato farms. They would dig up the potatoes, and we children in the summer would have to put them in baskets to go to market. We also worked on a raspberry farm picking raspberries, which I really didn't like because it was back-breaking.

But going back to the potato farm, I had close girlfriends, and about seven or eight of us were looking for work. This man said, "Oh, yes, I'll dig the potatoes out, and you can put them in a basket."

So I said, "How much?" I was always the spokesman, always the leader. I said, "How much?"

He said, "Ten cents a basket." That was 1939 or '40, like that, so that was good money then. So we said, "Okay."

So we did this and we had to go at five o'clock in the morning, because it was hot, very hot, and we would be out in the field picking up those potatoes. So we went out, we'd pick potatoes, and he'd pay us, and we come home. We'd be so happy. One day we went and we picked the potatoes, worked diligently, and the man gave us five cents a basket.

I said, "Wait a minute. You told us ten cents a basket."

He said, "Yes, I know what I told you." There were so many of us, I guess, and we worked so fast. So he said, "I'm just going to give you five cents." The girls were fussing. Well, I said, "Okay, that's fine. We'll see you tomorrow morning." So when we left his farm, they said, "Olivia, what are you talking about?"

I said, "Don't worry, we're going back tomorrow and we're going to get even."

They said, "What we going to do?"

I said, "We're going to put the straw and stuff in the basket, fill it up with that and put potatoes on top so you can't see it, and we get our money and leave."

Some [one] said, "I'm scared."

"Don't be scared, just be with me."

So we went on and that's what we did. He paid us and we come out of his farm and we got on the road just laughing and joking, and wouldn't even walk that way for a long time, because we figured he'd be looking for us.

Then there was this white man and his girlfriend. They had a raspberry farm. They wanted us to pick the raspberries. Here we were out looking for work. So here we are picking the raspberries, and here goes my name again. The man said, "Hey, Susie. Susie. You missed some on your row."

I knew he was calling me, because this was my row, but I just kept on working.

He said, "Susie, don't you hear me talking to you?"

I said, "I told you before, my name is Olivia. Olivia. Can you say that?"

He said, "Don't be so 'd' smart."

I went back and picked what he said I missed. It wasn't that I was working badly, I just overlooked it.

Well, another day he did the same thing. "Susie, I want you to work down this end, and I want you to work with them." I just kept on working.

He said, "Do you hear me telling you?"

I said, "Do you know my name? Can you learn my name?"

He said, "All right, whatever it is. I want you working down there."

So one day we went through this name again, and he said, "Get the 'h' off my property. I don't want you working for me at all."

I said, "Fine, because I don't want to work for you, but you have to pay me for the work I have done."

I already computed the amount, and he told his girlfriend, "Pay her. Let's get rid of her." I don't remember figures now, but it wasn't the correct amount. I said, "No, this is not right. You owe me such-and-such cents."

"Pay her. Give her anything so we can get rid of her."

So she paid me, and I stepped out on the highway, and I said, "Come on, you all, you don't want to work for him. He doesn't know how to treat you." They were standing there working and scared.

He said, "Get away from here. Get away from my property."

I said, "Wait a minute. I'm on the highway. My mother and father paid taxes for this highway. This is not your highway." I said, "You leave me alone." And I went home and told my mother.

She said, "Oh, Lord. They're going to kill my daughter. I know they're going to kill my daughter."

I worked for a lady one time in town that refused to let me in the front door, and I'd go to the back and call her and come back to the front door. I refused to go to the back door. My reason was, my mother had to go to the back door to keep her job. Not that I was better than my mother, but I was avenging my mother.

One day I had cramps, one Saturday. Mother said, "You going to work?" I said, "Yes." Because I didn't have a phone, I couldn't call [the woman I worked for] and tell her I wasn't coming. She was depending on me. So I said, "Yes, I'm going to work."

I had to walk then, it was quite a long walk, but it helped me. I knocked and rang, and called her. She never did come, because she was determined for me to come to the back. I went home and went to bed, and that was the end of that job. I saw her in the grocery store a week or so after that and her little boy come calling me and "Hi." She snatched him away and acted like I didn't know her.

So one day I caught the bus going to one of these ladies where I had to go through the front door, [and I] wouldn't go to the back. The bus driver, a woman, this was during the war, '42, passed the stop. She passed the stop and the stops were blocks and blocks away. I said, "Didn't you hear me ring the bell back there?"

She said, "What?"

I always looked younger than what I am, so she thought I was a snotty-nosed kid. She said, "What's wrong with you, gal?"

I said, "I rang the bell, and the stops are too far between anyway."

She said, "You better get the 'h' off of my bus." [After that] I wouldn't take the bus anymore, because I was afraid I was going to run into her. I would walk all that way to work. But those were the things you had to put up with.

Mandie Johnson was born in 1913 in Cruger, a community in Holmes County, Mississippi. Raised by parents and grandparents who farmed, Johnson began working in the fields at a young age. The structure of southern farming—dominated by sharecropping and low cotton prices—created perpetual debt and made it hard for the family to break even. The family's financial survival was tested even further by her difficult marriage. But after she "quit" her husband, Johnson and her children made ends meet through a combination of farming, domestic service, gardening, and sharing with neighbors. Although Johnson's interview reveals the challenges that women faced, especially those raising children without a husband, she also demonstrates the importance of sharing with community, a value that even those with few resources shared.

I had a pretty tough time after I married because I had eight children who lived and four died. So I had kind of a tough time then, because I had to work. I didn't have anybody to help me work for my eight head of children. My husband, he wouldn't help me. I had to quit him. He would sit up all night long and cuss and go on. See, I was working, he wasn't working. I was the one working. He would just go across town to the whiskey place. He would get drunk, and sit up and cuss all night. I couldn't rest. My nerves got bad. You can't put up with that and then go to work too. I had to work. I'd get up there at my house and cook breakfast and clean up. Then I'd go to the white folks' house and cook and clean up there. Sometimes I had to cook three meals at their house—breakfast, dinner, and supper—and then come home and cook supper. And that was hard on me. Then I had to stay awake all night with him, drunk. I just got tired of that. I just walked on out. Went to my brother's and stayed with him awhile. I left all the children with my husband until the police got me and told me to find me a house and take my kids. So I did and I moved down there in Sidon. He had quit us. He quit first. Left the children naked and barefooted.

And I made it. After I quit him I had a good time. Yeah, I didn't suffer for nothing. I worked all the time and got my children up old enough to help me, my boys. [I] had six boys and two girls. So they helped me. Mostly I worked as a cook. I was a good cook and I would keep the house, laundry washed and ironed. I worked ·a long time for different people, white people in Cruger and Greenwood. Everyone I worked for wanted me to cook. They said I was a good cook, you see. It wasn't much they were paying then when I was working, not like it is now. Just could not live off of it, if that was all you had to depend on. They weren't paying much, only twenty some dollars a week back then. Sometimes $17 a week. You know that wasn't anything. I got more working in the field picking cotton. Sure seems like I picked 300 pounds a day. That'd be $8 I made a day, picking cotton.[10]

When I was in the country like that, I raised my stuff. I didn't have to buy meat and lard and meal and stuff like that. I raised peas and butter beans and okra and all that. Sweet potatoes. Irish potatoes. Pop corn. I raised all that. Greens. See, I gathered up all of that and had them when winter time came. In my days they planted sorghum molasses and they would squeeze that juice out of the cane and cook the molasses off. So we didn't have to buy molasses. I didn't have to buy anything like that when I was in the country. I just had to buy some flour, and sugar, and rice, and coffee, salt and soda, and baking powder. I raised my hogs. I used to kill as many as eight hogs a winter. I'd get two 50-pound cans of lard and two 25-pound cans of lard. That's enough lard to last me all the year. And I sewed for my children. After I married, my grandmother gave me a machine and I used to sew for them. I used to make little shirts and little overalls for my boys and dresses for my girls. I used to buy cloth, cut it, and make stuff on the machine. I used to quilt on the machine, piece quilts. We made it all right with what we raised. We made it all right through the year. If it wasn't for that, we wouldn't have made it from one bale of cotton to the other.

At one time they were paying 50 cents for a hundred pounds of cotton. A hundred. You pick a hundred and you wouldn't get but 50 cents. You didn't get anything then for working a crop. Sometimes we would make twenty some bales of cotton and come out behind. We didn't clear anything. The only way we could make it was to go back and borrow some more money for the next year. We borrowed money from the man where we worked to make our crop. They wouldn't just give it to you, [but would] take it out of the next year's crop. [People] would have to do without, or would bring sacks and things to gather my beans and stuff. I usually shared with folks. I didn't raise stuff all for myself. The Bible says I have to divide it. And that's what I did. I raised my something.

In Chapter 1, Corinne Browne describes her childhood on St. Helena Island, South Carolina. She moved to New York after high school, doing a variety of jobs before and during World War II. In 1945, she married and returned to the South to raise her family. Shortly after her return, Browne started a child care center on St. Helena, one of the first for the area's black farming families. She faced considerable resistance, however, before convincing residents of the benefits the center could provide their children. She speaks here with obvious pride of the accomplishments of her young charges and the positive difference the child care center made.

After I graduated from Penn in 1936 I went to Hampton.[11] I went there to be with Leroy. We were just friends, that's all, just friends. I think I was almost more in love with him than he was with me. So when he went to Hampton I just wanted to go to Hampton. I shouldn't have gone. But I went and we were okay for a couple of months, and then we broke up and went our ways. I didn't graduate. But I [had been] back and forth to New York with my mother after my grandfather died. Before I used to go just for the summer, you know. But after I left Hampton I went and stayed about five years. I worked in the post office. I worked in the doctor's office and I did some domestic work also, a lot of things. But fate brought [Leroy and I] back together. We wrote, corresponded back and forth and stuff, and then we got together and the next thing I knew he was coming up to New York. He came on up there and we set this date and got married. I stayed up there I guess about four or five months until I could get my resignation in and stuff and I came on down in 1945 and that was it.

I didn't work the first few years because I thought I wanted to pursue my education. But I started having the children and then I stopped. See the oldest girl was born in 1946, and I took a couple of courses and stuff and I said no, it's not going to work. I was always interested in children and this new couple had just come to the Penn School, and they were getting programs started and something just kept in my mind that I would like to run a day nursery. That was one of the programs that they were thinking about setting up. At that time a lot of the older children had to stay home to keep the smaller ones and we saw a need for a daycare. And so we got together, had meetings and so forth, and they said, "Well if we set up a daycare, who would run it, who would direct it?" So it was me. So I directed the Penn Nursery School.

It was really the first daycare center in Beaufort County. In 1950 we set up that daycare and it wasn't the easiest thing to do because people didn't hear or know nothing of that at that time. And they were so afraid and some of the people tried to discourage them, said, "You can't have all those children there at one time. Somebody's going to kill somebody," you know. Yeah, that's what they thought. We went around, we combed the islands and interviewed parents and asked them if they would be interested in sending their children and they told us, "Yes, okay." We'd set up and expect them and the next week or so we'd go back and, "No, no, I can't send them, I'm scared, I'm scared." Anyway we pursued it and the opening day we started with about seven, I think. We worked at that. They weren't paying but two dollars a week when they could, and we tried to get transportation for them. That was 25 cents a day because they were so far and scattered. But anyway, we worked at it until we made a go of it. It was pretty hard. It was pretty uncertain and everything. The Penn School helped with the facility and helped us to get commodities, and that came in quite a bit of help, you know. They would give it to us to help us.

There were only two of us, the girl who was going to do the cooking and stuff [and me], and we got three dollars a day. We carried it on for twenty-seven years; I stayed there for twenty-seven years. Different ones would come in sometimes and volunteer and help, you know. [At first, it was just farmers who sent their children.] Later on the teachers, especially those who had no place to leave their children, they decided to take advantage of it and that made it a little bit easier because they took over with the fund raising and all that sort of stuff. They would bring their kids there every morning, around six o'clock and then I would take them on [to my house] in the evening until they'd pick them up. We had babies coming with diapers. We had to change diapers, give them milk bottles, all of that.

You just kept going all day long. You'd put them to sleep and while the younger ones were sleeping, you'd be working with some of the others or having them out on the yard or something. We had a little graduation [at the end of the year] with caps and gowns. The first year was made of paper. A lady here had a pattern and some of them got together and made those little paper caps and gowns. Then next year the teachers took over and bought caps and gowns.

And I also worked in the very first Head Start program here. The teachers [at] the school used to just about fight over the students because they had such a head start, you know. [By the time they left the daycare, the students] knew how to do quite a bit; they knew how to write and spell. They could count. A couple of them came out reading.

In Chapter 1, Cleaster Mitchell describes her childhood in Blackton, Arkansas. Mitchell started working as a child, helping her family pick cotton and accompanying her mother to private homes where she learned how to clean and cook. Although her mother taught her what to expect when doing domestic work, Mitchell chafed at the abuses she endured. Eager to avoid these horrible conditions and to make more money, Mitchell migrated to Chicago in 1945, where she found greater opportunities and escaped the worst exploitations of segregation.

I learned very early about abuse from white men [when working in people's houses]. It was terrible at one time, and there wasn't anybody to tell. Sometimes the wife knew it, but she was scared of her husband, too. You could go to the wife and she'd say, "Oh, just don't pay him no attention. Just don't pay him no attention," because she would be scared. They'd say, "Oh, don't pay Mr. So-and-so no attention. He was drunk. Don't pay him no attention." A lot of people that worked left on that account, because you had no alternative. To go to the law didn't mean anything. And I'll tell you, one time in the South, it's bad to say, white men was crazy about black women. They would come to your house. They would attack you.

But every bit of this went on. That was no joke. See, some of the people you worked for, they worked you all day, and said, "When you get through with such and such, I want you to do so and so and so." It was something all day long. In '43 I was only making $2.50 a week. I washed, I ironed, I took care of the baby, I worked the garden, I mowed the yard, I took care of the chickens, I pumped the water for the animals, I did everything. I got $2.50 a week.

But at that time, I knew how to maneuver. I'd get through with my [house] work and I'd go to the field and I would work. I'd go chop [cotton] until eight o'clock or nine, and I would get paid by the hour and I would make extra money. And on my off day, I would go and work. So I always found a way to earn something to take care of my own self, support myself. I'd get off in the evening. I'd go and I'd pick cotton. There was a farm nearby and I'd go over there and I'd pick 100 and 150 [pounds]. I got maybe $2.00 a hundred pounds. That was a lot of money then. I got my room and my board at the house, and I didn't have to spend my money for anything.

When I was twenty-two years old, in 1945, I moved to Chicago. I was tired of working for nothing. We had made a crop and never cleared a dime, and I just said to myself, "There's got to be something better, got to be something different." And that was one thing my mother taught us. She used to always say, "I would know how to make a living if I was in England. If I was in England, I'd know how to feed myself. I'd know bread in anyplace." She'd tell you, don't be afraid to try something or to do something different. And so I said, "I'm not going to starve to death, so I'm going."

I got on the bus, I got on the Greyhound bus, and I went to Chicago. I got there on an Easter Sunday morning in '45, and I stayed there thirty years. I worked and I learned how to do a lot of things. I accomplished something that I dreamed about when I was a kid. I like to design things, and I just went and had an opportunity to put into action my thoughts and my dreams. I designed hats, and I had my own store, custom-made hats and everything.

My sister went first, and then I went. She went in February, and I went in April. She was the only somebody I had there. We first both left and went to St. Louis. We both got on a bus and went to St. Louis and didn't know anybody. When we got there, we missed the lady that was supposed to meet us. We knew the name of another lady in St. Louis, and we looked in the telephone book and found her and called her up. She came down and got us.

We didn't have but $7.50. But, we made it fine. We were job crazy. We got there, we worried everybody about a job. She said, "Just give yourself a chance. You're going to get a job." We went down to 8th and Pine and got our Social Security cards. We both wound up working at the same laundry. She worked about a month, and she left and came to Chicago. I left and went back to Arkansas, and then I went to Chicago in April.

So many people were leaving the South at that time, because it was during the war. A lot went to shipyards. A lot of people left the little small jobs they had and went to bigger jobs, and all these little jobs, so you didn't have a problem getting a job working at a hotel, laundry, or restaurant. All those little jobs were just there for you. You really didn't have to have a lot of education to find a job to take care of yourself, to make yourself independent. You learned how to survive easily.

When I first made $20 a week, I was just shocked, because I had just left a job making $2.50. That was a whole lot of money. People saved money. You don't see how anybody saved anything out of $2.50 a week, but things were much cheaper. And then they had a little something they'd fix to put savings in, and they would keep it. They just wouldn't spend it for nothing. You had to be critically ill or something or other for them to spend it.

Dorothy Fletcher Steele was born in Washington, D.C., in 1907, and grew up in Reading, Pennsylvania, where she was one of the few black pupils at her public school and at the normal school where she trained to become a teacher. In contrast to Cleaster Mitchell, who followed the Great Migration stream north, Steele left Pennsylvania and moved south searching for work and community. In 1929 Steele settled in Charlotte, North Carolina, where she found a good job and enjoyed a busy life of activism and social events. Steele dedicated her career to ensuring her students' success and to breaking down segregation in education. Her job also led her to consider teachers' responsibilities in their community and to confront the troubling realities of poverty and class differences among African Americans. In the 1960s, Steele was among the first teachers in Charlotte to desegregate the public schools when she was selected to instruct in a new program for gifted students. There, she realized that she detested segregation of all kinds, including the kind that tracked students of differing abilities.[12]

I came to Charlotte in the fall of '29 seeking a job. I grew up in Pennsylvania, was educated in Pennsylvania, and went to a normal school,[13] now West Chester University.[14] But apparently I wasn't prepared fittingly to teach in Reading. The fact was that Reading had never had a black teacher, and there were very few of us there anyway. The black population was small, barely 3,000, [out of] about 75,000 in Reading at that time. It was the beginning of the Depression and I was the oldest of eight children. And it was just mandatory that I work. So after finishing the two years of normal school, I taught one year on the eastern shore in Maryland in a rural school where I was the principal and the teacher.

I had a friend who had finished West Chester a year before I and whose father's family was originally from South Carolina. [My friend, Florence] had made some contact with the principal of this Fairview School, Mrs. Davis, and [had] gotten a job here and then [Florence] had suggested that I write to the principal which I did. And she employed me sight unseen which she said she had never done, but she and her husband on their vacation had visited West Chester's campus and they were impressed with what they had seen. And they were also impressed with the work that Florence had done. And, so, that's how I got the job.

It seems as if long before I came to Charlotte it was a case of fighting injustices or feeling the results of the injustices most of my life and knowing it was quite wrong. My parents had their roots in the South. My father was a Washingtonian, my mother from rural Virginia, and they would tell about the life [of] blacks in the South, and I said, "I believe I'd like to go there some time." For some reason I never felt that Reading was the garden spot, was heaven on earth, which so many blacks, or Negroes, at that time, felt. I wanted more and my parents wanted more for me. Financially they were very, very, very limited in what they could [do], which meant that I was thrown on my own, but I didn't mind that. I never have minded that.

I knew I had to get out of Reading. Reading was stifling. Suffocating. I couldn't stand it. I knew I had to get out. I had to get out. So, when I came to Charlotte, I was amazed to see this large elementary school, larger than any in Reading, with thirty teachers. A brick building. It was five years old, I think, when I came. Fairview Elementary School was over in the section of Greenville. Mrs. Davis [the principal] was a very fine educator. I had never come across a group of so many fine, cultured Negroes. These were graduates of Howard University, Fisk University, Atlanta University, Spelman, Bennett, and that sort of thing.[15] At those black schools at that time, if you went there without culture, they instilled it in you. They gave you experiences that helped the students to develop. I liked that because, oh, well, the way we were brought up, we were brought up feeling that this was the way it should be and this was our background.

Charlotte was much larger than Reading at the time. Everything was segregated. You knew you weren't going to be served if you were thirsty or hungry. My contact with white Charlotte, of course, was very, very, very limited. Our white superintendent at that time, Mr. Hardy, did the unusual. He [would] call you with a title, Mrs. or Miss, and that was most unusual at that particular time. I had some contact with white Charlotte through the YWCA, which was just about as prejudiced as it could be. We had our little branch, the Phyllis Wheatley Branch, and a few blocks away, on Trade Street, was the Central Branch. And if they decided to be good Christians and have some meetings, some little teas with the Negroes, you couldn't sit down with them. Always a stand up and sip the tea affair. No, no, you didn't sit down together.[16]

Fairview Elementary School was in a modern building, but we did not have new furniture. I never had a new desk in my room until I was transferred to a white school. It was always the discards, and then the same thing was true with books. The old discarded books, which had been used. These books in the back had a label on them where every child each year who had used them had written his name. Often the space was filled up. At the beginning and then at the end of every year, the teacher was supposed to go back and check on the condition of the book and charge damage fees accordingly. I know so many cases I just paid a little bit out of my pocket. We knew that many of these children had come to school hungry. We had a school nurse and a so-called domestic science teacher, and also a shop which we did not always have a teacher for. Well, none of the other schools, black schools, had anything like that and everybody credited that to Mrs. Davis because she looked the way she did as you see.[17] I'm not going to say that didn't have something to do with it. And, she and Mr. Hardy, the superintendent, got along very well together. He liked her. But, as I said, I felt she knew education, having just come out of school myself. If she came in your room to observe, she knew exactly the steps you were supposed to follow and to take to have a good lesson. Well, there was no excuse for me. I had just gotten out of school. So, and she took a liking to me too.

I had always wanted to teach. Well, what were the other choices? I didn't want to be a nurse and I didn't want to sit in an office and be a typist. But nevertheless, I enjoyed teaching, and I enjoyed working with children. I started off with fourth grade, and then Mrs. Davis allowed me to move on with a group of fourth graders to fifth grade and then move on to the sixth grade. By this time, many of us wanted to raise our certification, to go ahead and get a Master's. We had to finish college, which I did. I went back in the summer time and finished at West Chester. And, incidentally, the state of North Carolina wasn't paying black teachers nearly what they paid the white teachers. So, our salaries were very low.

[When I got to Charlotte, I] boarded. No self-respecting female lived alone. You just didn't do it. So there was this place where I lived with four or five other girls, all teachers, and one social worker. So that's what you did until you married. Until some man came along and rescued you. Charlotte reached out to me. The place was just filled with social clubs of all kinds, and there was almost a fight to get you to join. So, I joined. And I got to know all of the teachers. We would have monthly meetings citywide for blacks, and you just got to know the people, and there were a lot of us new teachers coming and going, coming and going, and there were a lot of the so-called home town girls. That's one of the reasons Mrs. Davis said she hired me, because she thought there was too much in-breeding in the system.

I enjoyed the fact of having a job, although it wasn't paying anything, but at least I was employed. And the social life meant a great deal. I was starved for it. I didn't have it in Reading. Johnson C. Smith University, at that time, was an all-male school. That made things exciting. I'd never seen so many fine Negro men in all my life, just a gorgeous passel of them. I said, "This is the place for me." Smith had the reputation of educating only gentlemen. The cream of the crop and straight, I mean A & T[18] was all right, but the true gentlemen were at Johnson C. Smith. The sororities were very active and you would join at least one. To be honest that would be about all you could afford at that time, because you were expected to entertain the group once a year; and then every year the group would have a big dance, and you financed that. There were so many social clubs until once the season got in swing, there was just about every weekend a dance. And then on top of that, the fraternities were active, the Omegas, the Alphas, and the Kappas.[19] Each one had their house and they would have parties and dances. I just enjoyed it and some of the behaviors that I hear about now, you just didn't hear about it.

Respectability required no public disgrace of any kind that people would hear about. Not that things weren't happening, but people kept it right there. Of course, going to jail was a complete no-no. You definitely had to be a church member and a college graduate, and as I said, you couldn't have brought "any disgrace on the family." I'm sure abortions were going on and all that sort of thing, you see, but they handled it their way. I never heard about a social affair, disagreements, or arguments.

Then marriage was my goal like it was [for] most of the females at that time, and I always knew there'd be no problem in getting married whenever I wanted to, which I did. My husband was a scholar, which I admired. I learned so much from him. He taught down at Johnson C. Smith. For a long time, if women married they lost their jobs. That ruling was in effect when I married. When I discussed it with Mrs. Davis—after the fact—she said, "Well Miss Fletcher, you know we'll make an exception in your case." There were a lot of women around who got caught up in that and, therefore, never married.

I joined the NAACP in spite of Mrs. Davis. When they had a drive, Mrs. Davis had a meeting and said, "Don't join because you run the danger of losing your job. Don't join." Well, I was young and foolish and so I joined. This was strong in me. And losing the job didn't mean a thing to me. I thought, "Well, I scrub too well. I can clean a house too well." I wasn't fearful. Maybe I should have been, but I wasn't. My father was what they called a race man.[20] Both of my parents could be mistaken for white. My Grandfather Fletcher lived in Washington and that's where my father was born. He was a realtor. A prosperous one, no, but one never-the-less. I remember one of the last things he said to me is, "Dear, don't ever forget your grandfather and Frederick Douglass shared the same office at the foot of Capitol Hill and put their feet on the same desk."

All right, now I relate that to say that the spirit of Frederick Douglass has always been in my family.

Personally, I really have not been politically active. Given support when I could, yes. Financial support, yes. Moral support. I didn't get out in the streets and march. But I've always thought that I [had responsibilities to] the black community. How did I act upon it? Well, I've always been a little leery of being a do-gooder and I've always been very careful. I didn't want to rush in on somebody's so-called territory, so I guess all I've done is try to work around, and where I could help, I would. So, I've always felt the responsibility and, of course, I still do, but I also have a very helpless feeling too. I hate to say this, but [the Greenville section of Charlotte] was a different world. You know, that smells to high heaven, but I think you understand what I mean. These are people, who, like I, stand in the need of prayer. My contact with the parents was very limited. In my beginning years we were required to visit the home of every child in our room. Sounds good. But when you examine that, I have trouble. What right does that give me? Does that give me a right to go and knock on your door and visit you, and you in midst of I don't know what? First place, you're tired. You've worked all day long out there in Myers Park,[21] and here this old teacher comes around a knocking on the door to talk about Johnny, uninvited. So my argument was always, if you're going, that's fine, but can you have an invitation extended to us to come at such and such a time? I think it's very unfair for somebody just to knock on my door.

And, you'd see some terrible things. I mean, you'd see some horrible things. Some things I never dreamed existed. I mean, one bed and the mattress rotted through the middle and shoved together, and the other baby is lying up there on it sucking on this bottle with a sort of a pinkish looking fluid in there. And I said to the mother, "Oh, that's new formula." Stupid me to even make a comment. "Oh Lord, no, Miss Steele, that ain't new. That's just a little Kool-Aid." I had been teaching menus and good foods and healthy breakfast foods, asking students, "What did you have for breakfast this morning?" Then I'd go and see this one little heater in the kitchen heating up everything, and one pot on there. Perhaps, good beans in it or some cabbage, or maybe some beans left over in there with the cabbage and that's breakfast, lunch, and dinner. Incest. These things I would talk about with even some of my peers and teachers. "Oh, Dorothy, no, those things don't happen." So, when I talk about contact with parents, to tell the truth, they didn't want contact with me. They didn't feel at ease. There was no church contact. No social activities contact.

I learned a lot as a teacher. A lot. Many things I did as a young teacher, I did not do as an older teacher. Now I never was a paddle and strap teacher. Didn't believe in that sort of thing, although there was much use of it made. But I had a ruler and I have given some whacks with that ruler which I would never do now. Never. There are other ways of working with children. And I'm supposed to know those other ways. I had to learn that every child didn't take a bath, forget every night, every other night, or twice a week. There was such a thing as cold weather. The water pipe freezing. No water. No money for soap. I learned. I came from a so-called middle-class black family, I learned. I learned and I have very little patience at times with some of my peers. My patience runs short, very short, because I think they should be more understanding. A little less church going, if necessary. And working with our little black children is so different from working with whites. We were taught that basically we are dirty, and we are liars, and we'll do our share of cheating, and so on and so forth on down the line. And I didn't realize that I had bought somewhat into this. But you can't beat many of our blacks for just down right decency and integrity.

And then, when I was in a white school, that was interesting too. I was the first black teacher, you know, to go [into a white school in Charlotte]. In the '60s, five years before [Charlotte's] court ordered integration, about three days before school opened,[22] I got this call to meet with the principal of Myers Park Elementary School and with [the woman] who was heading up the gifted program at that time. That was the most prestigious school in the city then. Well, I met with them, and they wanted to test out integration, and they thought this might be one way to try it, to get a black teacher to come over to that school. I couldn't believe my ears at the time and I recall, saying, "Do you realize what you are asking me?" All of these years I had worked in a so-called underprivileged neighborhood with underprivileged children and I had to work in a certain way with them. And this special program was at Myers Park and at several other schools, and it included fifth and sixth graders with high IQs, and I was to teach the language arts. I was very reluctant at first. Well, anyway, I decided to go. Now why was I selected? You know some of us can be very unkind to each other, and some had said, "well, well, Dot, it's because of the way you looked, you know. You looked white, almost white." I said, "just don't be ridiculous." Now, I'm not stupid, I realize they did not pick a very dark-skinned teacher. I realize that. But I also thought I was a fairly respectable teacher too and late that spring I'd had some white observers in my classroom from downtown, and they were impressed with what was going on. I would try some of these innovative ideas that we got from Columbia.[23] I think I was one of the first teachers to get those seats unscrewed from the floor so students could work in groups, and that sort of thing.

Well, I went and it was a very enjoyable year. One deal that made me feel good about that year was Mr. Callaway who was one of our two black janitors. Bless his heart. My presence out there as a black teacher meant so much to this man. It meant so much to him, and I was always gracious to him. He was always Mr. Callaway. If I had to send a child, I'd say "you go and find Mr. Callaway." They knew who I meant. One day he said to me, "Mrs. Steele, you might go further, but you ain't never going to go no higher." I thought that was cute. Bless him, that's the way he looked at it. Now that was the epitome to him. That was the height.

So, I will say this, the parents were very warm and welcoming, but they were not poor whites. It does make a difference. I can't say as much for the teachers, but that didn't bother me. The principal always said the teachers were so steeped in tradition and some of the old ideas that he wanted someone to come in with some new ideas. But the parents were just great, and the first PTA I thought my room would not hold them all. They were curious to see me. And then my husband died that year in January. Well, they came out here after that; they kept my kitchen spotless. They filled my freezer, refrigerator with smoked turkeys and hams, and things like that. Anyway, but at the end of the year I requested a transfer. Now you might ask, why? Does anything hit you as to why I might have? This really went contrary to all I deeply believed in. Segregation of any kind, thumbs down so far as I'm concerned. I don't believe in the tracking system at school. But I could never communicate that to them.

I thought the *Brown*[24] ruling was a wonderful decision. I wanted it to happen when the sun came up the next morning. But then I recognized how slowly we as people move and how some of us can resist, and some of us are still resisting. Segregation does not satisfy me in any way. Not in any way. Yet I know I cannot make you accept me, but then the law will say you will respect me.

In Chapter 1, Theresa Cameron Lyons describes her childhood in Durham, North Carolina. Dubbed the "capital of the black middle class," Durham was home to numerous black businesses, including the North Carolina Mutual Life Insurance Company, reputedly the largest black-owned business in the world during the Jim Crow period. As the child of sharecroppers and the grandchild of slaves, however, Lyons reaped few benefits from the city's reputation. Expected to work from a young age, she longed for a job other than farming—a goal she achieved, thanks to her connections, luck, and persistence. Here she describes the benefits and the challenges that she experienced as an employee of the Mutual and a participant in Durham's large and well-connected community of black professionals.

After I got married I continued to go to high school. I wanted to be a nurse, and when I finished high school I got a job, and then I went to take the test to go to nursing school. That's when my husband and I, we started fighting, because he didn't want me to quit the job. We argued and argued, so I just gave up the idea because I knew I couldn't do it if he was fighting me. So I just quit the idea of going to nursing school. I guess there was not a wide variety of things that women could do. I knew about nursing and I knew about teaching, and that was just about all I knew. But I didn't want to teach. So I worked in a dental office for two [black] dentists on Fayetteville Street. I was a receptionist: I typed and I worked in the lab and developed x-rays and cleaned instruments and just did everything. When I left there, I went to Duke University[25] and worked three and a half years in the records library [at the Duke hospital]. At that time I was one of the first blacks to work at Duke. I worked at Duke for three years, from 1953 to 1956, and the records library was a very segregated department. Betty, the person who hired us, was from either Alabama or Georgia. She went through the interviewing process to find some black people, because she said she thought it was time to offer some positions to black people. We were the first black people to have any kind of office jobs there. Miss Harnett, the head of the department, was always mean to her because she had made that decision to hire black people. There were about eight black file clerks. We did all of the filing and the pulling of the charts.

Miss Harnett had the black girls come to work a half hour early and clean the records library, even though this was the job of the janitorial staff. But she wanted to make sure that we remembered we were black. I remember once there was a cobweb over one white girl's desk, and we were in the back, pulling charts. She came to me and said, "Theresa, Miss Harnett said for you to come and get that cobweb over my desk."

I said, "I'm not getting the cobweb down."

She said, "Well, Miss Harnett said."

I said, "I don't give a (hmm) what Miss Harnett said. If you want it down, you get it down. You tell Miss Harnett she'll have to fire me, because I'm not getting on that desk to get any cobweb down." She never came back. But I was happy to get the job, because I was ready to get out of that dental office, and it was more money and it was a job that I knew I had security and stability there. Saying that you worked at Duke and that you worked in the records library was more prestigious, because at that time people knew that blacks just didn't get jobs like that, working in a library. Plus, working at this dental office, you had to work on Saturday, and I had Saturdays and Sundays off working at Duke, and I loved that. It was more money.

I worked at Duke from '53 to '56, and in '56 I came to the Mutual and started as switchboard operator. I got hired at the Mutual because the woman who was the human resources clerk was [married to] the manager of Mutual Heights [where I lived].[26] When I was on the switchboard, there were three of us. We operated the switchboard and gave tours to visitors. School children, dignitaries, foreigners, they knew about this black company and they wanted to see it. I guess it was just novel for them to come and see that blacks could run a business. We just had tours all the time. All of us who gave tours were light-skinned. A lot of people still feel that way. They have said that I hired my secretary because she was light, but I care nothing about what color anybody is. And Mr. Collins, our president, he looks like he's white, and we have people who come through the company all the time and say, "I thought this was a black company. Why do you have a white president?" He's not white. He just looks white.

I went to college later.[27] My second husband was very supportive, and I could not have done it if he hadn't been, because I had a daughter from my first marriage and was going to PTA and going to the library and all the studying. I went to college[28] for three years, year 'round, but I was still working full time at the Mutual. I had a boss at the time who would allow me to go to school the hours I needed to go, and then I could make up the time in the evening, so he really was very supportive also. It really didn't matter to me what my degree was in, as long as I had a degree, because I honestly feel that going to college just broadened my knowledge of everything. But it really didn't help me with my job, because I came from experience anyway. What helped me with my job is we have a curriculum of life insurance courses here that you get and you take examinations, national examinations. Then you become known as a Fellow, Life Management Institute,[29] if you pass all of these exams. I did that to also show that president that I was not a dummy. One woman had done it before me, but as soon as she got her FLMI, she left. I was the second woman. I wanted to let him know that not only men could do things; we could do it if we wanted to.

I've seen a lot of changes [at the Mutual], because I remember when women couldn't wear pants here. I remember when they talked about if you wore eye makeup. I remember my boss spoke to me once, told me that he thought it was improper. When eye makeup first came out, I thought it was nice. He told me that he thought that I shouldn't wear eye makeup, that his daughter said that I shouldn't wear makeup on my eyes; it was improper. That was like a "lady of the night." I said, "Well, consider me a lady of the day."

[More women than men worked at the Mutual], but most of the men [were] in top positions. Women were in the clerical and secretarial positions; they were not in the professional positions like accountants and actuaries. They were not in those positions. Miss Vi Turner[30] was my mentor. She was a very strong lady, a person that everybody admired. She had a very keen mind and she went after any job that she wanted. She went after it, and it didn't matter to her that she was a woman. She became financial vice president when it just wasn't popular for a woman to be that. She knew stocks and bonds, and I thought that was just something—a woman who could talk about Wall Street. We all just went to her for advice and for guidance and for leadership, asking her what should we do if we wanted to do this. She was our mentor. She would call a meeting of the women, and she would tell them things that weren't proper and things that were proper, and what they shouldn't do and what they should do. She was just something. She was a great lady.

For a long time I had a terrible inferiority complex, I guess because I had come up so poor. Then when I started working at the Mutual, I was put in an environment with people who I thought had a lot, and they did. Like Dr. Cleland, the only black pediatrician in Durham. His wife worked in my department. So her desk was here and mine was here, and here she was wearing all these fancy things and all this stuff. She was the most beautiful person. In the beginning, I just felt like I was so poor; I had clothes, but not the kind of clothes she had. I liked working for the Mutual because I was able to dress up, to wear heels and to wear makeup and to come to work and leave every day and still not be all sweaty. I thought it was just a great job. My mother was proud. She was happy. "My daughter works at North Carolina Mutual." She knew it was a good, stable job, and I could help her if she needed it. I never have had a lot of contact with whites, because I've worked for this black company since 1956. I think because I have been with this company for so long, I have more pride in the company than if I had worked in a big white corporation.

Hortense Spence Williams was born in Emporia, Virginia, in 1928, one of fifteen children. Choosing to never marry and inspired by her father, who started and managed a trucking business, Williams was economically independent and opted for self-employment. In 1958, she opened Hortense's Barbershop, in Norfolk's black business district. Williams used her shop and her financial smarts to make a contribution to her community. She helped establish a business league for other African American merchants; she coordinated fundraisers through her church; and she made it a priority to hire men released from prison to work in her shop. These activities were good for her business, bringing positive publicity and visibility, but she also intended them to strengthen the black community against the conditions brought by segregation.

My father owned a truck line. He was able to manipulate and use politics and get close to this white man, Mr. Harrell. He could see something in my father, as far as making money for him, also. But my father was so aggressive and smart until he worked his way in. He worked with this white man until he was able to get his own franchise and named it Spence Truck Line. But he had to work in through the white man, as all of us did back in those days.

But I highly respect my father, because he did not have an education. He just had what most of us need: good common sense, vision. He was very aggressive and a very smart man. He was able to send all of my sisters to college. I had one brother to go. The rest drove the trucks. After my father passed, we weren't able to carry on the truck line, because all the sisters, all of us, finished college and moved away. In the meantime, my brothers had other jobs and three of my brothers passed and so we sold the franchise.

When I went to college, St. Paul's,[31] I took teachers training. I changed my mind the second year. Majored in industrial education and took cosmetology. I never thought about cutting hair and I never dreamed that this day I would be in this kind of business, which I have been in thirty-seven years.

I moved to Norfolk in 1948 because my oldest sister lived there. I really hadn't decided what I wanted to do, even after I finished school. So I started out manicuring and specializing in facials in these barber salons. Back in those days there wasn't such thing as a unisex shop. I worked in several shops before I went into business. One day, something said to me, "You've got to do better than this." I knew that I had the wisdom and the vision and the aggressiveness to do like my father. So a young man came along and said, "Hortense, let's go into business. Let's go into business." Well, he was more financially fit to do it than me, but we made an agreement, and I decided to go into business.

So in 1958 I started Hortense's Barber Salon. I had the largest business for a long time, because on one side of my shop, we cut hair, and on the other side, the barbers processed hair. It was located on Church Street, where there were many barber salons and beauty shops. All our black doctors and lawyers were on Church Street in the same area that I had my business. Because of segregation, they could not go downtown and open an office. A good friend of mine, the first black lawyer to go downtown and open an office, told me that even after the Civil Rights Bill[32] was passed and he moved down there, they would come and take the name off his door, spit on his door, and still wouldn't accept him for a long, long time.

There was a time in Norfolk that black barbers worked in the white shops. They were the operators, but no blacks could come in for service. We had a lot of professional barbers cutting white people's hair, taking appointments, but black people could not go in the barber salon. Same goes for beauty shops. There's a beauty school right downtown today that refused to take minority students. Back in those days, black women were using straightening combs and all like this, and [whites] didn't know how to teach the students. So they refused to allow black students to come to the school. I can't down the white man for not knowing how to cut black hair, as a black barber has always been able to cut white hair, because the black race has every grade of hair in the world in it—every grade—the straightest, the most straight, to the most kinky hair. So we had to learn how to cut every grade of hair. But they had no reason, really, years back during slavery time, before the Civil Rights Bill was passed, to know how to cut our hair. Now, when I was on Church Street, I was the only one that was willing to hire a white barber. But he finished the black barber school—Jenkins Barber College. I hired him. He didn't work too long, but he was pretty fair at cutting our hair, because he finished the black barber school.

As I said, I'm like my father. I have my father's instinct, and by working in several hair salons before going into business, I had a sense of what it was like to run a shop. I love people and I wanted to be in business. I was able to meet another party that wanted to go in business, and then I bought him out two years later and was on my own. But by my father being a businessman, [I knew that] businesses sometimes, if you're weak, you better not go into it, because you'll run into a lot of surprises. There are times that my employees would get in trouble. The public won't use that person to cut their hair, and if you have an employee, a barber [who] has the majority of the business and if he gets in trouble, there's nothing for you to do but go and help try and get him out, because he carries your business. It's not like a McDonald's or something that has the name McDonald's. You build a name, like I built a name, Hortense's Salon, but your employees, the stylists, are the ones that bring the business. This is who you have to depend on. I can't run this business alone. I have my clientele and my barbers have theirs. That's what makes a business like this successful.

I've always tried to do what I can for my people. That's why I have a reputation for giving many black young men jobs that come out of the penitentiary. Someone has to do it. I believe in giving you a break the second time, until you come out of there. I have one who was in the penitentiary; he could have been in there just about all his life. He came out and this was the third time I'd given him a break. He stayed here about six weeks when he went back and broke his parole. So I told him I was through with him. "I'll give you two breaks, but three, four, five, I can't, because I feel as though you're not ready to follow the system."

Well, the black community was very much together [in the 1950s]. We had to be in the same community as far as business was concerned. Back in those days when I was on Church Street, there were very few minorities that owned contracts like they do now with Burger King and McDonald's and all.

Most of the black businesses in Tidewater came in through the minority organization. That's how they got the contracts. Because Lyndon Baines Johnson proposed all this money. I hired a young lady once that was on the welfare, and they had a program called the WIN Program.[33] For people on the corner, had no education, they were on the welfare. The welfare would send them to barber school, cosmetology, nursing, whatever. But when the Republicans took over, that was terminated. After Ronald Reagan took office, that's when we had a lot of downfalls where minority [business] is concerned—cutting back and terminating a lot of these organizations. So things change as time goes on. I can see more and more conservatives coming back in America. Like [with the demise of] affirmative action, it's getting harder and harder for us.

When the Tidewater Area Business League started in 1964, [I was the first woman and the only woman.] But I have never had a problem in approaching people and them accepting what I have to say to them as far as joining an organization. I think that's why I was made chairman of the membership, because of my personality. I love people. We formed for minority businesses to get some of that $66 million that Lyndon Baines Johnson had proposed. So I'll never forget the first meeting that we had. I was the only female, and there were several black men. With the vision and the aggressiveness and mentality to push on to help our people, we formed up this organization. We went around and got so many business people—professional people—on the board. We formed a large board—twenty-two people. I was made chair of the membership committee. In public life, I knew a lot of people. So I went around and brought strong people in, strong leading people, to build up the organization. So we started to meet once a month. We went on and on like that for two years, and we started growing until we said, "There's more money out there in Washington. We can have contractors." In the beginning, most of the contractors still weren't bonding.[34] So we merged with the contractors of Tidewater so they could get bonding and receive some of these contracts from the government. So we named it the Tidewater Area Business and Contractors Association, and it got larger and larger. Now it's one organization.

Today we have two black-owned shopping centers in the area where I started my business on Church Street. So we were able to get some of that land and reinvest, some blacks were. But I can say, we as blacks, we have to think more for ourselves. We cannot go ask the government to finance us. My church, First Baptist Church, is a great church, and we have a lot of programs in there for the youth. We have a great tutoring program. We have tutoring every Thursday evening, headed by my pastor's wife. Through this program I've been able to get computers, books. I'm always trying to help the underprivileged kids. But I feel as though we need to reach out more, because if you look at our youth today, if we don't do it, who's going to do it? The world owes you nothing, although I know we've had a hard time. We haven't always been treated right and everything, but we need to look up more and look at ourselves more. I think we've a mind sometimes to look back to that slave mentality: divide and conquer. Well, it's time to get away from that. That's what I try to do. Grow more and more and help your community and the underprivileged, someone who's less fortunate than I am.

Flossie Fuller Branchcomb was born in Norfolk, Virginia in 1933. Her father worked building the supply center at Norfolk's Naval Operating Base and her mother cared for the family's seventeen children (Flossie was number ten). In addition to her father's job at the naval base, the large family survived with the money he brought in from gardening in the neighborhood and from her mother's resourcefulness as a tailor and manager of the family budget. In the 1960s, after she had married and become a mother, Branchcomb entered the work force as an apprentice welder, breaking (and running up against) race and gender barriers that prevented black women from doing—and succeeding in—this work. She worked as a welder and supervisor at the shipyard until she retired, fighting when she was passed over for promotions. Her access to this occupation came thanks to the 1964 Civil Rights Act, which made sex and race discrimination in employment illegal and helped open new vocations to black women workers.

I was born in Norfolk, Virginia [and] I was number ten of seventeen children. My mother only went to the third grade. I think my father was fifth grade. They were from Princess Anne County, the New Light section, which is now Virginia

Beach. They owned that land down there but they lost it due to not knowing about taxes.

My father helped construct the Naval Operating Base supply center. He was more or less a laborer. I think he started working there in approximately 1916 or '17. My father [told] us about coming in contact with the different nationalities coming to the base on the different ships, which was very fascinating to me. He spoke mostly of the Nigerians and the Ethiopians. He never complained about Jim Crowism; he never complained about it to us. I think he more or less kept us safe from that type of conversation. To help support the family when he was not working, my father would go around the neighborhood getting plots of land that weren't being used or that nobody knew who it belonged to. He would get the men in the neighborhood to plow it and he would grow vegetables all over the community. He grew corn, butter beans, collard greens, all types of greens, string beans, sweet potatoes, all types of vegetables. In the back yard, my mother had the condiment garden, which would be parsley and rhubarb and radishes and sage and all types of spices. All of this was grown to feed the family and to share with the neighborhood.

I went to Booker T. Washington School. I was in the National Honor Society, but I wasn't fortunate enough to go to college. I didn't know anything about scholarships. The wealthier children and the children who were in the know, as we called it, got scholarships. My parents were not in the know as far as what benefits were out there, and I was naïve. I was very, very intelligent, but I was naïve. After that, I wanted to go into the service. But my brother was in the Navy, and my other brother was in the Army. My mother and father wrote my oldest brother to tell him about my desire to go into the service, and he wrote back and said, "Don't let her go. It's not the place for her." So I couldn't go.

Then I didn't know really what to do. I took on a little job, but it wasn't a job that was really worthwhile. I was cleaning house. I worked at a dress shop a little bit. Like I said, I was so naïve, I ended up like a lot of young people today. I met a young fellow who was way above my head and I ended up getting pregnant. The dad went into the service and he sent some money home to help out. I continued to do those little jobs.

I got married the second time in '61. As you know, Norfolk has been a transient town for military, especially sailors. I happened to marry a sailor that I met here in Norfolk, and he was getting ready to go to Puerto Rico and we went to Puerto Rico and got married. We had two children while we were there. After two and a half years, he was being transferred, so we came back this way, and we decided to buy a home. I had another child. I worked for GE—General Electric—for a couple of years, and then I took the apprentice test for the Navy shipyard. I began working there in August of '69. I was an apprentice welder. It's a four-year program training you to be a journeyman in the trade. It was very scary. I had never experienced anything like that in my life. It wasn't my choice. I didn't choose that as a trade; it was chosen for me after I got there by the human relations office.

It was weird for the men to see us women coming into the work force. There had been women there before, during the war,[35] but since then, there weren't too many women in there, except in white-collar jobs. This being a blue-collar area, it was very strange, and they were watching and swore we weren't going to make it. So when I got my hands-on training, I was scared, because there's fire, you get burned. It was weird. I was fearful. For a long time after that, the men looked down on us. They looked down on us because they didn't think we belonged there. They felt like we were taking a man's job. A man could be in there on that job, but here we were, women. But economically, we had to survive just like anybody else. They made it miserable. It took a lot of will power, a lot of strength to stick it out. We had to do ten weeks, twice, of academic training at Tidewater Community College. In that time, I passed all the academics. As a matter of fact, I was on the dean's list. That still wasn't enough. I got hands-on experience as I began to work. There were two of us ladies who were put into the welding program at the same time. Of course, I was the older one, I was about thirty-seven years old, and Eloise was about eighteen years old; she was just out of high school. But we studied together and we worked together, and we were able to succeed and excel in doing what had to be done. A lot of times officials would be walking through and they'd watch how we were doing. They were shocked that we were doing so well. As a matter of fact, some of the most tedious-type little jobs that had to be done, we would find them giving them to us to do.

But when it came time for promotion, they didn't want to consider us. Once my training period was just about up, I decided to put in an application for promotion to see just how it would come out, and I put in for supervisor. I came out as highly qualified. I was shocked because I was just coming out of training, although I'd had the hands-on work experience. So I made highly qualified. That was in '73. I didn't get that job and I didn't expect to, either. I let it go by. Each year, I would put in for all different types of positions, and it seemed like I was just passed over on everything. I couldn't understand why, because they had a negotiated agreement in the manual that stated that 95 percent of all the promotions were made from ex-apprentices. That's the way the program was set up. But as it turned out, I had to end up fighting for a promotion after I tried so long. I got serious; I really wanted to get a promotion now. Everybody else was getting promotions and moving right on, and I'm still back there. They refused, because I was a woman, and because I was black, too, I believe.

I belonged to the Metal Trades Council[36] and they had to fight for advancement of everybody. They had to fight for any cause that arose that was questionable. Finally, I put in a discrimination complaint and it took five years, but I won it. I filed the discrimination complaint in 1978. I won the complaint in 1983. So it was a fourteen-year period since I started in 1969. I didn't file any more promotional complaints, but I had to file complaints against upper management for things that they had done that [were] not really right toward me. So by the time I became very proficient in supervising and management, they offered me to take another management thing that would take about four years. In the meantime, I was doing the duty of a general foreman. I was still supervising between thirteen and eighteen people, while taking care of all the safety meetings for my whole shop, about 800 people at the time.

But then I got to the point where I knew I was getting older and I would hope one day to retire. So I wouldn't put in for promotions again. It was very difficult in dealing with that, if you wanted to get ahead. Yes. It made it difficult. But if you didn't care, didn't mind, you just wanted to be passive and just work and work and work and work, and just do that little bit, just do what they say do and that's all, it's a different story.

Rodie Veazy was born in Tunica, Mississippi, in 1940 and her family moved to Memphis after World War II. From a poor family, Veazy was introduced to work at an early age, and as the only daughter, she assumed responsibility for household chores while her mother, father, and brothers worked outside the home. Veazy graduated from high school and married young. After she separated from her husband, Veazy found employment in Memphis' mattress factories, where she worked on assembly lines and became involved in unions. As Veazy recounts, work in the factories was hard, but the unions provided some aspect of equality and a way for workers to exercise their rights.

I was born in Tunica, Mississippi, and my family moved from there when I was five years old, in 1946. We moved to Tennessee because my mother got a job up here in Memphis. Some rich people down there knew she was a good worker and through them she got a job at a hotel. I had three brothers. My father worked for the railroad and had a good job. He was a veteran. But he drank himself to death. He was alcoholic. And it killed him. Yes. It messed up his liver. So he died at the age of 55.

We had a hard life. My mother worked hard for us day and night. I can remember she worked so hard she couldn't sit up the rest of the night after she got home. My responsibility was head of the house. I was the lady of the house. I was the only girl so I had all the chores, the cooking, so forth, to do because she worked all the time. I had all that to do. The boys you know aren't going to do too much housework. They aren't going to cook. That is for sure. And my two oldest brothers dropped out of school to help my mother to support us. They dropped out to go to work. It was pretty bad. I started cooking when I was about ten. My grandmother taught me how to cook. I learned how to cook, wash, iron, clean house. I had that daily. That was daily.

We did not have any relatives in Memphis. Just us. We lived in south Memphis, close to the state line of Mississippi. It was just poor people like us. Work hard and survive the pain. Go to school, come home and work. That is all we ever knew. That is all we ever did. I was determined to get an education so I wouldn't have to work as hard as my mother did. My ambition was to get my education. Get me a good job. Get my own home. That is all I wanted. Something of my own. I always wanted something of my own. Drive me a nice car and have a nice home. And that was it. That was all I wanted out of life. I knew I wasn't ever going to be rich. I just wanted a good education so I could get a good job, a better job, paid more than what my mother was making. But I have worked as hard as my mother.

I got a job when I was sixteen at a restaurant down on Union so I could buy my school clothes. First job I had. I married at an early age. I married when I graduated at seventeen. Had two boys. I met my husband at work. He ate there a lot. Older man. I just got fast and wanted to get away from home. I shouldn't have ever married. I was married about three years and then I had my first son. I was just fast and wanted to get away from home. I made the biggest mistake of my life. Crazy. We stayed together six years and I had to get out of it. It was too much for me, I was young for that. I hadn't lived my young life and he was an older man.

At first I was scared to leave but I made up my mind that I can take care of my own boys and I left and I have never looked back. I am glad. But I had to work hard. I started working in '63 at Sealy Mattress and Upholstery. I didn't live too far from Sealy at that time. So some friends and I just got together one Monday morning and went looking for a job. I was going to school at night for sewing so I was the only one they did hire. I worked at Sealy six years and I left there and went to the job I am on now at Serta. I worked two jobs. I worked guard duty for twelve years, on patrol, riding around and checking buildings. I did that when my two boys graduated out of high school. I worked that twelve years. So I worked hard all my life.

Yes, I have been a production worker for twenty-eight years. It was pretty tough at Sealy. They made everything when I first start working there: mattress beds and upholstery. Every piece I sewed, I got paid for. I worked hard. I worked an assembly line, to sew and build mattresses. We just made them from scratch, the whole thing. I built the mattress from the springs. They built the springs in the back and brought the springs up there and you went around a long table and you stapled. Then you threw them over there and another guy taped around the edges of it, put the binding around it. We worked hard. We earned what we made. Yes, we did.

Sealy was not a union job when I first went there. As a matter of fact, everybody who talked about the union got fired. That is the way it was when I went there. And these big guys would come in and talk about union and, of course, the company could not do anything to you while they were there. But the minute they left, if you discussed any union, you were out the door. It used to be when an employee needed money, before the union came, you could go to the boss and say, "I am about to lose my home or my car. I need $500." The company would lend you that money, take it out of your salary. But after they got the union, they cut out all that. They just didn't want the union at Sealy. A lot of firing and a lot of everything during the time they were trying to get a union. The company can scare you and threaten you and do everything they want to. And they did a lot of people that way because they were determined not to have a union. Said they were doing fine without it and they had been in business fifty years so they didn't figure that they needed a union. But they got it because the people wanted it so they could have their rights. Yeah. Before the union, the bosses could pick favorites, no matter about seniority or whatever. Whoever they liked [would get picked] to work. You could not do anything about it because it was nonunion. That was it. But I didn't ever have problems. I kept my position, you know. But I was a hard worker, always have been.

I only worked there six years and the year I left, they got the union in. But when I first went to Serta, they already had the union, Local 282. Serta is the oldest mattress company in Memphis.[37] That was one of the first factories forty-one years ago. So they have been in that Local 282 that long. With a union, jobs were divided by seniority. Seniority rules. It didn't matter what color you were. If I came in here and got hired today and you got hired tomorrow, I had more seniority than you did. So I was really impressed, you know. Because I never worked at a factory before with the union going behind us and telling us all that, and boy we got more rights than we thought we had. But it was a whole lot of difference. The union played a big part in your job.

[In terms of racial prejudice] Sealy was a little better than Serta. The boss, a multimillionaire, he was real nice. He would give parties, Christmas parties and things, and he would mingle with the people as a whole. He would have big meetings. I don't think he was that prejudiced. Some in the office might have been but he didn't seem that way. He would come out there and sit and eat with us just as big as he would go and eat with the white. You know that was his way. He called it one family, because we were one community. And we were the one making him richer. That is for sure. Sealy did not have too much prejudice. Not that I know of. At Serta there was more.

[I got active in the union because] I would always speak out. If somebody was trying to be more than he is, or trying to run over another one, or somebody trying to take somebody's job, I would be the main one to speak out. I was never afraid to go to the boss with a problem. So, therefore, I was Miss Big Mouth and I got elected Steward in about '84. And for the last three years I was Chief Steward. Chief Steward means I was all over the plant. So when they had a problem, because I was more familiar with the contract and I had been there the longest, the stewards down in the departments would always come to me for advice. I would show them how to fill out grievances or whatever until they got used to it. It was a big deal because we had a lot of problems with younger people. They'd come to work and then you wouldn't see them for two or three days, and you'd have to go in and speak for them and they would have all kinds of problems. It got to be a headache, trying to teach them and tell them what is right and what the contract says. But I still had to file for them and go for them even if I knew they were wrong. And so I played a big part. Any kind of problem they had, they would come to me. I have been through all of that. Right up there with the big bosses and the lawyers. Trying to fight for these people's rights.

I remember in '68 when Martin Luther King got killed I was working at Sealy. They announced it on the radio. Everybody walked out of the plant. We all left the plant. I didn't know too much. I just knew he was a big man and he got killed in Memphis so, therefore, everybody was mad. I went home like the rest of them did. I didn't understand why anybody wanted to kill him. I didn't understand why nobody wanted him to have rights. This is something I never understood. If I can do as good a job as you, I think I am good as you. If you can come in here and I have just as much education as you have, I am supposed to have as good a job as you. That is just as simple as that. But people don't do it. They don't want to do it. Let's put it that way. I have always thought I was just worth as much as anybody. I have always wanted to have something of my own. And I wanted my kids to have the best, to not have as hard a time as I had. I wanted them to have a good education so they could get a good job and never have to worry about not having enough education to get a job. I wanted to see those diplomas.

I have always been able to speak out for myself. I was just always the type of person to speak out and say, when you go to the bathroom you are going to do the same thing I do and if you get cut, you are going to bleed like me. You aren't better than me. I was always able to speak out for myself and go right ahead. I have always felt I was just as much as anybody. You know I might have been poor, but I still was a human being and I let them know right up front they weren't more than I was. Nobody is. I have always been able to do that. That is why I stayed put on my job so long because I would always speak out. I was never afraid to go to the big man or whoever he was to speak out. Speak up. That is the main thing about life. You got to speak out for yourself.

Children and teachers at the West End School, Durham, North Carolina, 1906. Courtesy of the Durham Historic Photographic Archives, North Carolina Collection, Durham County Library.

Vermelle Diamond Ely, crowned queen of the Queen City Classic, 1948, Charlotte, North Carolina. Ely is pictured with the principals of West Charlotte and Second Ward High Schools, the rival teams that played an annual football game in Charlotte. Courtesy of the Robinson-Spangler Carolina Room, Charlotte and Mecklenburg County Library.

Midwives Association, New Iberia, Louisiana, 1920s. Members include (*left to right*) Mary Pratt, Mary Guant, Mrs. Prezeal Simon, Virginia Compton, Mrs. Laninia, Mary Traham, Mary Anthony (unidentified), and Patsy Moss. Courtesy of the Iberia Parish Library and the *Behind the Veil* Collection, Duke University Special Collections Library.

Penn School students selling vegetables at the Farmer's Fair, 1939, St. Helena Island, South Carolina. Courtesy of Lula Holmes, Ernestine Atkins, and Louise Nesbit, and the *Behind the Veil* Collection, Duke University Special Collections Library.

Margaret Rogers interviewed by Kara Miles, Wilmington, North Carolina, 1993. Courtesy of the *Behind the Veil* Collection, Duke University Special Collections Library.

Susan Kelker Russell playing checkers with Florida A&M College president, John Robert Edward Lee, Tallahassee, Florida, circa 1930. Courtesy of Sue K. Russell and the *Behind the Veil* Collection, Duke University Special Collections Library.

CHAPTER 4

A Society Totally Our Own:
Institutional and Cultural Life

"Everywhere you went," Ruthe Lee Jackson of Mississippi recalled, "Blacks had a place where they'd go. Whites had a place where they'd go. You didn't mix. You didn't mix with the white people." Similarly, Virginia's Celestyne Porter remembered that African Americans "developed a society totally our own....The way of life in our society," Porter explained, "was with each other." Porter and Jackson's lives differed in many ways, but they shared similar memories about the segregated communities in which they lived. Segregation kept African Americans separate from whites and forced them to deal with unequal conditions. But black people did not view segregation itself as the problem. In fact, racial separation generated spaces where the black community existed away from the unwelcome gaze or supervision of whites. Behind the veil, African Americans developed a world of neighborhoods, schools, churches, clubs, businesses, and professional and voluntary associations. Each institution served multiple purposes, fulfilling community needs for assistance, security, support, and encouragement. As protective public spaces, neighborhoods provided youngsters a sense of belonging in contrast to the outside world of degradation and insult. Black businesses—including shops and stores, beauty parlors, barbershops, night clubs—not only served black communities economically, but also provided secular spaces where people met to socialize, seek information, and absorb community culture.[1]

African American women were critical to the development of black spaces. Here, narrators describe the specific ways that their roles in the home and within the family extended outward to their roles sustaining their communities' institutions. As culture carriers and curators, they passed on knowledge as diverse as biblical teachings, history, recipes, and remedies. They served as missionaries and mothers of the churches, teachers and counselors in the schools, customers and owners of shops, and members and leaders of voluntary associations and political groups. In this way women were the exemplars of upbuilding and uplift. Determined that their communities should be all they possibly could, despite the circumstances of racism, they not only started institutions, but they also created and deployed programs to provide social services denied by Jim Crow. They showed particular concern for children, the elderly, and the disabled or infirmed. In these interviews, women describe small armies of church women who, with their children in tow, made home visits to read the Bible and sing to those homebound by illness. Strikingly, however, none of the women recall being visited in this manner, an omission that may reveal the extent to which women internalized their role as caretakers and not recipients of others' attention.

In these interviews churches constituted the central community institution. A site of lifelong affiliation, the church proffered political space and meeting place, as well as spiritual retreat Among the first things communally built at Emancipation, churches bound freedpeople to each other. It was the one institution that African Americans could call wholly their own, epitomizing African Americans' aspirations to live independent of whites, in terms of distance and autonomy.[2] Whether rural or urban, the church provided the focus of most community activity, joining people for fellowship on a regular basis, virtually every Sunday even when no minister was available.

In addition to its significant role in connecting segments of the community, narrators stress, the church influenced their personal and spiritual lives. "I've been in church all my day," Ruthe Lee Jackson declares in her interview. In her experience, churches affirmed black Christianity as a daily practice—a way for people to live and a way to manage crises. As communal space, the church relied on its congregants, especially the participation of women. Leadership positions in churches might go to those without significant economic means. In fact, one could come to church with no resources and find respect and dignity, social capital for even the poorest of congregants. People might be active in multiple churches, and even have affiliations with multiple denominations. In a different church one might practice faith in ways other than the ones they learned as children. Yet, our narrators explain, they reconciled beliefs—those of the Methodists or the Baptists, for example—with their decisions to participate in churches that resonated with them personally. For many women, church became the one place where they could put their personal needs above those of the family.

In spite of their articulations of unity and mutual aid, our narrators' discussions of the internal dynamics of black communities and institutions in the Jim Crow era throw the spotlight on not only the differences among African Americans, between urban and rural experiences, for instance, but also between classes, genders, and neighborhoods. As interviews with Dorcas Carter, Celestyne Porter, Harriet Wade, and Emogene Wilson demonstrate, the clearest delineations of class among African Americans emerged in cities. Wilson's interview reflects on her family's relative privilege, the result of her father's self-employment as a doctor in private practice. Segregation confined professional and elite families to the same neighborhoods, churches, and schools as laborers and the under- or unemployed. Porter addresses this diversity, suggesting that African Americans in Virginia never "had any seriously bad attitudes about living together as black people." Still, Porter's narrative points to class differences and to the limits of cross-class alliances.

But even when middle-class women in urban areas enjoyed privileges brought by a degree of wealth or security, they also recognized the dangers they faced. As Carter's interview suggests, prosperity could be achieved, but it was never ensured and it was often endangered if whites refused to tolerate black wealth or power. It is useful, for instance, to recall not only lynching and harassment, but also race riots where whites destroyed vibrant black communities across the South in order to limit or, more drastically, to wipe out black wealth and reassert white supremacy.[3]

These interviews convey a persistent undercurrent of frustration with Jim Crow tempered by affirming comments about their segregated communities. Indeed, racial hostility greeted black women on the other side of the color line. The safety zone was behind the color line where women could make measurable contributions to the larger community and find satisfaction and fulfillment in these roles. For adult women, black spaces provided important opportunities for leadership and for organizing activities, businesses, and programs that reflected their interests and concerns. In their memories of community and cultural life, black women detail few changes in those roles over time. Despite expanded opportunities in the desegregation era, African American women continue to volunteer time in their churches, to support their communities through a range of activities, and to remain affiliated with black institutions. In this way, although interviewees express aggravation and anger at the results of segregation, they demonstrate the continued importance of spaces they call their own.

Dorcas E. Carter was born in 1913 and lived most of her life in New Bern, a small port city in eastern North Carolina that had been home to a free black community before Emancipation. Here Carter remembers New Bern in the 1920s and 1930s, describing a prosperous black neighborhood that a fire gutted in 1922. Even more devastating than the destruction of black properties, according to Carter, was the impact of the fire on the African American community's sense of cohesion and security. In her memory, the fire became a turning point, marking the loss of innocence about race relations and forcing her to confront the realities of racism in her community.

As a child I grew up in a very dedicated family community where there were children, my peers, and church-oriented people and many of the people in the neighborhood in which I grew up were members of my church, St. Peter's AME Zion Church. I was just a stone's throw from another church, Rue Chapel AME Church. I used to lean my head out the window and I could hear the services going on. Of course, I felt that St. Peter's AME Zion Church was the grandest church around.

I felt as a girl that [black New Bern] was prosperous. We had tailors in that community; we had butchers in that community; we had merchants in our community; we had a blacksmith in our community. We also had a shoe maker in our community and my father was a home site builder, contractor, and my mother had taught formerly for five years but when she married my father she did not teach any longer. She went into home making. Everybody was busy and everybody was doing something. No handouts. In the historic section of New Bern, on George Street particularly, the houses were very historic and the people dressed so modest, so cultured. When they were walking down the street, you could see the men escorting the ladies by the arm and lifting them up to the street level or the curb level, all dressed with their walking canes and their derbies. George Street at that time was a very popular street and it was mac-adamized.[4] We could walk to our corner and get a trolley and go down to my grandmother's house. You could ride for five cents. You had all of these things around you, and the men in the community were self-sufficient people because they had their own enterprises. These were the people whom I knew as a girl until I was eight years of age. Then when I was eight years of age the big fire came and it destroyed this.

But one startling experience that I had just before the fire. After supper my parents had given my brother, Sylvester, and me pennies to go to the store. Our neighbor had a little shop on the corner. It wasn't quite dark because they would not have allowed us to go that distance [after dark]. We were going on down holding hands and I looked and coming up George Street were hooded men on white horses. When I saw those I became aghast, you know, and I got my little brother by the hand and we ran back down to our home very hurriedly and I was exasperated, I fell. My father said, "What is wrong, what is wrong?"

I said, "Daddy we just saw some men hooded." And my father explained to me, those are [white] business men from downtown.[5]

He said, "They're coming to," he said this word, "intimidate" the black man. And he named these men. This stood out with me. And not very long after that incident the big fire came. And I always felt that they always wanted us off George Street but they didn't know how to do it. They seemed to have envied that section of New Bern because it glowed, all these beautiful homes, and people would come out, you know, looking graceful and dignified. So to prove my point is that after the fire of December 1, 1922, the city proclaimed an ordinance that this area was condemned and nobody in a given footage could go back and build. I always wondered why we could never go back.

Another startling thing was [about] two valiant blacks. One was a pharmacist and he had just restored a beautiful home before the big fire and he had invited us down to a birthday party, my brothers and me. This was the first time I had ever seen a light switch that you could turn on, because we had oil lamps. And when I wanted to go to the bathroom they turned on this switch and it lighted up all the stairway, and I thought this was the most beautiful home that I had seen. He had just finished this before the fire. Dr. Kennedy was his name. And another one was Mr. Sawyer who was a tailor. Each one of them started rebuilding and when each would get up maybe to a second level [white officials] would make them tear it down. Dr. Kennedy fought and fought. In this time I think the blacks had become intimidated, wouldn't come forward like they do now. If he even had men to join with him and fight this struggle, we could have gone back into our areas and rebuilt. And I guess my father didn't take a stand and maybe no one took a stand. Finally he became so disheartened until he died, Dr. Kennedy did. Mr. Sawyer had got up to the second flight [of building his new home], they told him again to tear it down. When he tore it down, he got some more lumber and he built again. But when he got back to the second story they told him if he did it again they would imprison him. So then he just went to live with his father and never tried to rebuild. Now I know that these were the only two men that tried to rebuild. The Red Cross came through and it gave you like $200 to start anew and it was so devastating.

So then this was really a turning point in my life as a little girl because I had to relocate. You had to get in another community. You have to meet new friends. Looks like my life has been just that way. The day after the fire my three brothers and me, we asked Mama could we go back and see our homesite and she allowed us this privilege. And I remember I was sitting there with little tears coming down [my face]. My grandmother did not know she had two daughters who were fire victims [and] had already taken in a family whose baby was eight days of age. [So we had to stay in this field.] After we got in this field, my father got our living room chairs which we had salvaged and our living room rug and put it down so we could, like little Eskimos, go in there and spend the night. But by this time some white woman had told my mother that she had a basement in this area and that we could sleep the night there. Mama didn't want to impose. But my aunt told Mama, "Well, Sis, we have one room and you can stay in there." And we had these high back beds then and Mama and Daddy put them in there and that's where we stayed for nine months until we got some place to move.

But then life, well it changed. We relocated out in this area and I met another section of people. These people out here were not near as enterprising as the people whom we had left. They were home builders. We had a merchant out here, two merchants out here to be exact. Little girls and little boys and the plum trees and the apple trees and the peach trees and the gardens and all of this. This was a new type life that you could play in the ground. Then we were about a mile from school and we would have to walk to school. I liked this section because it wasn't as large as the area in which I had born. But anyway, we still would tread down to St. Peter's each Sunday to our church.

The fire brought a lot of disheartened people wondering now how could they reshape their lives. Many of them migrated to New York City because they felt they could make a place in life there. We lost a lot of our church members who left and never returned to New Bern, you know, just disheartened. Then a few people gathered themselves together and started businesses. See the fire lessened the prosperity that had been for the black man. But he reestablished himself and by this time the 1930s came and the big Depression. This was another disaster, you know, this big Depression. And this brought low incomes, but thanks to Franklin Delano Roosevelt and the NRA and the WPA[6] and so forth, I saw men making maybe like a dollar a day turning bricks over, just giving them something to do. And work didn't altogether boom for my father. There was a lot of devastation and a lot of people just weren't able to rebuild.

So then I guess by relocating I really started to see differences in the races. Right after the big fire, I was still living at my aunt's and Mable and Louise Havens and I were coming from school. We were coming along singing and running and I was about eight years of age then, maybe turning nine. Mable and Louise were girls older than I. And this white girl called us "black niggers." And my two friends went into her and this girl went running. I ran all the way three blocks to my aunt's home. I was so frightened I didn't know what to do. I mean frightened. I said, "Oh, Lord, I think this is going to be a lynching." I got home and my aunt's porch was high and I ran under the house. Eyes this big. I know they must have been. Just shaking. Nobody knew I was under the house. They had what they called a Black Maria then, an old paddy wagon[7] and they'd put you in there. It passed by my aunt's house and I knew they were seeking me. Lord, pitty-pat, pitty-pat, pitty-pat. When my girlfriends saw me again they named me scaredy cat, but I didn't care because I wanted away from trouble. But they felt that they had as much privilege as anybody else did. They were ready for the fist. They're going to fight back. "Black niggers!" And they pushed her. I cut out. And, honey, you talking about running. Honey, I got wings in my heels and I mean I ran. I went away from there. I don't know whether I ever related it to my parents. I don't know that I did. But, honey, I was one frightened girl. Because then you couldn't strike anybody white. I knew about lynching. I thought they were going to put me in that paddy car and maybe go to jail.

The white man was prosperous downtown. That was a very prosperous area. It often seemed when you would go in a store to be serviced, you could feel a little tinge sometimes. They would have dressing rooms that whites could go in but I could not go in. But you had to be very scrupulous to know the difference. And you would go in a shoe store and you could sit, but in a little place toward the back. See as a little girl, I wasn't discerning all of this. But because of the fire I had grown up. Mama [would] take me downtown and I could feel little things, a sign in the store that said white/colored over a water fountain. This got to be devastating. Go in the bus station, white/colored. And you weren't even allowed in a restroom in the bus station. You would walk on the street and the whites would be coming down the street and they would try to take all of the sidewalk. And then they would call you "black nigger" in a pair of seconds. I didn't go through all of this because I was a very passive girl, and I always tried to stay out of the way of trouble even if it meant I would walk off the sidewalk, you know.

Ruthe Lee Jackson was born in 1909 and raised in Crystal Springs, in Mississippi's hill country. The members of her family were farm laborers, hired by the day to work picking and packing a variety of crops for market, including tomatoes, cabbage, beans, beets, watermelon, and carrots. The family moved to the Delta in 1924, working on cotton plantations and sharecropping. After marrying at a young age, Jackson started doing domestic work, staying with one family for more than fifty years. In her interview, Jackson discusses aspects of the spiritual life of her community, including her participation in organized religion and people's belief in "haunts" and spirits. She describes other community customs, such as those that directed planting, health care, and safety from storms.

We've been going to church all our days. Mama raised us up in church, just me and my sister. Mama carried us to Sunday school until we were big enough [to go by ourselves]. We got a little catechism and she carried us as long as we were little small children [and when] she didn't feel like going, we went by ourselves. So we were raised up in church. I was born in 1909 and in 1918 I was converted. When I joined the church at Crystal Springs, it was a Baptist church, [Good Hope Baptist]. But my mama was Methodist and she couldn't take care of us at two churches. So I waited until I got married [before joining a church], because I wanted to do what my mama said to do. [When I married] I came on up here and I joined a Baptist church called Saint John's and was baptized in the river. I was happy because the Methodists sprinkle [when you're baptized] but I wanted to be buried[8] and I wanted to go in that water. And when I got married I came to the Delta and joined Saint John. And I was buried in the Yazoo River. And I [have] been happy, happy, happy ever since.

I've been in the church all my days. My sister has been in there all her days and our parents were. We didn't know anything but Christians. There wasn't as much going on in a church as goes on now. We had church and Sunday school and revival, and that was all. But you know now they have all kinds of reunions and guest speakers. And I'm a missionary for the Lord. I stand at the table. I teach Sunday school. I'm a missionary and I'm president of the missionary society and I was a matron of the Eastern Star.[9] And I just love the Lord. Yeah, and

I work, work, work. I just work in the Congress, in the conventions, and in the churches, and in the missionary I represent [the church] in the convention and things like that.

We used to sit around and hear people talk about haunts and spirits. That's all they talked about. They would tell us about the haunts and tell us about bears and all kind of stuff like that. They would talk about the haunted houses and what they heard in the house, that they heard something fall and they did that and another. Somebody would hang a horse shoe up over the door and that would keep the haunts out. We listened to all that kind of stuff, but I forgot a lot, because after we got grown and people stopped telling us about those stories, you know. So we quit. It might near passed my mind.

People used [to take] an ax and they'd put it in the ground to turn a storm. We never did it, but some people do it. They said they changed a storm, but we never did. But some people did it. They [would see] the way the storm was coming and they would stick it in that direction. But when the Lord said storm, it was a storm, and you stuck that ax any way you wanted to.

People used the signs to plant. "Don't plant now. If you plant now, it's a bug day," or "If you plant now it's so and so." And they would wait until a good time and then everything would work out all right. And then some people used the moon. There's a certain time of a moon when you plant certain things. Some call it the growing moon. If you look in that almanac and it's a bug day they'll say, "Don't plant today cause this is bug day. The bugs will eat up your stuff." So people would do that. They do that now.

When anybody died, you had to bury them the next day. We didn't have undertakers. The people would go and sit all night and drink coffee and put this person on a cooling board, you called it. [You had] some planks and you'd put him on them and put nickels over his eyes. Put nickels over his eyes and put a little old dish of something with some salt in it over the mouth. [That would] keep their mouth and eyes shut and keep him from purging from the mouth. Then the next morning we buried him. But you'd sit up all night. If somebody passed, a woman, they would always get my mother to come and give this person a bath. If it was a woman, Mama would always go and give that person a bath and comb their hair and get them ready for the funeral for tomorrow. [That was when we lived] at Crystal Springs.

[My mother and grandmother could get plants out of the woods and make tea.] When we had the flu or pneumonia or something like that they would use tallow. They would save tallow when they killed cows. They would use this tallow and a piece of red flannel. You would heat that flannel and just grease the bottom of your feet and all like that and it would heal. They had so much in the woods they would get and make. They would make sassafras teas through the spring. And you would eat poke salad through the spring. You could mix it with your vegetables or you could cook it by itself. And they had another thing you called simmer leaf. We'd make tea. Mama would put that down by the fireplace. We'd pour some hot water on it and then when we'd get ready to go to bed at night, they'd give us some simmer leaf tea. Well, that would help you. That was also to help you keep your bowels moving. Then it would help you otherwise.

There were plenty of black businesses, and there were plenty of places where [it] was whites only in the Delta. And, you know, that was all up and down everywhere you went. Everywhere you went, you know. Blacks had a place where they'd go. Whites had a place where they'd go. You didn't mix. You didn't mix with the white people. We called the Delta the devil, because we heard how they treated people. In the Delta, [white people] took advantage. They didn't want the blacks to have nothing.

Essie Alexander recalls the specific work that the church women in her family performed. Alexander was born in 1927 on a plantation in Sunflower County, Mississippi. Her parents were sharecroppers who had seventeen children, with eight surviving to adulthood. Alexander's parents provided powerful examples for her; her father attempted to negotiate with landowners for more favorable economic arrangements, showing his willingness to relocate the family if a landowner failed to agreed to more beneficial terms. Her mother, a member of a missionary church, spent time nursing and caring for the community's most needy members. From the time she was a child, Alexander accompanied her mother to care for sick members of their church, a responsibility shared by all adults and children, although with roles distinctly defined according to age and sex. Alexander recalls her reluctance, and then eventual acceptance, of this role, a position she came to understand was an important demonstration of community commitment and spiritual faith.

My mother was a strict Christian woman. My father wasn't but he became a Christian later on. My mother was a member of a little church, the New Jerusalem Church and when we moved to another place, my mother joined North Mount Olive Church. At that time, I was eleven years old and I joined Mount Moriah. I reckon you're wondering why I wasn't at the same church with my mother, but the church that I joined when I was baptized, it was right by our house. But it was a kind of large membership and my mother said that she was needed at the little church where they didn't have anybody. But she didn't object to me joining there. So on first Sundays, my mother would be there [at Mount Moriah] with us, and on fourth Sundays we would go to her church, because we only had one Sunday out of a month that we had a regular pastor day. But we always had Sunday school. I taught Sunday school, I think starting when I was fourteen. I became an usher at the age of eleven and I've been an usher ever since.

As I said, my mother was a strict Christian woman, and she was crippled. She had had rheumatism five years before I was born. But she walked on a crutch, sometimes seven or eight miles to see about sick people. My brother and I, we had to go with her. She formed a group of ladies that would go and do that kind of thing. In the middle of July and August, until about the fifteenth of August, there wasn't any work for the women to do [in the cotton fields].[10] The men went to the woods and cut wood for the winter, and the women just quilted and did whatever. So if there were sick people in the community, my mother would get that group of ladies and they would go and visit in the daytime. If there were men that were down sick, the women took care of them, too; but at night my father and some other men would go and sit with that individual until a couple of hours before time to go to work, and then they'd come home and get ready to go to work. We were Missionary Baptists and that was part of their mission to go and help people who were less fortunate or were ill. If there was somebody in the community sick who couldn't go out to church, my brothers and sisters who were members of the choir would go and read the Bible. The adults would read the Bible and the young people would go and sing. So that's what we did then. I still do stuff like that in the community, get together with ladies and do stuff like that in the community. I always said when I got grown I wouldn't do it, but I wound up doing the same thing, but even more.

I got married on July 17, 1944, when I was seventeen and my first child was born a little before I was nineteen. I moved out of my parents' house and my husband and I, we also did sharecropping. We farmed, just like I did when we were at home, and my husband drove tractors and things like that, baled hay, and I chopped and picked. We were married almost three years when I had children. I have three children, one born in the hospital and the others were delivered by midwives. Really, midwives did a lot more than doctors, because the doctor, once that baby was delivered, you were on your own. But the midwife would come back and check [on] you and that baby until that baby got four or five weeks old.

Unless a person got hurt real bad and had to go to the doctor, we used home remedies. I'll tell you what we used to use for cuts—coal oil, kerosene. That would get the swelling and soreness out. And if the cut was deep enough where it bled a lot, you took the soot out of the chimney or out of the stove and [got] sugar and put it in there and that would stop it from bleeding. I mean, you had to nearly get your head cut off to have to go to a doctor, for real. For fever they had a type of fever weed, peach tree leaves and all of that. For diarrhea we used to boil kookaburra roots. For sores, there was a weed they called milkweed. It had little fine leaves and you broke it off, white stuff would come out like milk, and that's what you put on your sore. For colds and whooping cough, we made tea out of the hoof that comes off the pig's feet. We put it in the stove or down in front of the fire and baked it real hard, put a little sugar in it and boiled it. For mumps and stuff like that, we got sardine oil to rub [until the] mumps [went] down.

Some of these home remedies were passed down from my mother and other people. But things also just came to me to try this or try this. Because although I was a young woman living out there on the plantation, I had to take care of everybody else's children. When somebody's child got hurt or got sick, for some reason they would call for me and I had to figure out something that wouldn't hurt them, that would help. Nine times out of ten it worked. Then, I was a real observant person. If I went to the doctor with somebody, and the doctor told about home remedies, I kept it in my mind and when I got home I wrote down what the doctor said. And just anything I would hear an old person say they used, I'd write it down and I would try it.

Most of my associates were older women and that's how I learned a lot of stuff. I really didn't associate with younger women that much, because I was kind of old fashioned for them. And I was into church activities and a lot of younger women my age just weren't into all that kind of stuff. Everything just changed about women. They wore shorter clothes; they did different things and got jobs, which we didn't have at first, unless you worked in white people's houses. Time brought about a change, a big change. But I was just more of a traditional person. There was nothing wrong with it. Just because I didn't change, there wasn't anything wrong with other women changing.

Aurie Flowers was born in 1907 in Milford, Georgia, in rural Baker County. Her father died when she was an infant; still, she managed to finish high school and attend college, earning a degree in elementary education. A teacher and wife of a minister, Flowers was at the center of a lot of community activity. In her interview, Flowers talks about broadcasting a radio show to publicize news and information about black churches, organizations, and schools in southwest Georgia, work that she continued for more than forty years. Flowers' broadcast was one way that African Americans in southwest Georgia kept in touch with their institutions.

In 1952 the radio station WGRA was expanding and thinking of some way to bring Negroes, the colored people into it.[11] Back then we didn't have TVs; we just had the radio and we were proud of it. WGRA was the only radio station within Grady County. They thought how would a program do among the colored people giving highlights of the community news? And someone told the station manager about me and he called me, and we talked by phone, and then I went out to the station and it was decided that I would try it out. He gave us fifteen minutes on Sunday mornings from 9:45 to 10:00 to give the highlights of the colored folks news and so I accepted it. Now that was somewhere back then in the '50s and I've been doing it ever since and now it's forty years.

I was the first black working there. On Sundays, I'd get up and give the news, and then I'd keep on round to church for Sunday School and remain for morning worship services. I have missed but mighty few Sundays. Sometimes I have had to ask somebody to take over for me, but most times I have compiled it. When it first began, people thought that there was some compensation in it, you know money. But when they found out that I was just doing it, I haven't had too much competition because nobody wants to take the trouble of compiling the news and going out there.

The Beauty Culture League sponsored the show and then after that Rutherford's Dry Cleaners sponsored me for a short while, and Cloud & Son Funeral Home after them. When they were about to let go, the manager of the radio station at that time said it was a good program, such a nice program, that he would let it go as a public service feature and that's the way it goes now as a public service feature; no one sponsors it. The sponsors paid the amount that the station charged and they furnished transportation at the beginning. All the sponsors furnished transportation, to get me out to the station just outside of Cairo Highway 84 and back for those fifteen minutes.

The community responded real well from the beginning. I received news weekly from different organizations saying that our organization is having such and such a thing and would you please announce it through the third and fourth Sundays. I gathered all the churches in the community and in the county, notified the people to give me information. Like Lutheran Primitive Baptist Church held services third and fourth Sundays and what time and what other services were held, if there were any services like Sunday school such and such a time and morning worship services at a certain time and evening worship at a certain time. If something happened in their community that they wanted to relate, if they were going to have some kind of meeting or something, they would let me know. If they sent me a card telling me such and such a thing is going to happen then I would read that on air. I do church news first and then outstanding community news next and then social news next. If things were happening at the school, I'd read that. And I did that for as many churches as I could. I did mostly church news but other local news too that we considered important. I didn't get into sports much, but if something very outstanding maybe was happening with the school then I would mention that. I also mentioned social gatherings, funerals, and deaths.

Now we don't have a black newspaper but our news comes out in the *Cairo Messenger*, a Grady County paper, and we have a space in there. Betty Williams, she lives in this brick house down there, she does a column called the Ebony News that comes out once a week.

Helen Howard was born in 1909 and raised in rural Arkansas, growing up in a small community known as Dark Corner. She worked as a farmer and seamstress. In her interview, Howard recounts the community's cooperative activities during the Depression, when women from area families ran a collective kitchen. Built on black-owned land near the church and started with government support via a New Deal demonstration program, the community kitchen expressed the neighborliness that already characterized the small community.[12]

I was born January the 26th, 1909, here in Cotton Plant, out in the rural area in a little place down there they called Dark Corner. It was mostly a colored settlement. All families would want land, and if you didn't own the land, you rented so many acres and worked. Therefore the houses were close together. There were two churches down there and both of them would be full of people on a Sunday. And we would walk to church and Sunday School and to school everyday, about three miles. And the schoolhouse was right on the campus with the church.

The families would have from three to six or seven children. And, you know, some had more than seven. My family was seven, seven children. And we had a place not far from us where we'd go fishing and have fish fries right on the lake, right there. They would have all the children out there for a fish fry.

We had that Depression in Hoover's administration, let's see, it was '29 and '30, somewhere in there, when the crops burned up so. And the people had to go out in the fields and cut the corn, what little corn got up about waist-high, and cut it and pack it up, and make fodder for their livestock. And if you rented, the landlord would hire you to pick that cotton for $4 a bale. That's what you got for that if they hired you to pick it.

[We] had a place there they called the canning kitchen. The government furnished a cooker. At first, when they demonstrated, they gave [you] some cans, tin cans. That was on up in the '30s when they had this canning kitchen. And the children had school for four months during the winter and two months of summer school. And during the time the children were in school in the summertime, well, the families would be at the canning kitchen, canning. The next day, the next two families would go there and can. After the government gave them so many cans, then we had to buy the cans. And then the community bought a pressure cooker and then they bought this thing that they sealed the cans with. And that was down through the '30s and on into the '40s. The government [also] demonstrated making mattresses.

[The canning kitchen was] down the highway at Mount Pleasant Church, out on that campus, just north of the church. The school campus was east of the church and the canning kitchen was north. At that time, it was wasteland, water stood there when a big rain came. And they just built a log cabin and fixed it up nice and made the canning kitchen. Had a stove out there and tables, you know, where you could do your work. Mrs. Idella Lee Darby owned that land then. She was a colored lady. [And] the community [owned the kitchen.] Mrs. Clemens, Mrs. Darby, Mrs. Bullard, and Mrs. Childress [were over the kitchen.] Mrs. Childress was a younger woman than the others I named, and she would go there earlier. You know, they always said "old people for counsel, and young people for work." So she had a group, Mrs. Childress had a group, younger than she was, working there. [And the older women] saw that it was kept up.

Margaret Rogers, who appears in Chapter 2, witnessed segregation in public accom-modations in the beach communities on the Atlantic coast near Wilmington, North Carolina, where she grew up. She describes the ways that African American residents created their own recreational spaces, such as Bop City and Sea Breeze, beach resorts on the southern coast of North Carolina. Rogers also talks about having to raise funds for the public high school, including money for the bus to take students to school. In her discussion, Rogers highlights resistance and conflict, including children's efforts to rectify inequalities and exact justice against those individuals—sometimes com-munity leaders—whose actions they considered contrary to the public good.

I was born in 1939, so I was here during World War II and beyond. Wilmington during that time was a relatively small place. Most of the people knew my mother and they knew my father. There was discrimination in this area, a lot of it. But it never really, really bothered me to the point that I felt violent about it because I like to use my education and turn the discrimination against them. I would do little things I knew would aggravate them constantly, but I was never hostile in doing this.

During the 1940s and 1950s when you went to Wrightsville Beach[13] you were stopped at the bridge tender shack. If a colored person came to that bridge you were stopped and asked where you were going. You had to give a person's name and a telephone number and they would call them to see if indeed you were going [there]. And if that person said, "Well, yes, I know them but I was not expecting them today," you didn't get across that bridge. Or if they said, "Well, no, I have no idea who this person is," you did not get across that bridge. And so to this day I still don't go to Wrightsville Beach. That's a public ocean and it always has been. But blacks had a problem getting on Wrightsville Beach. Even if you worked there you weren't allowed on the beach. This is the Atlantic Ocean and you were not allowed to walk on that sand out there.

The north end of Carolina Beach at that time was called Freeman's Beach or Bop City, and we had Sea Breeze. Sea Breeze was a very, very famous black resort.[14] Bus loads of blacks would come here from as far away as California. When you went to Bop City, you had to travel through Carolina Beach. So the parents would always say, "Now you know we're getting ready to go through Carolina Beach so let's be quiet. Let's not make any noise." You couldn't eat at the restaurants at Carolina Beach. You couldn't stay in the hotels. But if you went into one of the stores at Carolina Beach to purchase something you knew that you had to leave. But you didn't get that feeling that you did at Wrightsville Beach, you know. The people [at Carolina Beach] were at least civil to you. But at Wrightsville Beach they didn't want anything to do with you, period. They didn't want you there at all.

Bop City was interesting. We called it Bop City because of the rock and roll, the dance steps. There was a building there that was called Monte Carlo by the Sea. It was a restaurant with a big dance floor and an outside deck and it was right on the beach. The churches went down for Sunday school picnics and the band went down every year. We would go to Bop City one year, go to Jones Lake one year, go to Topsail[15] one year at the end of the school year as a treat for the band. So we all stayed, you know, in our own area unless you stopped at the gas station or the fish market or to purchase something. And they let you purchase it without a problem as long as you behaved. You go shopping. You get what you want. You pay for it. You leave. That's what I mean when I say you behave.

There were whites around who did not allow their employees to be blatantly mean to black people. They went along with the segregation and the Jim Crow to a point, but then there were whites who did help. We had a lot of little [white-owned] stores in our neighborhood and usually we were treated kindly in those. As children we played our pranks on the store owners and they knew it. There was one man who had a store on Castle Street and he kept his empty bottles, soda bottles, outside in crates propped against the building. We used to sell him his own bottles over and over and over. We'd come in with two or three bottles, you know, and we'd sell them to him. He'd give us the money and we'd turn around and buy cookies. Cookies were two for a penny and bubble gum was two for a penny. And he'd tell us "Okay, when you leave, put them in the crate outside," and we, of course, said, "yes, sir." And we'd put them in the crate. And we'd leave and a few of us would come back later and get those same bottles.

Of course, we did that with a paper drive in the 1950s. Williston High School[16] was having a paper drive to raise money to buy band uniforms. We went all over the city on this one particular Saturday with flatbed trucks picking up newspapers, and we'd take them down to the paper company and sell them. Well, what they did was, they estimated the weight of the kids on the back of it. Then they subtracted that and that gave them the weight of the paper and so they'd pay us for the paper. So then we were to back the truck in, throw that load of paper off, go back and get another. Well, we'd throw about half off each time and we'd leave the rest on there. Put a tarp over it and kids would get on it and we were playing and cutting up and the guys were telling us to be careful, not paying attention. We'd sell them that same load of paper five or six times.

But this was necessary because Williston, like all other black schools in the South, received the used materials that the white high school had [cast off]. When funds were allocated, the white high school got the new books and new equipment and then they gave us the old equipment. If we ever received a textbook that we opened that nobody's name was written in it we knew it was a brand new book. This was exciting but then we realized that we received that new book because the white high school was receiving revised editions. These books were now outdated.

There was one incident. The students had raised money to buy a new activity bus and they turned the money over to Professor Rogers, a principal at [Williston] high school. He was supposed to go to the school board with the money so we could get a new bus. Well, Professor Rogers turned the money over to the school board. The school board bought a new bus and gave it to New Hanover High School,[17] and New Hanover High School gave us their old bus. This was in the late 1940s. The highway patrol, the police department, and the sheriff's department had to be called in to escort Mr. Rogers from the school because the students were going to kill him. The high school boys came to the elementary school and they walked down the hall, which was something that was not done. Teachers when we were going to school were more like gods. You did what the teacher told you to do or else. These guys walked down the hallway and they stuck their heads in each classroom and they said, "Let the children go home because there is going to be trouble." And we went! We all ran home as fast as we could.

But where I lived, in an area they called the Bottoms, we watched and then with [some] adults went back over onto Eleventh Street to see what was going on. And they had to get that man out of there safely because those kids were going to kill him. So there was such an outcry until the money was given back. Professor Rogers knew exactly what would happen. He was what a lot of the [white] superintendents referred to as one of the "good ole boys." You know, "He's a good ole nigger over there. He doesn't give us any problems. He does what we want him to do so everything's fine. We love Professor Rogers." Sure. But that was the problem. A lot of the problem during that time was that you had what people called "the Uncle Toms." They made certain that somebody knew what you were getting ready to do. Most of the Uncle Toms were people who were in a position to help. Instead of helping they did more harm. But that incident with Mr. Rogers I just really remember because it was so unusual. It was just so unusual that instead of trying to help us to do better, he was after his job and he felt that by turning us in, that protected his job.

Harriet Wade was born in 1928 in New York and grew up in New Bern, North Carolina, where her relatives gained prosperity by working as barbers and beauticians, opening and running the first barbershop in the area that served African American customers. As a high school student, Wade worked in her aunt's beauty parlor; she later attended cosmetology school in Washington, D.C., and then opened her own shop in New Bern. A prominent business owner in the town, Wade participated in the state's cosmetology association and in numerous community organizations. Her interview, like that of Hortense Williams in Chapter 3, describes the role of beauty parlors and barbershops in African American communities. As black owned and controlled spaces, such businesses were important gathering spots, where people shared gossip, news, and fellowship in addition to getting their hair done.

My grandfather's first barbershop was downtown on South Front. The oldest man in New Bern would probably tell you he went to Vail's Barbershop and he took his son and his son took his son and his son took his son. We had a barbershop and beauty salon combined. My uncle and father and cousins were trained by their father standing on boxes, and I feel sure they were Pepsi Cola boxes. Later in life the women became beauticians.

At one time the Vails were one of the most prominent families in New Bern and it was a rare thing for a black to be in business for himself. You might find a carpenter. I think those were two of the first professions. I can truthfully say that my family was considered wealthy. They tell me the house on South Front Street had three back yards. The middle yard was a pecan orchard. The front yard had the toilet and my dad's workshop. And the back yard, waterfront, we had a walk and a motorboat and a car, which was something in those days. But they tell me my aunt, my dad's sister, was the only black girl in New Bern who had her own horse and surrey. And that was the same as a Cadillac today.

At one time, if you didn't go to Vail's then you didn't have too much of a choice. I believe it was in the 1930s they combined the barbershop and beauty salon. The barbershop was in front and the beauty salon was in the back. My aunt, Alberta Vail Allen, ran the beauty salon. She finished beauty school in New York in the 1920s. A cousin finished Stark's Beauty School in Raleigh. This went on until my uncle, Seth Allen, retired in 1976 at the age of 84, I believe. I was the last one to come along and no doubt this is the end, because no one else is interested in the profession.

I can remember the barbershop being on Broad Street in the area where Smith's Drugstore is located now. [It had] about five chairs, a dirt floor in the back room where the toilet was. And in the window at the front there was a shoe shine stand. I'd sit on the shoe shine stand and listen to the men talk. It was more of a meeting place. We had a doctor here, Dr. Mann, and [his] son was the first black football player for the University of Michigan. I was just a little girl but I had a crush on Bob. It just thrilled me to sit and listen to them talking about Bob's touchdowns and what Bob did.[18] And the ladies would pass and the men would whistle. And, of course, during that time, Saturday was the big day. People would come in town from the country on their horse and wagon to get their hair cut, do their shopping. Some would get drunk and fight, you know. But everybody in New Bern knew us. They respected us.

During the Depression, my family, the men, the barbers, went to New York because there was no work here. The men went to New York to work as barbers and the women stayed here. I don't know how my family salvaged property and things but they didn't lose their home. They just left everything and went to New York and worked and sent money back here.

[After my father died] I came back to New Bern to go to three years of high school. [My sister and I lived with my aunt and uncle and] we were servants really in my aunt and uncle's house. We had to do all the work. We acted as maids. And we were not allowed to stay home alone, so we had to go to the beauty salon. Everyday we had to clean the beauty shop and the barbershop. On Mondays we had to wash the towels. [My aunt had] three to four [beauticians] besides herself, employees, working for her. All the girls who worked in her shop were from the country and they [boarded] with us in the house. So every morning we had to get up and go out to the store and get breakfast and bring it back and let her cook it, then take it to the beauticians, then come back home and wash dishes, eat and then go to school late every morning. December, November, we'd hang out the windows, washing the windows and her house was spotless. My sister and I were her maids. We had very little social life. For Easter, I remember how beauticians used to be at the shop, they'd be working and we had to be out there because we couldn't stay at home. We would be going home when people would be going to sunrise service, going home from the salon.

And of course I was doing hair at twelve years old. I gave my sister Shirley Temple curls. And I swore when I got away from it I wouldn't ever touch hair. But it's just natural. It came natural.

I came back here in 1966. My marriage broke up and I had one daughter entering Howard University and I had one in the fifth grade and I knew I had to get out of D.C., and that's when I decided to go to beauty school. It was my desire to move back to New Bern and I knew if I took a trade I wouldn't have to look for a job; I would have a job. When I came I rented a booth in my aunt's shop for $10 a week and [then I opened my own shop,] Vail's Beauty Center. I introduced the styling to New Bern in 1966 that they're doing now. I brought with me my big floor dryer, the gooseneck blow dryer on a roller, and eight curling irons [of all sizes.] All of these were brand new things for New Bern. It was then that New Bern was really introduced to styling. I didn't realize they were not familiar with rolling their hair and most people in the area wore wigs because it gave them the style they wanted. And, of course, I took them out of wigs and started styling. Then I ran into the problem by them not knowing how to roll their hair to keep the style, and so then I went into an educational thing and taught them how to care for it. I sold my shop in 1986 and most of my clients had been with me from the time I moved to New Bern.

Years ago the beauty salon was a source of gossip. You know, you'd walk out, they'd talk about you. You'd come in, they'd stop talking. Having moved here in 1966, I was not accustomed to people sitting around telling their personal business and talking about people. [In] D.C., we didn't have time for that and people didn't know each other personally. We have worked very hard to change it. But the beauty salon and the barbershop were gathering places for information like the newspaper is now or like television. People spoke of their accomplishments, bragged on their children, and talked about how hard times were. You know, during that time people [would] go to work, come home, and the men would walk out to the barbershop. And that was their entertainment. In most barbershops, they played checkers. It was rare that a woman went into a barbershop and got a haircut. And I guess it would have been considered an insult for [a man to come into the beauty parlor.] In fact, they didn't even come in when their wives were getting service.

Most [beauticians] were in organizations like the Elks or the Eastern Star. They were very active in church. Going back to my teenage years, I've known the younger gals to leave work on Friday night or Saturday night, go home and get dressed and go on to the dances and dance all evening. They were involved. Of course, I've been one of the most involved people in New Bern. I owned and operated a business. I was on the YWCA board for five years. I had a radio program every Saturday and Sunday morning. I was secretary of the Black Progressive Business Associates. I went around to the schools and I talked to the kids. And all of this at one time. And people used to say to me, "How do you do it? My God, don't you ever get tired?" And it wasn't a chore to me because I always felt that I was different from the average person. I just always have been a super busy person.

Emogene Wilson was born in 1924 and grew up in Memphis. As the child of a physician and school teacher, she enjoyed many privileges that her less well-off peers were denied. She married a journalist and became a mother, allowing her to pass on many of these privileges to her own children, including opportunities to participate in social organizations with others of their own class. Here Wilson discusses some of the organizations to which she belonged and the roles that they served in Memphis, and, in particular, how these associations operated to benefit black women.

I grew up in north Memphis. My father was a physician and he had his office in north Memphis on Bellevue and Jackson. He was originally from Baltimore, Maryland, and was a graduate of Meharry[19] back in 1911. My mother was originally from Tuskegee, Alabama, and her family had moved here. She was a teacher.

Growing up was a very pleasant thing except that we lived on the north side and my parents had always done everything socially on the south side of town. Most of the people in north Memphis had migrated there from the rural areas. So you had a really different mix of people. Everything was in a separate world. And black people, for the most part, operated as though they were in a separate entity. We had our own stores. We could go to the white store, but for the most part, you had people who went into business for themselves. Black businesses were flourishing more then than they are now. They had their own parks and everything was separate. It was a way of life. Most black people had to live in run-down areas because most of them didn't have that much work. Half the people were domestic workers and they depended on white people for their livelihood. But we never felt, what should I say—subjugated? Because I guess we were more or less independent. We didn't have to go through the business of being angry because the paycheck didn't come. Whatever my father didn't get, he had to blame himself, you know? So we didn't grow up feeling anger in the fashion that we would feel it if somebody was always on our back.

There were [many] women's groups that organized for the help of black women. My mother was one of the founders of a club that I'm in today. It was established in 1923. And all of these women were either wives of professional men or they were themselves professional. They were either teachers or something like that. And they used to organize cultural kinds of things. You [also] had clubs that were organized among women who were nurses.

A number of clubs formed during that period. For the most part, fraternities and sororities sponsored the bigger things. They would sponsor a national figure to come to town because they had the funds. So some nationally known people came to Memphis because the sororities and fraternities took the forefront in providing the means to get them here. And our church provided the auditorium. The national Jack and Jill Club[20] organized because of the lack of outlet for the black children of middle-class America who had the means to go places, but were deprived of going places. I was a member of it when my daughter was born. It's mostly for young parents. Somewhere where you know the families, you know the parents. You have three or four friends who have children and you'd like for your children to play with those children. And the club was a good outlet for that and for people who thought alike about going places and doing things. It's kind of an elite thing, but at the same time it was another way for black women to get together and share a lot of common things.

The National Council of Negro Women[21] sponsored cultural events. They sponsored lectures. They sponsored things that people wanted to do but couldn't do in the white world. You know, concerts, fashion shows. And anything that's uplifting, anything that promoted women. A lot of women were also second-class citizens. A lot of women needed to go beyond just rearing a family. And in some cities, maybe it was the cooking of foods that brought women together. For some women, sewing was the thing. Now since the early days, things have shifted where women are more into working, going to school, and being educated. So the emphasis of the National Council of Negro Women has escalated into a voter rights kind of thing. They do education among groups on voter education. Civic kinds of things, showing them how to organize for political purposes. Sometimes it's a religious emphasis. It depends on what is necessary in the life of women in that community and what their focus is. And they raise funds. The National Council of Women is something to help women to come into the forefront and come into their own rather than be Mrs. So-and-so, rather than just follow their husbands.

Most of the women [who joined these organizations] were women who were already out there anyway. It wasn't a thing where, you know, [they said] "Ask my husband, do you think I ought to join that club?" The women who were married, many were teachers or their husbands were in the world of business and were probably involved [in other things.] They were already out there and meeting other women. A lot of the women were single women. You find a lot of single women are the ones who do things with the Girl Scouts and the YWCA. They're the ones. So they needed a group that would give them that vehicle through which they could operate.

Celestyne Diggs Porter was born in 1911 in Mathews County, Virginia, where her family farmed. As a teenager, Porter went to live with her older sister in Norfolk in order to complete high school. In Norfolk, she benefited from the resources provided by her extended family, including the relative wealth enjoyed by her uncle, a prominent lawyer, and an aunt who taught at Booker T. Washington High School, Norfolk's only high school for black students. Porter attended Hampton Institute, graduating in 1933 and commencing a teaching career that lasted more than forty years, mostly spent at Norfolk's Booker T. Washington High. After teaching, she served as supervisor of social studies for the Norfolk Public Schools from 1969 to 1977. Here Porter recounts her many community service activities, efforts that date back to her years in college and reflect the burdens she shouldered as a member of Norfolk's black middle class. Like Emogene Wilson in Memphis, Porter and other black women of means supported the African American community in Norfolk through their voluntary activities and organizational work. But in Porter's telling, these were not burdens but opportunities to serve the community and enjoy the company of other women.

We didn't feel the impact of the Depression. We didn't feel it. My uncle was a lawyer and he was an outstanding lawyer, one of the outstanding lawyers, and, possibly, the outstanding one in Norfolk. We lived up there on Boulevard Terrace, a big white house. We had two cars. My aunt had a car and he had a car. I don't know that we felt the Depression as such; I mean the same as you didn't have this and you didn't have that. But as a race, we had always learned to live at our level, you know what I mean. The churches took care of [people] and you gave to the churches. For instance, in schools kids didn't mind wearing hand-me-downs. If an aunt had a nice dress and passed it to you, you didn't mind. It was a nice thing to do. The churches helped. They took care of large numbers of people who did not have anything. And then as the war progressed [and] people began to move across borders and into industry and all that sort of thing, then you began to understand what the Depression really meant, because then people made more money and they began to get more economic security and things went on in that way.

We had learned about black history before I finished high school because my aunt taught about it. She talked about men like Benjamin Brawley,[22] men like [W.E.B.] Du Bois, [Booker T.] Washington, all of the people who contributed things to the development of the American story and black history. We could call names, you know what I mean, and we could drop names of people. And then Dr. Woodson would come to speak each year to a group of black teachers and professionals called The Book Lovers in Norfolk. Dr. Carter Woodson was a friend of our family's,[23] and he stayed at our house every time he'd come to speak. This was in the twenties, the mid-twenties through to the mid-thirties, early forties. Dr. Woodson was very nice to have around. I used to have to fix his meals for him, and during that time my aunt used to have us serve coffee to the guests upstairs in the bedroom before they got up, and I had to carry him his coffee. He was always so gracious. Dr. Woodson was a lovely person to talk to. He could talk with children just as well as he could talk with grown people. He was a very experienced character. He left us large numbers of the first editions of his books. When my uncle died, we gave all those books to Booker T. Washington High School, and Booker T.'s library has one of the finest collections of first-edition black history around. They've got first editions—Dr. Benjamin Brawley's work, Booker T. Washington's work, Frederick Douglass' work, Du Bois' work, and the younger Countee Cullen, his poems. Oh, all of the newer ones, Langston Hughes' poems.[24] Langston Hughes used to come here every Christmas to Norfolk, and a close friend of mine, her brother and Langston Hughes were classmates at Lincoln. It was nice to meet them.

[At Hampton] we had lovely social groups. The fellows had their clubs called the Olympics and the Omicrons. Then we had a group called the Phyllis Wheatley. They were girls. And then YWCA, the Hampton Players, the dramatic club, and then the debating society, and I was on that. I was in the debating society and the Hampton Club and the Phyllis Wheatley. You had plenty of organizations and things to go to.

During the age of separate and unequal, we developed a society totally our own, and I don't think that we had any seriously bad attitudes about living together as black people. You knew that you didn't live on the other side of town. You knew that you had to sit on the back of the bus. You knew that you had your own churches, your own school, your own everything. For social life, it was your house and friends' house and families' houses and clubs, and this is where we met. There were no places to go, so you went home. And as a result, people developed home and home society, and that was the way of life in our society when it was separate. It was with each other, like that. That's all the good time we knew. So we organized our clubs. We did things for people. Now, that happened throughout the country, not just here in Virginia. It was typical of the United States.

As soon as I came out of school, I came here, Norfolk, to work. I worked with King's Daughters Hospital, Children's Hospital. They had a black wing and a white wing. And I found out as I went in and did volunteer work, they treated the black children with serious diseases just as well as they treated white children with serious diseases. It was three of us that were with the King's Daughters, and we'd go down after school in the evening and we'd go on Sundays to read to the children and to show them pictures and carry them bunnies and make things. It was quite an experience.

Oh, I belonged to everything. Let me see what it is that I didn't belong to, [that] I could tell you better. Well, I belonged to the Moles Club. I was their first national president.[25] Now, the Moles gave the first operating table at Norfolk Community Hospital when the hospital was built,[26] the first black hospital. We sold [raffle] tickets for the first operating table, and that was dedicated in 1938. The social clubs played every kind of role you could think of. We were fund-raisers and we attacked the needs of the community.

Then I belonged to another club, the Kiski. We were all over Hampton during the Depression and we met at the YWCA and formed our club. So we were fund-raising, and we gave the first ambulance to the community hospital, the first ambulance. Then after we had been organized over a long period of time, we organized another group called the Kiski Connections, which were younger girls to carry on our name. They do fund-raising and they make serious contributions to Children's Hospital, because that's my bag and I sort of work with them on that.

[I was also active in] the Women's Interracial Council. I worked with them and especially in the Jewish community. [The Women's Interracial Council] contained large numbers of Jewish women. The Jewish community has yet to be given the credit that they should have in the integration movement. We did much in trying to ease the situation [of desegregation]. I sponsored the National Honor Society at Booker T. Washington High School for twenty-five years. We got the first charter member in 1929 at Booker T. Washington High School. When I came back to teach, I sponsored the National Honor Society, and we'd meet with the children at the other schools, the white schools, and we tried to ease the contact between the children. We didn't live in white neighborhoods. Black children didn't live in a white neighborhood. Very seldom did you go to white churches. You went to your own church. So therefore there was no line of communication, and going to school there was no line of communication. All the white children saw of black people were domestics, you see what I mean, and all black children saw of white folks were those in the shops and around and the plumbers, like that. It was a strange but challenging lesson in humanity, in learning about people, and I should think they did fairly well.

I don't know whether I get carried away or not, but I'm so interested in seeing young people progress and especially young blacks, and especially young women. I'm telling you, young women are coming on, and I'm so glad to see this, I really am. It just enthuses me so. It's nice to be able to be around to see young people do in areas where we couldn't do. You know what I mean? You just could not do anything but teach school. That's all you could do. And that was a prestigious profession for blacks. Some could be nurses, but the top line was teaching school.

Irene Monroe was born in 1912 in Vernon, Alabama, the youngest of eleven children and daughter of a former slave. Monroe became a teacher in a rural school where her job extended beyond the walls of her classroom and to many forms of engagement with the community. Unlike Celestyne Porter, who describes teaching as the best kind of work available for women, Monroe was eager for other opportunities. In 1940, she moved with her brother to the industrial town of Bessemer, on the outskirts of Birmingham. Her move from the rural countryside mirrored that of many other women of her generation who were drawn by economic opportunities and other aspects of city life. Monroe eventually succeeded as a business person, owning and operating a nightclub in Bessemer and a steakhouse in Birmingham. Here, she recounts with pride her accomplishments as both a teacher and business owner, and she points out some of the differences she perceived between black rural and urban residents. Monroe describes the ways that schools and cafes served as important gathering spots and provided recreational activities that sustained African American communities during Jim Crow.

I used to teach down in Lamar County. I finished high school in 1931; I taught nine years and I stopped teaching in 1940. First the supervisor started me off in a little country school where I taught first through sixth grades. See, in the country you had to teach all first through sixth grades. Later I was at Sulligent, Alabama, and we had four teachers there. I [taught] first grade there. [When I was there] I had to board with some of the parents. [The] lady dipped snuff and you'd be sitting up there at the table eating, and if she wanted to spit, she'd spit right on the floor. So the supervisor told me I'd have to say nothing [because] people in rural areas think you're making fun of them. But the rural people were nice to you. They'd invite you to their house for dinner and the children would bring cans of pickled peaches and ribbon cane to school.

When I got my little school I organized a basketball team. The children who had stopped school because they finished the sixth grade, they wanted to start back because they wanted to play ball. So the supervisor asked the superintendent if they could come back, the grown ones. He said [it would be all right] if they were willing to abide by the rules and regulations and not do things in front of the little children. So I organized a team there, and those boys came back to play ball, but I told them they'd have to get their lesson, too, their English work. They didn't want to write, but they learned how to do work and then play ball.

After I got a team, we didn't have anybody to play against. The supervisor asked if I would go to other schools and organize teams so we'd have somebody to play. So after school I would go to these other schools and organize a basketball team so we'd have somebody to play, and people came out to see their children play ball. The fathers made the back boards and put up the hoop.

When school was out [in the summer], I'd come home to Bessemer to my brother. After I taught nine years, I asked Lamar County for a leave of absence to come to Birmingham and finish college. I had two years in college. I started the Madison Nightspot in 1940. My brother had it built, so when I came from school, he said, "You won't have to go back down there in the country and teach this time because I've got a job for you." I got out of school in April, and I started the Madison Nightspot in May with a barbecue pit and all that stuff. It was a one-stop place. I made barbecue, hamburgers. I had beer, whiskey, and I sold soul food. Coca-Colas were 6 cents a bottle then. Beer was 11 cents. The sandwiches were 15 cents back then. Hamburgers were a dime or something. I had a lot of white customers. I had them come in convertibles and back up to the door, and they would sit there and eat barbecue pork sandwiches and [drink] beer. I served beer on the curb out in the front. They'd sit right there and eat pork sandwiches as fast as I could make them. I didn't turn down anybody. Whites would come in. The blacks didn't pay them attention. I had two or three houses.[27] I furnished beer by the case, bootleg. I'd sell them a case of beer, especially on weekends. They'd run out on Friday night. They'd come down here on a Sunday. They'd put one in their trunk and go on about their business.[28]

My brother and I had a farm and we raised everything. We had chickens, hogs, geese, ducks, cows. We had everything. We killed it all and raised all kind of vegetables—corn, potatoes, peas. My brother managed the farm. We'd milk cows and bring the milk here, and my sister would churn it with the dasher and she'd sell all the buttermilk she could get. She'd do all the cooking here at the house.

[To book the out of town performers,] you'd have to buy about four or five dates on them. I had three places in Montgomery [where I booked performers], the Catfish Club and the Sawmill Quarters and another place.[29] It just kept me on the road. Every night I'd have somewhere to go with the band. I'd get a little shut-eye, strike out that evening about five o'clock. I'd always leave early to get in town and let them know that the band's there. I'd come back that night when it was over with. The band would come back and they'd stay out here, because they didn't have anywhere else to stay. They couldn't stay in the white motel. I had B. B. King, Ray Charles, Louis Armstrong, and Nat King Cole. I'd carry them to Selma to the Elks and another little old place in Tuscaloosa. They'd just bring a big crowd to their place to get to sell to them. That's the way they made their money, selling food and drinks.

When I first started, I got some contracts that were $300, some $350. I paid Ray Charles, Little Junior Park, James Brown, Ivory Joe Hunter. I'd book them from New York and from Houston, Texas. B. B. King was my sure bet when I wanted to make some money. B. B. had a lady, a black girl from Memphis, the first time he came here. Her name was Evelyn [Young]. I never will forget her. She could blow. She'd take that solo. She could blow that horn.[30]

I had reserved seats down at the front and [put] a fence around it. Other people sat in the booths and outside. They'd come out to dance. One time I had the Sweet Arthurilles. They were white girls, and I didn't know it. New York folks sent you a poster, they didn't tell you whether they're white or black. When they got here and they were white, I had them out there in the motel. I said, "I didn't know you all were white."

They said, "It ain't no different."

I said, "Well, will you all mind putting on a little pancake makeup?"

They said, "No."

I got some pancake makeup and made them brown skin, light brown, put it all over them. But they had on little white blouses and little bow ties and the girl that was blowing the horn got hot and she opened up [her blouse]. One fellow said, "She's white! She's white!"

I said, "You shut your mouth, nigger. I don't want to hear you say that no more. What difference does it make? Ain't you enjoying it?"

"Yes, ma'am. I'm having a good time."

I said, "Well, you go on and have a good time."

They played their dates, and then they left. I had a big crowd. Those girls could blow their horns. Yeah, they could blow.

I didn't have trouble. All the people out here would watch the cars for me. They'd say, "Just open that window where we can hear that man play that guitar. The man reminds me when I was down in the country trying to get my row out. Let him play that horn." B.B. would get on one of them songs with a guitar, "Lucille" and "Had a Little Girl." Boy, he would flail that thing, and they'd just jump.

CHAPTER 5

I Like To Get Something Done: Fighting for Social and Political Change

"Women can have a more powerful impact on some things...than men can," observed North Carolinian Florenza Grant, reflecting on decades of civil rights struggles. Grant—along with members of her family—challenged local white authorities to obtain voting rights and to improve schools in their rural community. Not intended as a criticism of men, Grant's observation states her understanding of the different obstacles that Jim Crow presented black men and women, as well as the distinct resources and specific strategies women could marshal to assert their citizenship rights as blacks and as women. Grant and the other narrators in this chapter reveal how women and girls sought to resist and fight against the humiliations and inequities of the Jim Crow South. They speak with anger as they remember the exclusion and hatred they faced. At the same time, however, they speak with pride about their unyielding commitments to the black struggle for social and political change.

The array of activities recounted here reveals the constant assaults that black southerners mounted against Jim Crow. Because few African American southerners could vote before the 1960s, the electoral arena proffered only one mode of political expression. As we see here, African American women's protests expand the definition of politics. Everyday acts of refusal, resistance, and rebuttal illuminate modes of collective protest. Their fight was sometimes a spontaneous reaction to an injustice, and at other times part of a broader assault against apartheid waged by a community or organization. Frequently, however, these forms of activism were connected. The interviews show how women were moved by personal bravery and their refusal to sit idly by as others fought for justice.

The stories included in this chapter depict the breadth of issues to which these interviewees devoted their time and energies.[1] African Americans considered achieving access to the vote a fundamental goal and viewed enfranchisement as a basic citizenship right. The wall of requirements instituted by southern states— literacy tests, poll taxes, understanding clauses, and grandfather clauses—formed both a bulwark protecting white supremacy and a barrier that prevented most African American men and women from successfully registering. Fear often kept the small number who broke through that wall from actually showing up at the polls to cast a ballot, especially when polling places were located in police stations and other spaces controlled by unfriendly whites. Some of the women who tell their stories here recall pivotal moments when they tried to register or first voted. For many, these efforts constituted their earliest involvement in the political arena. Their interests in voting and citizenship rights, however, had been spurred much earlier by teachers, family members, and community elders.

Inasmuch as the black freedom agenda extended beyond the Voting Rights Act of 1965,[2] it also preceded the mid-50s. African American women pushed for changes in deplorable conditions of many black schools, segregated transportation, inequities in wages and working conditions, and the conditions that prevented black families from gaining economic security and holding onto land. In waging these battles, black southerners drew on their sincere beliefs in American democratic ideals and in their own sense of self-worth as individuals and as a group. They also anticipated—indeed, expected—that their families and communities would back them up with understanding, bail, protection, or other forms of support that might become necessary.

Just as the desire to vote was rooted in lessons taught within schools, churches, and families, so the activity of registering and voting was rooted in women's social connections, especially their personal relationships with each other. The narrators here recall joining—or leading—groups of women to the courthouse, the polling place, or an official's office. Working together in grassroots campaigns and in electoral organizations, they found in each other a source of strength and support, as well as common interests in the welfare of their families and communities. Indeed, personal relationships, more than political ideology, led them to take action. Efforts to desegregate schools and defeat other forms of racial oppression were often motivated by the desire to protect children or to ensure opportunities for future generations. Other women were drawn into action by their own children, who took risks that inspired mothers to follow.

Some of the narrators explain that gender shaped the roles women played in political struggles.[3] Florenza Grant asserts that black women were less vulnerable to physical assault, making them able to join protests when men demurred. In her experience, black women were relatively immune from economic repercussions that might result if they challenged the status quo. These observations, however, should not detract from the extraordinary bravery required of women when confrontations occurred. Nor should readers ignore the real threats that women faced: as many of the interviews detail, women suffered along with other family members when their homes were attacked, relatives were assaulted, or jobs were eliminated in retaliation for activism. And like all of the African Americans who survived the Jim Crow South, they bear witness to a hard racial past.

The support women gained from other women and from their families sustained them through the troubles that could result when they pushed against the South's racial order. In addition, neighborhood organizations, churches, coworkers, and social clubs provided structures and spaces that supported political resistance. Places controlled by African Americans were critically important: black-owned businesses, including the establishments described here by Julia Lucas and Alice Giles, offered safe spaces for people to voice anger at racial oppression, express wishes for the future, and organize for the present. Churches, colleges, universities, and even high schools became activist centers where one generation guided the next. Yet schools and churches could be conservative, as several of these interviews reveal. Representatives of public institutions sometimes tried to prevent political involvement, fearing the reality of white backlash. Also, we hear in these interviews early anxieties that desegregation might result in losses for the black community, not only for black teachers and children, but for the ideology of black education which reached beyond the classroom.

Finally, but significantly, the interviews show the connections between the mass movements for civil rights that emerged in the 1950s and 1960s and the messages of resistance and defiance women had learned as children. These descriptions of activism span from the 1920s through the 1990s, offering a reminder of the continuing fight to ensure that justice is served and equality maintained. They also remind us that the civil rights movement neither began in the 1950s nor ended in the 1960s. Instead, inspired as young women, these narrators remained active around contemporary issues like AIDS, apartheid in South Africa, poverty, and community development into their advanced years. Showing few signs of fatigue and articulating a lasting commitment to their endeavors, some narrators wonder whether younger generations will pick up where they left off, concerned that the post-segregation generations do not share a sense of urgency about citizenship rights. Lanetha Branch worries that black children no longer learn the importance of freedom and democracy from schools and community events. Yet, the interviewees are not pessimistic, assured by signs that younger generations are "going to stand up for themselves." As to the old Jim Crow, "It's not that way anymore."[4]

Harrieta Jefferson was born in 1916 in Leon County, Florida, and grew up on a farm, picking beans and cotton and helping with the family's cattle. Here, Jefferson describes Emancipation Day, an annual celebration held on May 20.[5] As Jefferson details, the celebration included food, fun, and an opportunity to express both racial pride and faith in American democracy. Thus, even at a time when southern states effectively disenfranchised most African Americans through the imposition of poll taxes, literacy tests, grandfather clauses, and other measures, the celebration of Emancipation Day remained a way for black communities to remember the past, express their patriotism, and stoke children's democratic aspirations.

We always had a picnic on the 20th of May. Emancipation Day. There's a special place down by the side of the road that my daddy had for the picnic. And he would always lime and whitewash his trees. And then we would all gather there for Emancipation. And my daddy and all the community would get together, and they'd make this great big barrel of lemonade. We would all say speeches. My brothers, Carter and Henry, would always say the Emancipation Proclamation. And I remember one speech that my mama taught, and I never did learn that speech right, but it was "The Negro Will Be In It."[6] And we were always taught as kids why we were having the 20th of May. That is from the day that people were freed, black people were freed. We would march and dance behind the drummer. Carter and Henry would beat the drums and they would just start that morning at the sunrise. They could really beat those drums. And my mama would have a Maypole. She'd have a Maypole wrapping with all red, white, and blue strings on the pole. And about the first of April, we'd start practicing how to wrap this Maypole. All the children out of the community would come from miles to practice twice a week, every Monday night and Friday night. And we'd learn how to wrap this pole.

We never paid that much attention to the Fourth of July, the only thing we would really celebrate would be the 20th of May, and people for miles would come and celebrate. White people would let you off work if you were a maid. They'd let the men off. All the men got off on that day. They would drive their wagons. Around seven o'clock in the morning we'd look down there and see wagons and horses and things tied around and people would get out with all these loads of children. My daddy made this great big 60 gallon barrel of lemonade. Everybody would come with their baskets and all those beautiful table cloths and the women would spread them on the ground and they'd fix the food, a pile here and a pile there and all over the place. And then when lunch time came, children would sit down on the ground. And after the dinner, the first thing we'd have would be the speaking. Everybody would say a speech, and then we'd march and we would have the wrapping of the Maypole. They'd walk and talk and eat and talk and eat all day long on the 20th day of May.

As the years progressed, the younger colored people didn't want to let people know they were celebrating the Emancipation. But in remembrance of my mother, every 20th of May we still have a big picnic and the grandchildren tell the reason for Emancipation Day, you know. And we still have the wrapping of the Maypole. But people won't participate. The neighbors won't send their children now.

Susan Kelker Russell was born in 1909 and grew up in Milton, a sawmill town in Santa Rosa County, Florida. Because public education for black students ended in the sixth grade, her father, a brick mason, and her mother, a teacher and stern disciplinarian, insisted that Russell and her six siblings move to Pensacola and stay with relatives to attend high school. Remarkably, all seven children finished high school and attended college. Russell attended Florida A&M College;[7] after graduation, she stayed at A&M, where she worked for forty-two years. When she was a college student, Russell joined protests organized by her classmates. Through their struggle against segregated practices—even at an African American institution—Russell and her friends expressed their frustration with an elder generation's unwillingness to push for change. Her participation continued into the 1950s and 1960s, when she refused to comply with segregation on buses and attended rallies supporting civil rights activists.

I didn't expect as much segregation as I found when I came to college. But I remember it very vividly. We used to have vespers every Sunday evening. Doak Campbell was president of the Florida State College for Women[8] and he would bring eight or ten of his girls out here to A&M for the service. And we would be sitting in the middle aisle and the seniors would be in the front. When the white women would come in, we were supposed to get up and move to the right and leave the front row seats for them. And we did that for over a year or so. But one Sunday afternoon, Eunice Golden decided she was not going to move and she sat there. Mrs. McGuinn, the Dean of Women, kept waving her hand until the rest of us just moved on back. But Eunice sat right there and she did not move. After [Mrs. McGuinn] did that so many times and Eunice didn't move, then Doak Campbell pointed to his girls to sit, stay where they were.

Eunice hadn't said a word about it. No. In fact, we hadn't discussed it. We just accepted the arrangements. When we saw them come in, we just automatically got up and moved. Nobody thought anything about it. But I guess Eunice had been thinking about it. She was very fair-skinned herself. She didn't have very good hair,[9] but she was very fair [skinned] and she was adamant about it. So evidently she had been thinking about it, but she had never said anything to us about it. And we were surprised too when she didn't move, because the rest of us had moved. But after she took that stand then we decided to support her. Phyllis Frazier, one of our classmates, called us together in her room after that and told us what to do. And she said, "Don't let Eunice be alone in this now." Race, I don't say race riots, but race disturbances were running high at that point [in the late 1920s].[10]

The next morning, Monday morning, we had an executive committee meeting and they gave Eunice fourteen demerits. President Lee, Mrs. McGuinn, the Dean of Men, the Band Master, and the Choir Director formed the executive committee. Fifteen demerits would send you home. And all of us went to this executive committee meeting to see what they were going to do to Eunice. And when we went, I think they were hesitant to do anything to her. I think they had planned to give her the fifteen demerits. But after all of us who were sitting on that same seat went with her, they just gave her fourteen and told her if she got another one she would go home. She said, "Well, you may as well give me the other one now, because I'm going to sit there next Sunday and I'm not going to move." And we said, "If she sits there we're going to sit with her." There were eleven of us. And the next Sunday we made it our business to go early and we all sat there. But they didn't come, the [white] girls from Florida State didn't come that Sunday; but the following Sunday [Doak Campbell] brought them and they didn't ask us to move. So that stopped that and that was my first encounter with real segregation, but it made you real angry. Real angry. And we got real angry with our Dean of Women, Mrs. McGuinn, because she was white, so to speak. Her color was white; she was supposed to be black, but her color was white. And after that semester he didn't bring them out any more. So we weren't bothered with them any more. But we stopped that right there. At that time, it wasn't common for students to protest. It was just an occasional uprising. Our situation was the only one I remember at that time and it was just one of those things that was understood, I guess, that if this continues it will start something. So we'll just let it rest.

Later, in the 1950s, Eunice Johnson and I were coming from town on the bus. The bus was full with people coming home from work and we were in the front of the bus. We were both young working women then and we were coming out on the campus. We were living in dormitories. Two whites wanted us to get up and give up our seats and we wouldn't. We hadn't planned to do this and didn't know the bus driver was going to ask us to move. We said, "We are getting off right soon," but he said, "You have to move now because we don't have a seat." And we just sat there. So the bus driver turned around and carried us on down to the jail house. And, Marion Johnson, who had a barbershop, he was the mayor of French Town.[11] He was a very good friend of ours. He looked like a white guy himself. We called him. He came down there with my brother-in-law, Porter and raised sand and got us.

I'd always avoid confrontation if I could. And that was the closest confrontation I ever had, but shortly after that they started this bus boycott.[12] That was a restless time. It was when Martin Luther King[13] started the bus boycott [in Montgomery] and people were afraid to go different places and what not. Whites were almost as afraid as blacks were because you never knew what was going to happen. And they had marches. In the '60s we used to have speakers and all. It was a restless time. A very restless time, but it began to taper off and get straight. I remember I went to hear King over at Bethel A.M.E.

and Abernathy[14] came here and spoke. I would always go to his speeches. The churches were always opened for meetings because that's about the only place they could have meetings. I know Bethel A.M.E. was one of the main meeting places. But I never marched or anything like that. In fact, I was working and I just felt that I couldn't. When they would have rallies and ask for money to help, after they put a lot of kids in jail and what not, I would support things like that. Give them money to help get a bond or get the kids out. I would always give them financial support when I could, or if a mother had to come up here and see about a child in jail, I would always let them stay with me or something and all, but that was the kind of aid that I gave.

Julia Lucas was born in 1912 in Warrenton County, North Carolina, the middle child in a family of eleven children. In the early 1930s, she followed her sisters to Durham where she attended North Carolina College for Negroes (now North Carolina Central University) on a scholarship. Lucas married a barber and became his business partner and bookkeeper. Here Lucas recounts the importance of their barbershop as a safe place for black workers to discuss their efforts to organize unions in Durham's tobacco factories.

Herndon's barbershop was one of the better barbershops. It was real close to downtown, and it was kept neat, nice and clean. We did have a lady barber in the shop. And we had pool tables in the back. My husband didn't allow betting on pool tables, but it was a form of recreation. At that time, all of the businesses downtown that had young men, the tailor shop or whatever, had a dinner hour or time off at noon, and the barbershop was their place for recreation. So they'd come in and play pool for that hour. At the time, too, the American Tobacco Company and Liggett and Myers employed a lot of black people. On their lunch hour, a lot of those fellows would come down and play pool, get their hair cut, or a shave. It just became a place to meet people and I was right in the middle of it.

People talked about everything in the barbershop. Everything from who went out with whom, where you go to church, who are good church people, and who are the nothings. They talked about it all. Back in the '30s, too, the unions in the tobacco company were organized.[15] This was something especially the younger men and women who worked in the factories would discuss. For many older black people, it was kind of like a hush-hush subject. They were so afraid that the wrong white people would hear and hinder them. But people were so proud [to be] a member of the union. They'd talk about what they were going to organize and what they were going to ask for. It was the beginning of a revelation to me, how blacks would say, "I'm all fed up, and I can't take it no more. We're going to do something about it." And they would discuss it.

The barbershop was a place where they gathered and talked about a lot of things and knew that it was secure with the people with whom they were talking. We didn't have that many private places, other than churches, where we could discuss anything that concerned black people's advancement and where they felt secure. A place does make a difference in how you express and when you feel free to express something that you know is controversial. But the barbershop was one of the places that people could go.

Florenza Grant was born in 1921 in Rich Square, North Carolina. After she married and started a family, Grant and her husband purchased a farm in Tillery, North Carolina where the family augmented their income by running a gas station, barbershop, and other businesses. Economically independent as landowners and entrepreneurs, Grant and her family became crusaders against Jim Crow and strong proponents of their rights as farmers and citizens. Here Grant talks about her experiences when registering to vote in the 1950s, her activism to improve her children's educational opportunities, and the impact of women pushing for change.

My grandfather was a white man and he was respected as a white man. And my grandmother had Indian blood in her. We were poor but we had a good home environment. My daddy believed that if you want something you have to work for it. And he was good as anybody else, that was another thing that I admired about him. My daddy was a sharecropper and he talked back. The white guy that owned the land came in the lot one day, we had a big lot, and he told him, "Hey, Henry, hadn't you better go out there and get that hay in 'cause it's going to rain?"

My father said, "I'll tell you, you go out there and get your half and I'll get my half when I get ready." So we were inclined to speak out and some of the kids would say we spoke out because we were yellow[16] and stuff like that. But I got my nerve from my daddy.

In North Carolina in the 1950s, we were having problems with black folks registering in Halifax County. My husband and my brother and five or six other men got together and would go up to try to register to vote. I didn't go, but one or two other women would go. Three or four carloads of people would go together. And they got turned down every time. So one Saturday my husband came back home and said, "Flo, will you get dressed? Look nice now. We are going to send you back with Mrs. Manley to register." Nobody had been able to register yet. At that time you had to read and write a portion of the Constitution. But we had been having classes, studying, and the NAACP really encouraged us to register. And I went up to try with Mrs. Manley. We went in together, but she acted like she didn't know me, because she was going see what they would do to me. I said I wanted to register. And the registrar asked "are you willing to abide by the rules and regulations?" I told him I was. He said, "The rules and regulations, not your rules and regulations." And at this time a little old white girl, about eighteen years old, came in and walked up and said she wanted to register. And he didn't put her through any questioning. So, then he said, "Are you ready?"

I said, "I was ready before she came in here."

He said, "She registered under the grandfather clause."[17]

I said, "I've got a grandfather, too, and he happens to be a white man." Then he just got shaky, and said, "Are you willing to read a portion of the Constitution and write it?" I said yes. And so he started reading one article and he was mispronouncing words.

So I said, "Man, you're not pronouncing that word correctly." And I corrected him. He turned red. He was really angry at me. But Mrs. Manley was sitting back there. Now Mrs. Manley had been up there with the men before, but she was sitting back there listening and she wouldn't have done what I did. But anyway, I got registered. At the time, there were only three blacks registered in Halifax County. And Mrs. Manley and I made five. Then another black lady got on [the voting rolls] the next Saturday.

One time we were trying to get school buses or something. Our children were walking to school every day, from way back where they lived. So we got a little committee together to go up there protesting. And all the women backed out except three of us. So I and two others went up to the courthouse to do something about getting this stopped. And this old black man was walking behind, talking about how he was going to get buses for black children. But when we got ready to go in the courthouse, he stuck right up behind me, right under my dress tail. He said, "I'm going to stay right behind you, because they aren't going to hurt you."

I said, "I won't promise you that." But we went in there and we got the buses.

Once our children had been at the elementary school for three weeks and they didn't have seats [for every student]. The children came home and said, "We had to go outdoors and play because we didn't have enough seats" and so and so. It was cotton-picking time and so I really didn't have time to go out there. But I got five women together in about an hour. I was shocked; a lot of things you can do if you go at it the right way. And we went out there and nearly scared the principal to death. And he said, "Can I help y'all?"

I said, "You sure can. I want to know why school's been going on now three weeks and there are no chairs for these children to sit in?"

He said, "Well, well, well, they're going to bring them any day now, any day now, any day."

I said, "That's not good enough, not good enough." The other women just supported me and let me speak, you know. And so we gave them another week and then we went back out there. I asked if they had gotten the chairs. And the principal said, "No, not yet, but they're going to bring them any day now."

I said, "Okay, we'll go up here to Halifax[18] and see how come we can't get some."

And the assistant superintendent up there was black and he knows me, he had learned about us the hard way. So we went up there and I said, "Mr. Young, we are up here to see why we don't have some seats in the school for the children."

"Well I tell you Mrs. Grant, I really don't know," he said.

I said, "It's because they are little black children. I bet you don't have white students around here with nowhere to sit." And he was so tickled he didn't know what to do. And two of the ladies that were with me belonged to his church up there in Halifax. Well they were not vocal, but they were standing strong behind me, you know.

He said "Mrs. Grant, if you'll just be quiet, I will have chairs in there before the day is gone." And he got them. You see, you just have to go at things like that. But the principal, he didn't want to rock the boat. So I found out that women can have more powerful impact on some things, more than black men can.

Lanetha Collins Branch was born in 1935 and raised in Memphis. She attended Fisk, LeMoyne-Owen College, and the University of Arkansas in the 1950s and 1960s, earning her teaching credentials. During several decades of teaching in Memphis, Branch observed attempts to integrate the schools by bussing African American children and transferring black teachers to the previously all-white schools. Here Branch recounts her experiences as a "rebel child" and an activist, when she flagrantly disregarded some rules of segregation. She also notes the people who were helpful in inspiring her resistance and discusses the structures that sometimes inhibited African American action against inequality.

I had always been taught by my mother—because of the neighborhood we lived in, we were the first blacks there—that we were not better than anyone else but we were as good as any one else. And so, therefore, I might have had a different concept of black and white than others. And, of course, my mother considered me her rebel child. I was not a fighter but I would do things that she felt one day I'd get in trouble for doing, such as drinking out of white water fountains and these type things. I'd do that for spite.

During the time of Jim Crow, it was just unthinkable that you'd drink out of white water fountains in the department stores. And I would do that. And the thing of "yes, ma'am," "no ma'am," this type of thing, I just didn't do it. Because of the fact that Mother had said that I was as good as anyone else. And I felt that if I must do that then they'd have to do that for me too. And so, she would always say that I was her one child that would argue with a stop sign. I guess my activeness, if she had lived, would not have surprised her at all.

You know, here in the South, no matter how far back you sat, if a white person got on the bus and there was not a seat for them and you were sitting in a seat, you were to get up and let them have a seat. And so I had done that on the buses here in Memphis, not getting up. I was eleven, twelve years old. I think when you are a child, [whites think] that you don't know what you're doing. But I knew exactly what I was doing. The bus driver told my mother what I did. She just told him "Thank you very much." And that was all.

I can recall when I first went off to college at Fisk University. That was 1953. A group of us were coming home for Thanksgiving and we decided we were not going to get on the back of the bus. And, of course, the bus did not move. The bus driver said he was going to call the police. I still didn't move. I used to do that on the buses here. I would not get up and give up my seat. I would sit in an area that I felt was in the middle of the bus and if the bus was crowded and there was another [empty] seat, I would not get up. But I guess some of my classmates got a little afraid so they convinced us all to get up. Of course, anyone who sought to right injustices at that time was called Communist. You didn't have restroom facilities and what have you. And so, I just always felt that those things were wrong. And I would voice those opinions. So this is why [my mother] would probably say I was her "rebel child," because I did not conform to the status quo.

Mother was the type of person who usually would get along with anyone. They used to call us the "uppity niggers" on our street because of the fact that we had a car, and we were able to dress well, and we always had food on our table. And my mother taught us that you're important; you are somebody, and nobody can tell you who you are. She was very religious. She would say "All of us are God's children. And so, therefore, you're not better than anyone but you're as good as anyone else. And don't let other people decide who you are. You must find that yourself." I guess that's the lesson that's always stayed with me. That number one, where there's injustice, I have no fear speaking up. And then, to have empathy for all people, recognizing all people might not be at the same economic or education status that I am, but they're still people and they have something to offer and they have something to give. And that's the attitude I take toward all people.

There's one teacher that I remember very vividly, my eighth grade social studies teacher. And she was a very strong woman, as most black women were during that time, very strong. Very forceful. A strict disciplinarian. But also always telling her black students what their possibilities were and not making them feel that they did not have the possibilities to do anything. And then, another of my instructors at Booker T. Washington High School, my twelfth grade history teacher, really helped us to keep in perspective who we were as well. And to think positive of our blackness and not negatively of it.

They have said that we are a matriarchal people. And that black women were able to get things done when black men couldn't. And then black men had been so dominated that they did not talk a lot. I guess they were told to "keep your mouth closed and you'll be okay." Well, in this particular area, here in the

Delta, opening your mouth about any little thing might necessarily mean you were lynched. And we are not too far from an area about two blocks up where some businessmen were lynched.[19] And it was not unusual. On many of the corners in this area, black men have been lynched. And so you had black men at that time who were not stepping forward because of the fact that they might well be killed for any remark that they made.

One of the things that people feared in this area was people who got information and took it back to the white population. This was always a fear. And many people did that because most anything that was done in the black community, the white establishment knew about it. And so sometimes people were not as open as they might have been because they did not know who was going to be taking what back. I really think it was things that were just passed along and people just started doing it. Pretty much like during slave time. You had no leaders necessarily, but the message got around just from word of mouth that this was what you were going to do. And that you couldn't identify who your leader was but yet the message was there.

As a teacher in the city school system, I took part in some of the boycotts that we had. At that time I worked in the Memphis public schools. Of course, there were some of us there who worked there who had been activists and been in the marches and what have you. We had what we called Black Mondays, an attempt to get representation on the Board of Education. And black parents were asked to keep their children home every Monday.[20] And the Board put pressure on the black schools; the children had to have an excuse for why they were absent. And you know, in Tennessee, you get your funding based on the number of children who come to school. And, of course, the Superintendent made a statement that I caught right on to. He said he could not assure our children's safety if we kept them at home. And, of course, if you can't assure my child's safety at home then you can't assure it at school. And so I wrote [a note] to that effect, that since your Superintendent cannot assure my child's safety, I'm keeping [my son] at home. So they couldn't do anything with that. And I'd send that to school with [my son]. And in the mid-sixties, after they saw that we were not going to change the Black Mondays, they finally appointed two [black] people to the Board of Education.[21]

We also took up money for the sanitation workers during the garbage strikes.[22] They asked us not to put any garbage out on the street because they said, "if you put it out on the street, we'll [have to] pick it up." Oh, I should have taken a picture of my back yard. It was horrendous! But they had asked us not to put it out on the street. My job at my school was to take a dollar from each teacher every week because the sanitation workers didn't have any money. And really, during that time, if you looked at garbage men's salaries, they really would have qualified for welfare because they were making so little money. And it amazes me now how fearful people were at that time to even give a dollar. They were so fearful. We had close to forty people in my building and only seven of us would give a dollar a week. People were fearful that somebody might find they gave a dollar. They were so afraid of losing their jobs. Some people were afraid of being associated with the movement and were afraid to be around Martin Luther King. Now, you know, we celebrate his birthday and all those things now. But you have to recognize during that time there were many African Americans who did not participate, and did not believe in what he was doing. Because some African Americans also thought that he was a trouble maker. People were afraid to attend the meetings down at Clayborn Temple and Mason Temple.[23] They were afraid to go there even in support. But yet, it mobilized people that ordinarily would not have been a part of that structure. There was a gang in south Memphis called the Invaders who really, virtually controlled that area. They became a power of the civil rights movement. And it changed their lives. So it changed people in many ways. Yes, it did. In the movement, you had to make a decision one way or the other. Either you had to join or, as they say, get out of the way.

And I can recall after Martin Luther King's death—I had been in Mason Temple the night he had spoken. It was an eerie feeling. It was very eerie. When I say "eerie," you know, it felt like he was somewhere else. Then the next day, we heard about his shooting. I was at school. We were at an in-service training. We had a principal who was not the best person in the world. He remarked, "Well, we have to finish the workshop." I told him I would not stay, because I had been following what had been going on all the time. In fact, the tension was so high we were sure something drastic would happen. And some of us felt that just really something was just in the air and that something dreadful was going to happen. Because prior to that, some young people had gotten to march and started breaking out store windows on Beale Street.[24] And that's what the police were waiting for, for something to happen. They were prepared for something to happen. And some have said that that was a plan anyway. That was something they had planned to happen anyway so that they could move in with the billy clubs and call out the National Guard and all those kinds of things. It had been quite difficult during those times. And then, after that time, the white establishment stepped forward. What the sanitation union was asking for was not unreasonable and could have been done. But once the city broke out in riots after [King's] death, then the decision makers who were not in public office, those who really [were in] control and told other [whites] what they will or will not do, then they stepped in and said, "You will do this." But you can't change history. It was going to be that way anyway. Maybe to draw the consciousness of this nation to a point. I think that King's death did draw the consciousness of whites and blacks to the predicament that America was in. The land of the free and the home of the brave. Democracy. What did democracy mean to whom? And so it made people look at race relations in a different way at that time.

But now we have a young generation of African Americans and white Americans who haven't the slightest idea about history. One of the pet peeves I have is that we know so little about our history in America. We put it on the back burner. And yet, you can go to most countries and the children can tell you about their history. We have no custom about our history or what the government is all about, or what history is all about, or what this country's all about. Democracy does not mean you can do anything you want to do. Democracy means that you must work harder than any other kind of government in order to make it fulfill itself. And we don't have the right understanding of what democracy is. And the fear is that no one is really teaching the children.

Essie Alexander appears in Chapter 4, explaining the ethic of service she learned in her family and through the Missionary Baptist Church. Alexander married in 1944 and in the early 1950s moved with her husband to Greenwood, a small city in the Mississippi Delta. Here she describes her first experiences as a voter and the ways that she encouraged other women to join her in exercising their rights as citizens.

I believe I registered to vote in 1954 or 1955. I liked to read, and I read a lot of information about being a citizen and your right to vote and what have you. I remember way back, if you didn't own land or something, you could not register and vote. So after things changed, whether you had property or not, that was your right that you could register and vote, so I felt like I had that right.

We were living in Carroll County and only a few of us had registered to vote. I think the others were afraid. Of course, where we were living on the McCarty plantation, they didn't try to [prevent] us. Mr. McCarty told my husband, Henry, and another little guy that was a tractor driver, and my cousin, Ben, he told them, "If it rains one day this week so we can't work, you all need to go to Carrollton and register." So he encouraged the men to register. I think maybe he knew eventually they were going to register and vote or what have you, so I think that's one of the reasons he encouraged them to go on and do it.

So I felt like if the men needed to register, then the women did, too. But the first time, I had a time trying to get the other women to go. We went together to register and to vote. I went with my cousin's wife and one or two other ladies to Carrollton. Of course, our husbands had already registered. I can't remember who was the clerk up there at the time, but she wasn't too nice. She asked us what were we doing at the courthouse. The others were hesitant about speaking so I told her we came to register, and she said, "For what?"

I said, "So we'll be able to vote." She asked, did we think it would make any difference? I told her yes, because you win by the count of the ballot. If I didn't vote, then somebody would be less one vote. We voted.

[Many people who were] registered at that time, they were just afraid to go up there and try to vote. Other than our husbands, I think about four women went up there to vote. Maybe it's bad to say, but I was kind of the spokesman for those few women, because they were kind of bashful. But whatever I thought was right, then that's what I pursued, whatever I thought was right. Nothing to start no fuss; I never got into anything like that. But if I had that right, then I thought I should exercise my right, always. And it worked. I never had any problem. After that first time, then it just came natural that whenever there was an election, then we knew that without any problem we could go and vote. I've been a registered voter ever since.

The NAACP got active in the early '50s and '60s around Memphis and Clarkson, all up around in those areas, and Jackson and Greenville. Then it became active in this area. In the '60s there used to be groups that would come to churches and speak. They weren't all black. There were some whites with them. It was a mixed group with the NAACP, and they would come to churches and wherever and talk about your rights. So a lot of people took advantage of it. That's after people started listening to radio; a few of us had TVs, and listened to different reasons why we should [vote], to be a citizen like anybody else. We had that right. And unless we took advantage of those rights, we really weren't full citizens, because my vote helped make a decision. So we were decision makers, once you got to be a registered voter and voted. If you are registered and don't vote, you still aren't doing any good. Whether it's a bad decision or a good one, you helped make it.

A. Elizabeth Harris Pointer was born in 1927 and spent her childhood and adult years in Macon County, Alabama, not far from Tuskegee University. Here, Pointer recounts how her family and teachers shaped her views of politics. She demonstrates the personal aspects of political activism or, in this case, how her unwillingness to participate in the integration of Tuskegee's schools stemmed from her passion to protect her children. Assertive in exercising her own rights, Pointer understood the potential for repercussions. Her interview also points out the difference between memory and history. In recalling how a teacher inspired her to register to vote, Pointer describes how she registered at age eighteen, soon after she finished high school. But by connecting her high school teacher with her attempt to register, Pointer mistakenly collapses time; the voting age at the time would have been twenty-one years, not eighteen. These events, therefore, did not occur in the quick sequence that she remembers. She may have been inspired by her teacher to register, but not until she was twenty-one. Or, perhaps she did register, but the official would have thrown an underage registration away.

In high school, I had an American history teacher that talked so much about this voting thing, and it hadn't crossed my mind that they would prohibit me from voting. As soon as I finished high school I went down there one day, and said "I came down to register to vote." They said, "All right." And it was nothing. I just filled out a form telling my age and where I was born and all that sort of thing, and they sent it through the mail. And then it turned out I was the only registered voter in the area. So I registered to vote when I was eighteen.

I was on the executive committee of the NAACP for a number of years. But as far as me getting out in these marches and all of that, I never took part in anything like that. I never demonstrated for anything. But I always supported causes that were for the right, you know. If there was a case defending somebody that was unjustly treated, I would always try to give money toward that. But as far as trying to fight city hall, I've never fought city hall. Because a lot of people are in bad shape today on account of doing that. My father said, "Nothing hurt a bird but his bill." You hear what I'm saying? And if a fish didn't open his mouth he would never get caught. And so, my father said, really and truly, in a lot of instances, you let sleeping dogs lie.

I had children of age when they got ready to integrate that school.[25] Somebody called me on the phone, I don't know who it was, but they knew I had children of that age. "If you go to that school tomorrow morning, you won't get back," a whole lot of stuff like that. I just called the sheriff and told him about it, and he said a lot of people were getting those calls. I said, "My children are not going to that school at all. I may as well send my children to the rattlesnakes." And when they asked me about it, I told them right up front. I said, "Let me tell you something. I've got to work, and my children are not guinea pigs, they're not targets. And the only way I'll send them down there to that school is if I go every day with them, and I'll be sitting there with a pistol because if anybody touched one of them I'll blow their brains out." And I meant it from my heart, and I've got to die and go to judgment. I was not going to have my daughter mistreated, or have people throwing things at her like they did a lot of little children, because I'd have gone down there and they would have me killed or [put in] jail. Just everybody in that room, I would've put a bullet in them. And I know I would have done it. I didn't want them to get in trouble and I didn't want them hurt. And my daughter was just not the fighting type and I told her not to ever let somebody hit her. If they call you a name, don't say anything. And I had them trained like that. But if somebody walked up on and jumped on them, if some stranger knocked them in the head, don't you know I wasn't going to take that? I'd have been in my grave because I would have shot everybody down there. I sure would have. I'd set the damn place on fire and so I didn't have to bother with it. The Lord blessed me that I didn't have to. And you wouldn't want it either, you wouldn't want your child to say that they went to an all-black school or an all-white school to be mistreated, while you just sat back and said, "My child is in there."

Wilhelmenia Adams was born 1926 in Charlotte, North Carolina, the daughter of a cook and a chauffeur. A mother of three and an active member of her community, Adams was involved in the PTA, the missionary club and choir at Myers Tabernacle

AME Zion church, the Democratic Party, and neighborhood organizations. She spent decades doing domestic work in private homes, a job also done by earlier generations of women in her family. Adams considered this a respectable occupation, but recognized that household workers were often denigrated and exploited; in addition, they worked for meager wages and were denied benefits, including retirement pensions through the Social Security Act. In the 1960s Domestics United Incorporated hired Adams to organize domestic workers in Charlotte and to advocate for better benefits and working conditions. On the basis of her activism, Adams held a leadership position with the National Committee on Household Employment, an organization that brought together local groups of domestic workers to agitate on behalf of similar issues.

I had been very active in civil rights and I got this job through Domestics United Incorporated, training and placing domestic workers in domestic households. If you needed some help, you could call me, and I would try to get you a person. We trained people for postnatal child care. We went through the Red Cross to train them to go to a home with a new baby, to take care of the mother, take care of that baby and do light housekeeping.

In the 1960s, I was the first vice-president of the National Committee on Household Employment.[26] I was responsible for Mecklenburg County people in North Carolina and a lot of other states getting Social Security for domestic workers. We weren't covered under Social Security, and I'm the one that got that started. I had been a domestic worker all of my life, just about. During the civil rights struggle, I learned that domestic workers were not covered under Social Security. I never had paid Social Security, and nobody was taking it out. Some people were saying they were taking out Social Security, but they were not putting it in the Social Security bank, and so we wouldn't have coverage. So this is what we did. I took two bus loads of black women from here to Washington to sit in on Charlie Jones, our representative, asking him to support domestic workers and demanding that [employers] pay their Social Security. They passed that. We took buses of people from North Carolina to the National Committee on Household Employment convention. We also tried to fight to get sick leave and things, but that didn't materialize. Some people got it, but a lot of them didn't.

Household workers were making 75 cents a day and we got salaries raised up. It took us about six months to get that changed. We did it by scaring people. They thought we were going to strike. We had about 600 or 700 people active in Charlotte. We just told them that if they wanted work they had to join. And we stopped them from washing windows. Have you heard people say, "I don't do windows?" They don't. No domestic worker is supposed to wash windows. That's a special job and should be handled that way. There are women who go around and do nothing but wash windows, but that's not to be included in your daily schedule of household work. You're allowed to clean the kitchen, the stove, refrigerator, and bathrooms, and laundry. Some people want laundry and if you do laundry, then you don't do anything but laundry. My job got funded by the Charlotte Area Fund.[27] But eventually all that good seed money left and we couldn't get back the funding. See, we weren't strong enough to continue.

Brenda Bozant Davillier was born in 1941 and lived most of her life in and near New Orleans. After college, Davillier taught elementary school and worked as a housing advocate. Living in a region with a complicated history of immigration and racial intermarriage, Davillier understood race in a distinct way. Here she recounts her efforts to desegregate a Catholic Church in Slidell, an act that slowly changed seating practices in that particular parish but did not erase racism from the larger church establishment.

[In New Orleans] everybody was mixed up. You could trace your ancestors back, and many people did have French and Spanish ancestry and some married folks with German or English heritage. Some with Indian heritage. Some with African heritage. We have French in my family on my mother's side and my father's side. So in my family we have people of all complexions. I thought all families were like that. I guess in a way I didn't grow up with prejudice. I thought this was how all families are. You know, you marry who you want to marry. And you know, as a little child, I'd say I guess that's why they call us colored, because we have all colors in the family.

I'm Catholic, and in New Orleans we went to Corpus Christi Church, which was a black, colored church. We didn't have any integration in the church because nobody white came to the church. I remember when I was in tenth grade that I went to Corpus Christi Church and the priest read a letter from the Archbishop stating that there would be no more segregation in Catholic churches.[28] That whenever you went into the Catholic church you could sit anywhere you wanted to sit. So that summer I went to Slidell to visit my grandmother. In Slidell, the Catholics who were not Anglo Saxons were few and far between. Most of the African Americans were Baptist or another denomination. There was a church down the bayou where they spoke French and had the Masses in Latin, and the last two pews in the church on the right hand side were for black worshippers. I told my cousins in Slidell, we could sit wherever we want to sit in church now. We don't have to sit in the last two pews. So the way things were then in the country, we'd walk that mile to church and the church was always open an hour before Mass for confessions. So I got my cousins, all of them younger than me, and I said, "Now we're going to go to church early." I didn't want my older sister or anybody else to know what I was doing. "We're going to go all the way up to the front and sit in the first pew, and if anybody tells you to move, don't move." I told my cousin, my good friend, "Now you sit on that end and I'm going to sit on this end and don't let anybody out. If anybody tells you anything, just sit there and say your prayers and don't even look around." Sure enough nobody was in the church. We sat in the front row and then two ushers came early. You could hear them talking in the back. They came up and talked to us and said, "You have to move." We didn't answer. We just sat in church and didn't move. So they couldn't make us move. And as I told you we had all colors in our family. So we had all colors across the front of the church. Nobody would sit behind us. So there was one whole side of the church empty, and people were standing up all in church. A couple of people fainted because they wouldn't sit behind us. I was in tenth grade. My cousin was in about the eighth grade and some of the other ones were younger than that. The adults—colored, Negro, African American, whatever—none of them came and sat up there with us. They sat in the last two pews.

Needless to say, our parents found out. The only one who could go to church with me after that was my cousin, the one who sat on the other end. But every Sunday we'd go up to the front of the church, as close as we could get to the front of the church for the whole summer. And people wouldn't sit with us. They might leave the pew behind us empty, but they had to eventually start sitting behind us. When Father came in for Mass, why he couldn't say anything because the Bishop had given his letter. But he was a big man. He was fat and he was big. He would glare at us. It looked like he was about to explode, but he couldn't do anything. One of the Sundays I went to confession. I knocked on the rectory door. "Father, could you come hear my confession?" He slammed the door in my face. He refused to do it. He slammed the door in my face. And that was strange, you know. But you know what, God is good, because I just didn't even worry about it. I think this is where it's been a blessing that we grew up believing that we were just as good as everybody else, because I guess when I look back at it, I figured that's his problem. That's not mine. It really didn't keep me from going to church. In fact, I was even more determined to go early every Sunday.

Years later, I was working for Catholic Charities in their refugee program. At first I was doing employment counseling, helping refugees from Vietnam settle here. And the position of housing supervisor was open. I was asked to take it because I did have experience with the Housing Authority and a very good background. But I was told I had six months probation. There was a white nun who worked with me as the housing counselor. So after the end of the six months, I was told, "We want you to continue to do this work but we're going to give her the title of supervisor and the pay."

I said, "I don't think so." So I went through the channels, you know, wrote to the personnel department. Gave them a copy of the job description, copies of the work I had done, and I told them if they wanted me to be the housing counselor, I'll be the housing counselor for the housing counselor's salary and title. But I'm not going to do the supervisor's work and [still keep] the title and pay of the counselor. And I thought they would reverse her decision, but they upheld her decision and I was fired because I refused to do it. Now that was very traumatic for me. It was more traumatic than trying to deal with the father who slammed the door in my face, you know. I ended up filing an EEOC[29] complaint, and because they were getting federal funds for their program they had to hire a lot more minorities. It was very difficult for me though, because here I was suing my church, and I ended up dropping the suit. Things did change over there, but it was a very, very difficult time.

Alice Giles was born in 1920 and grew up outside Greenwood, Mississippi, on a farm that her father rented until the family was able to buy a house in Indianola. With other sharecropping farmers, he purchased a tract of land in the countryside and eighteen mules that they shared. In the early 1940s, Giles married and with her husband opened a small store, Giles Grocery, in their home. The Giles ran their store for nearly forty-three years. In the 1960s, they became involved in efforts to desegregate Indianola's schools and supported the work of civil rights activists from SNCC (the Student Nonviolent Coordinating Committee) and CORE (the Congress of Racial Equality) who were organizing in Mississippi.[30] In 1964, Giles' husband joined the Mississippi Freedom Democratic Party, which challenged the seating of the state's all-white Democratic Party at their national convention in Atlantic City. Alice supported the work of the National Council of Negro Women, which sought to unite black and white women to support the southern civil rights movement, and she helped set up one of the first Head Start programs in the state. For their efforts, the Giles were harassed and their business was destroyed. As Giles recounts here, violence and opposition frightened the family, but strengthened her resolve to work on behalf of social change in Mississippi. In addition to revealing Giles' determination, her interview also suggests the differences between men's and women's activities.

My husband and I opened up this little store in 1946. And across that road was a plantation, Garrett Plantation. And all of those people who lived there were plantation folks. They worked from sun up to sun down, but they weren't getting but $1 a day. When we opened up this little store over here, bread was just 12 cents a loaf. A soda pop, a drink, Coca-Cola was 5 cents. But they made $1 a day, a day, a day. Chopped cotton all day long for $1. And you know, my husband and I, we wanted to see government for the sick, young, for everybody's people. People were suffering back then.

And this store, the menfolks from the community would come and sit round here. Sometimes they'd just come and sit and stay late, sitting here till twelve o'clock at night, talking. They liked to talk to my husband. Every now and then somebody would come by and buy something, but Giles just enjoyed the company of it, the menfolks coming. Mostly they'd be talking about voting when they'd come together, and they would read the paper and see what was going on, you know. When war broke out, they didn't look for just white folks to go war. They called blacks, too. And people would say, "Black folks got to go and fight for the country and we are living in the country, why can't we vote?" My father would come around and we would have conversations about segregation, and he would tell us about when he was a boy coming up and how it was way back, how white folks would beat Negroes and kill them and drag them up and down the road and all that kind of stuff.

We were members of the NAACP. The NAACP auxiliary was here then and the Movement was going on. And, of course, we wanted to see the schools integrated so the kids could get a better education. [Whites] had better schools, you know, across town. Better than our kids had, and our desire was to see the government for our people. We woke up one morning, when school was beginning to start. That was in '65, I believe. And some of the parents organized a parents' auxiliary. And we were supposed to take our children to the white school. And I carried my two children over there to Lockard School. Now don't ask me whether I was scared. Yes, I was scared. I was scared, but I went. Because of their grade my kids didn't get a chance to go to white school. But some others did get the chance to go. They didn't get in that morning, they didn't get in that day, but my husband and other parents went to court over in Greenville, and they got an order to let them attend Indianola Junior High. But my kids weren't in the right grade.[31]

You know, during the Movement my kids and my husband led marches around the courthouse and picketed the courthouse. We marched around the library. We would have weekly meetings at different churches. Sometimes we would meet in Vernon, sometimes in Morehead, Indianola, and different places, all over the county, wherever we could use a church. Some church folks were scared to let us use the church because they feared [whites] might bomb the church. And they would, you know. And the deacons were just scared. A lot of people desired to take a part in the Movement, but they were afraid. And there were some whites, they knew that it was right, but they were scared to say anything because other whites would get them.

[Whites in town would try to stop us from being active in the Movement.] They would mostly talk with Giles because he was the man, and try to get him not to participate in it, you know. He had an offer from a leading white man here in town who told him he'd help him to build a big store. They would do just anything to tie you up in debt to keep you from participating in the Movement, you know. But, my husband, he never did like debts anyway, and he always wanted to be free from debts, and then he felt like he could be free to do whatever he wanted to do. Because if you owe, if you are wrapped up in debt to a bank or something, naturally they can put a clutch on you. But if you don't owe them anything, you're able to do what you want. Matter of fact, we had bought a new car before my husband left for Atlantic City with the Freedom Democratic

Party,[32] and they found out that he was gone somehow. And they did come back on us for a note[33] that we had paid, but somehow he got it straightened out. And then we went on and paid the car out and got that over with.

And whites were planning on getting us anyway, because we had got a lot of telephone call threats. People from the North were sending food and clothes and stuff to help the people here.[34] And we had gotten a big shipment of clothes and food and stuff, and they had put a lot of it in our store here for us to distribute. So, one night in 1965, I said to my husband, "they're going to get us tonight, because I'm tired. Don't wait for me to stay up and watch tonight. I am tired." So, we were sleeping over in the dining room, and I was up on the couch and he was on the floor. And they threw a bomb at the house. I was asleep, but the minute they lit that torch, I woke up. The Lord woke me up. And I jumped up and I said "Giles, get up, the house on fire. They got us." See, the Freedom folks that had been staying in here, they would stay here and [white officials would] watch our house; they'd watch the houses of the people that were participating. I ran through the kitchen to the store. And that bomb, it was a bottle and it hadn't busted. And the Lord was in the plan, because it didn't explode on me and burn me. But that gas just went all over this wall and everywhere, all back there and, and it just lit up. And I couldn't hardly get my husband up. Look like he just froze. I said, "Get up, Giles, the house on fire! Get up! Get up!" And finally he did move. He ran out the back door, and he got a hose and brought it in and started shooting water. And the neighbors across the street, they woke up. And they came across with their hose, and they busted glass out on the front and they started shooting water in. And so they got it put out. We lost everything. We lost all the groceries. We lost everything in the store. They set four houses on fire that night. And it was just about daylight before the fire truck came.

My husband talked to the FBI and they never did find anybody. They never did try. The fire ruined everything in the store. We had to haul everything off to the garbage. But we stayed on in business. We went right on back. We fixed it up and went right on back to selling. It seemed like the fire just made us more determined. Because, really, it's not right. Well, the way I feel, God made this world. And he put us all here in the world. And it seemed like the world should be big enough for all of us to share. So why, just why, do some folks have to be so mistreated? Just only because of the color of your skin? Why? I mean you're a human being and I'm a human being. And if my skin is black and yours is white, cut me and I'm going to bleed red blood just like you are going to bleed red blood. Nothing ever was investigated. We never did find who did it. But the Almighty God knows. So one day somebody'll have to take account of it.

Cora E. Flemming was born in 1933 in Starksville, in the hills of southern Mississippi. Her parents were landowners who raised ten children on one of the small farms that characterized the area. Miserable with farming, Flemming fled north when she was eighteen and returned to Mississippi in the early 1960s to care for her ailing mother. Flemming soon became involved in the Delta's civil rights movement, joining with other women to protest segregation, to exercise the right to vote, and to establish Head Start programs that would provide early education, food, and care for local children. Indianola, where Flemming lived (along with Alice Giles), was the birthplace of Mississippi's White Citizens' Council, a white supremacist group affiliated with the state and local governments and organized to oppose civil rights. The Council used violence and economic recriminations to try to squelch black activism. Here Flemming describes some of the forces that led her to become an activist and the ways that this work changed her, as well as her community.

We were reared in a community where we cared about others. We didn't take anything for granted. We took one day at a time. And with ten children in the household, we didn't have sufficient clothes like other young ladies had or young men had. We had to do the best we could. People would send a box from the North, and we survived that way. But we learned to care for others. We were raised to be independent, not dependent. We weren't raised on the plantation. We had our own home, our own land, and that made a big difference in our upbringing and the way we felt about the conditions. And we never went to town where the white folks were.

I left the hills in 1951. I went to the North. I lived in different states—Ohio, Michigan, Illinois—and I learned a lot. I didn't learn too much growing up, to be honest with you. I didn't finish high school at that time. I just finished the ninth grade. At that time, I was so miserable in the field, in that hot sun in the field, I married the first somebody that came along, and I left my home. I had learned a lot about segregation, integration, hardship, living pretty good at times and the rest of the time living rough. In '55 Emmett Till[35] was killed. I was in the North. But I learned a lot through reading the papers and the news just how bitter people really could be towards one another. That's when I really began to understand about the evils of segregation and the hatred that goes along with it.

Eventually, by the grace of God I got involved in the civil rights movement. My parents moved here in the Delta in 1952. I had come here to visit in 1960, and I went back to Chicago and packed my clothes and sold my stuff, and I headed back to Mississippi. After I got back, my mother got sick. One day we saw some of the people coming down the street, the civil rights workers coming down the street toward my mother. My mother said, "All you need to be going to those meetings."

I said, "Ma'am?"

She said, "You heard me. I said all you need to be going to those meetings."

I said, "Why do you say that?"

She said, "Because there's so much that you all need to know that you don't know. You have to mix with people and learn the ways of life and learn how things are going. You see, I'm sitting here sick today. My pastor hasn't been to see me. Very few of the church folks come by to see me. You've got to learn how to do things to help yourself, because when you're down, nobody cares anything about you."

I guess I'd gotten here about three years earlier, and I hadn't done anything much in the community because of the illness of my mother. So I went to a meeting that night. I got there, and I had a big time at that meeting. I made a speech that night. That meeting led to another meeting. They kept on meeting; I kept on going. They found out right quick what I stood for.

I learned how to rouse them up. [I'd say] "Having to work in the private homes, bringing home $20 a week, seven days a week, how many quarts of milk can you buy for your children? How many pair of shoes [do] they have? How many stockings [can you] buy? You look at that $15, you ain't got nothing. But that's what you work for. Earn it, but look to higher grounds. While you do that, keep looking for something better. Test yourself. Test your mind, your skills, your ability, things you can do to help yourself and help others in the community around you."

We marched with CORE folk, SNCC. We had a lot of involvement in the community. Some went to jail. I didn't go to jail, but I helped get them out. We fixed food for those that were marching. We bought pop and stuff and food for them to eat on a picket line. Everybody couldn't go to jail, so I tried to be one that didn't go to jail. My bedroom window was shot out twice. One time, the glass flew all over my bed, and I was in the bed in there. At that time, we had white people staying in my house too, civil rights workers. So, we were armed. I had a shotgun, a pistol, and everything. We had some disagreements about non-violence, but I always told them, "If you can stand to be slapped on one side and turn the other cheek, more power to you. But if you can't take it, more power to you. You can't take being slapped in the head, don't take it, but be sure you've got somebody to cover you, because they'll run off and leave you." And I think most other people had some kind of weapon to defend themselves.

We had been in the civil rights movement, and I guess they were checking out who had leadership ability. Now, these were some black people from COFO,[36] I think some from SNCC and different areas. And they decided, when the Head Start [centers started] coming through the CDGM[37] project, and they came and got me, Mrs. Giles, Miss Anna Mae King, and two other people. We got two more people to start the committee off. I became one of the main organizers of the Head Start program here. I helped to organize Sunflower, Washington, Issaquena, Bolivar county programs. We had got everything already together, had the money funded through CDGM, an organization that organized in all the counties around Mississippi. We got the program organized, got all the children enrolled and everything for school, and we thought for sure we'd have the Head Start in Bell Grove Missionary Church, my family church. But down in the Delta, they're fearful of everything. They'd had burnings here anyway, so they were afraid of being burned down or something. So they didn't let us have the church. We had to leave Sunflower County and go to Washington County in Leland, Mississippi, and get a church over there to have the Head Start in. Now I look back, I can't really blame them, because that's the way it was in those days. I can't blame them; they were afraid.[38]

During the time we were trying to organize, we had a big meeting down in Edwards, Mississippi. About 2,000 to 5,000 people there at that meeting. They had to have a chairman of that big meeting. They had about five or six different nominees for chair. When it ended up, I had to chair that meeting. It scared me to death. I had never been in stuff like that before in my life. I got up and chaired the meeting. I think I did a really good job. That meeting must have been pretty good, because they had a tape of it they used in different universities. I didn't know I could talk that much, either. And I stuttered a lot. I have a speech handicap. But I didn't know I could talk that much, either. You know, when I was starting to get kind of dry, kind of dull, I'd always think of some funny joke to tell. That would bring them back into the realm of the meeting.

I was living in this house here then, and I'd be complaining to my husband all the time that I couldn't buy a new dress every week. I had gotten accustomed to dressing in the North. The Head Start program came in and the civil rights movement, where I'd do door-to-door canvassing to recruit children for Head Start. I was going to different people's homes, and I looked in some of these people's houses I went into. In my household, some people had died and left us quite a bit of stuff. I thought everybody lived like that, you know, had pretty nice furniture, nice dishes and stuff. But when I began to go in people's houses to enroll children in Head Start, I was absolutely shocked at some of the things that I saw. A lot of people didn't have any place to hardly sleep that was decent. I went to their homes, and they had their beds on the floor. Some of them had rags in the bed for mattresses. Some of them ate out of tin pans and stuff, the adults and the children. I didn't know that people lived like that.

I came home that evening and I told my husband, "As long as I live, I'll never complain again about not having a new dress or new shoes, because I saw a lot of people today. I'm a rich woman compared to them. I live like a queen compared to those people." They didn't have anything.

A lot of people worked. A lot of people helped. The main goal for me was to make tomorrow a better day for our people, and my goal was to try to see it happen, to do what I could to make sure. If I didn't finish it, I would have started it. Just give them food for thought and let them try to meet on common ground.

I have seen a lot of things that I hoped for come to pass. There are a lot of jobs that they didn't have. Of course, they don't do quite as I think they should do, because once we get the job, we forget about from whence we came. [People] forget about the stepping stone they went over to get there, who helped them make the job they have. If it hadn't been for some of us in the Movement, they wouldn't even have integrated schools yet, wouldn't have anybody working in the bank and the gas and light place, none of those places. A lot of those people that have the positions in the community now didn't do anything for it. They just stepped in and took over, you know. But that's all right, too. They're moving up. But don't forget about the ones that they're passing by. Don't ever forget about them, because they're the ones that caused you to be there. That's my main thing. I just don't appreciate them looking down on some people, because none of us is any better than the other one. [We] may live a little different because the Lord has blessed us a little different, but you don't take your blessing and criticize others with it.

The best thing that I've seen so far really is black people can stand up for themselves. They will stand up for themselves now. Though they have these jobs and get ready to picket something or other or put on a boycott or something or other, they don't mind doing it. But before, they wouldn't do anything. But this younger generation that's come up since the older people have gotten away, they don't mind getting out there, do anything they have to do to survive, because they have children to take care of, and they don't want their children see them be weaklings. That's a wonderful thing. Because you can't let nobody come slap you in your face and you don't defend yourself, [or] let your child see you be slapped. They begin to stand up for themselves. I'm black. I don't run from you because you're white. It's not that way any more. They're going to stand up for themselves, and I like that about it. I like that.

Shirley Miller Sherrod was born in 1947 and grew up in Baker County in rural southwest Georgia in a close extended family. Partly due to inheritances from white ancestors, the family owned and worked a large farm, growing cotton and peanuts. In the 1960s, Sherrod's family and other community members fought valiantly to exercise political power in order to lift the economic and social repression weighing so heavily on African Americans in the area. Like Cora Flemming and many of the women in this chapter, personal relationships drew Shirley Sherrod into the political realm. But unlike many women who recall inspiring women or family members who encouraged their activism, Sherrod traces her political involvement to a personal tragedy, the murder of her father, Hosie Miller. His death motivated Sherrod to join the civil rights movement and organize African American residents in the South's small towns and rural communities. Here she recounts her involvement in movements against segregation and efforts to promote black land ownership in the rural South. In telling her story, Sherrod also demonstrates how "the personal is political," as she details the connections between her marriage and her activism and the ways that her political involvement changed her life.

I knew that the Movement was going on here in Albany because we didn't shop here because there were boycotts. And people from the Albany Movement[39] would come down to our church to raise money, and we would take up donations to help support what was going on in Albany. [When] my uncles and aunts would come home for holidays, I'd hear them talk. Because so many bad things had happened they didn't want to live there again. And I'd hear my parents talk. My father would bring us to the dentist in Albany and I would hear them. I know that they were talking about the Movement moving into Baker County. After my father was murdered I put those pieces together.

My father was murdered; he died March 25th of '65. My mother was seven months pregnant with what ended up being my brother. Like I told you, there were five daughters before that and my youngest sister was eight years old. We didn't know how we would be able to take care of ourselves because, you know, my father had been farming before that. And [we] had just moved into a new home. It was actually my mother's uncle, a white uncle, who murdered him. And then, the white people refused to do anything about it in terms of indicting him and so forth.

I think when he was murdered, it was almost like people thought, we need to react now. We need to deal with this now. White people had killed so many black people in the county.[40] And my father was a likable person. I think everybody liked him. He had five daughters so you'd think that's enough children, but he sort of did things for other children in the community. Their parents wouldn't take them to events at the school and he'd just load up the truck and take them. He was just a good father, not only to us but to others around the community. So he was well liked by everyone. And for them to murder someone like him was just more than I think everybody was willing to take at that time.

I'm certain the family was concerned about the fact that, you know, their youngest brother was dead and there is the wife and five children and one on the way. And they were looking at what could be done to help. I graduated from high school on the day my brother was born. And my aunt who lived in Atlanta was a principal at a school in Atlanta at the time. She wanted me to attend this pilot Upward Bound Program at Clark College[41] in Atlanta. So a couple of weeks after my brother was born, I went up to Atlanta. But I came home for the Fourth of July weekend, and by then people had actually decided to do something about my father's death, starting the movement. Everything had started and I could barely stay up there. See, on the night he died, I remember the house being full of people, and I can remember not wanting to be a part of a crowd, you know, not wanting to deal with people. So I went into the bedroom. And I can remember looking out the window and thinking that as the oldest child I should do something, you know. But what? I was thinking, I'm not a man. I felt a man would try to go and do something to the man who murdered Daddy. So I finally arrived at an answer, and my answer was that I would devote the rest of my life to working for change.

Before that, I had decided that I was going to go to school in the North, and I didn't intend to come back and live my life in the South at all. I just wanted out of the South. Out of Baker County. And I had this crazy notion that things were so much better in the North that I wouldn't experience the racism. So my answer to what had happened to my father was to say that I would devote my life to working for change. Had no idea how I would do that or what I would do because, I mean, I hadn't been active in the civil rights movement. I only knew what I had heard others talk about and had been able to observe, what was happening in the Albany movement. So to find that SNCC[42] had come to the county, you know, I could barely stay [in Atlanta]. I wanted to leave that program but I couldn't leave because I would have disappointed my aunt. So they agreed to let me come home for the Fourth of July weekend. So I got a chance to attend my first mass meeting that weekend. And I can remember standing in the church and just crying because the church was full of people and they had already had Bloody Saturday, I think, by then. And they call it Bloody Saturday because when they marched, you know, the white people beat them. And then, hearing my folks and other black people there in the county getting up talking and acting like they weren't afraid. And I can remember thinking in the church that night, this is the answer. This is how I'll be able to do it. So, I went back and completed that six weeks of school there and came back and just jumped wholeheartedly into the struggle.

Once I came back, a hearing was held at the courthouse in Newton because the jail was full of my relatives and other people, my sisters—two or three of my sisters were in jail [for participating in protests]—and aunts and cousins and other people who weren't related. So they were having a hearing at the courthouse to decide whether they would be released or not. And C.B. King,[43] who was our attorney, everybody's attorney it seemed, was down for the hearing. And the judge made the decision to let the juveniles out. And when the judge and the prisoners, so to speak, were led back out, we got up to leave and the Gator[44] just went and shut the door and said, "Sit your God damned asses down!" And then he stayed in there cursing and calling out names and carrying on until he got tired and then he got up and opened the door and said, "Get your God damned asses out." So we all went out and went down and got in the cars but, knowing Baker County, we knew we had to ride in groups. We couldn't just get out and go. I think about two miles out of Newton, the sheriff's son was stopping everybody saying, "You didn't stop at the stop sign back up in Newton." So they were doing those kinds of things to harass us.

I went to register to vote and the Gator was standing at the steps of the courthouse and pushed me back out. Sherrod[45] was with me and there were three others, I think, who also went to register. So I was up front and [the Gator] pushed me back from the steps and he also pushed Sherrod down, as I remember. So I didn't get a chance to register to vote on my first attempt. We had to go to Washington later that summer to testify [at] hearings on Baker County. But we had to secretly get around the county to raise money. I think some unions were also helping us. And we were going to take five carloads of people. We identified everyone who needed to go. So I think this was like August of '65 that we were leaving at the end of a mass meeting. And five carloads left Thankful Baptist Church, which is the church I grew up in. And we took a detour into Mitchell County and took the back roads north. We had somehow been able to keep this whole trip very quiet so that the Gator, and the other whites, didn't get word of what we were doing.

We eventually got an injunction against the Gator and once we got that injunction, you know, finally we were able to cool him down a little from some of all that he had been doing. I think the federal government had tried in some other cases to deal with him and they just couldn't. I mean, Gator was just terrible! You could walk by him on the street and if he didn't like the way you walked at the time, he would do something. So it was really a big thing for people to be able to say, "We just won't take any more" and stand up to him.

People who lived on the plantation were dependent for their livelihoods on the very whites against whom the whole community had grievances in many cases. And the impression I have is that the more visible protesters, the more active people, were people who [did not live on] the plantations, who were not dependent. And people who lived on the plantations as well as people who had public jobs, like school teachers, tended to be sympathetic and supportive to the extent of helping to prepare meals and doing things out of sight of whites, but were reluctant to stand forward on the front lines so to say. It was like black people decided in Baker County we just aren't going to take any more. And the fact that my father's death led to people coming together in the county saying, "We're just not going to take any more" really was the beginning of a new Baker County.

Once my father had passed, I didn't even know whether I'd be able to go to college or not. I couldn't go to school in the North any more. But I was able to get in at Fort Valley State[46] on loans and so forth. And so that September [1965], the white people decided to burn a cross in front of my mother's house. By the time my mother came out to see what was going on, they had come out in front of the house and put this cross up and were burning it. So she told [us] to turn all the lights out, and she told my sister to get on the phone and call the sheriff and to call some other black men in the area. And then my mother got the gun and went out on the porch and started shooting. She was also able to see and recognize some of the white people who were out there. And a lot of black men showed up out in the woods with guns. And they were actually almost surrounding the white people and started shooting. And the white people realized they were in danger at that point so they left right quick. And then eventually the sheriff came and the GBI[47] came and Mother named some of the people but, anyway, nothing ever happened with that.

My mother ran for office in '76. She was the first black elected official there in the county. And this wasn't all that much longer, you know, after my father was murdered. It's interesting, she'd tell you, about her first board meeting. The man who was Superintendent was really one of her [white] relatives, Eugene Hall. And he was asking her about different family members and she was asking him about different ones. And then when they got ready to start the meeting, the Superintendent said they were glad to have her as a new board member. There's an old white man on the board and the Superintendent was trying to tell him she was Joe Hall's daughter. And he said, "Yeah, the nigger Joe Hall. Best nigger I ever known."

And so everybody else was sort of cringing a little and Mother said, "That's okay. He's old." And she said, "I can kind of understand because he's old, but there are times when I might slip up and say 'cracker.'"[48] Because we used that too!

My work in the Movement was not only in Baker County. I had made this commitment then and I was committed to life to working for change, so I didn't just work in Baker. Although I've always tried to go home and bring change. So that's why back in '70 I organized the first preschool program for black children. And then I started branching out and working in other counties. While [I was] working in other counties doing voter registration, voter education, working on welfare rights and other problems, people were getting put off the land. So during the summer of '68, seven people went to Israel to study the kibbutz. They came back, and we started meeting and decided to start an organization that we would call New Communities, Incorporated. And New Communities would be a land trust that would go about the country buying land and holding it in trust and turning it over to local community development corporations. After I married, we lived on very little because we had a movement we had to try to keep going. And, therefore, any money I made went into a common treasury that we all lived out of.

So we got our hands on the first piece of land in '69. A real estate agent knew of the availability of this farm just north of here, about twenty-five miles north in Lee County. It was called Feather Field Farms, 4,800 acres of land. We decided to try to get that land. It was $225 an acre. As I remember it was $1,650,000, something like that. And an ideal piece of property because the main highway from Atlanta ran right through it. We had two and a half miles of highway frontage on U.S. 19. Had a railroad that went through it with a spur onto the land. Had about three creeks. This was during the years of OEO, Office of Economic Opportunity,[49] and the Nixon administration. And then another white person had 937 acres of land that he wanted to sell. So that piece of land was pulled in so it was 4,800 plus the 937, actually 6,000 more or less. So here we were with 6,000 acres of land. We got a direct grant from OEO to plan, to put the proposal together. So this company out of Washington, D.C. was hired. I'm sure they had connections with the Nixon administration somehow.

But we'd gotten a $100,000 grant and I think they got most of that to help us put this proposal together. So we had charrettes.[50] We had gotten about 500 families who signed saying they were willing to move onto the farm. So we brought people together to talk about the kind of community they wanted. So through the meetings, people decided what kind of educational system they wanted, what kind of health, what kind of industry, where the villages would be located. During that year of planning though, white people saw what was planned. They couldn't figure out how this could have happened. So we had incidents of shooting at some of the buildings. And then they started an attack, both from the congressional and state level. They started this big fight to try to stop what was happening there. The congressman from our area entered into the Congressional Record that we were Communists. OEO, which had said they would give us this direct grant, wouldn't do it. They were afraid by now. They told us we had to get local support and state support for this funding. When we met locally with white people, they had the TV cameras there to blast us all over southwest Georgia. And Lester Maddox, Governor of the State of Georgia, vetoed the grant.[51]

So at that time, people were saying it just wasn't possible to do what we had planned to do. Those of us locally decided that we had never had our hands on this much land, and we couldn't just give up just like that. So we decided that we would try to fight to keep it. And we fought off foreclosure for three years straight until we were finally able to get some better arrangements financially. In the meantime, we had started farming because farming was all we knew to do at the time. None of us had operated a farm that size before. And I'm sure we made some mistakes. We operated in a different way from most farms. We had a farm manager but we also had a farm committee. And all of the workers on the farm were a part of that committee, as well as the manager and three people from the board. So the work- ers, in a sense, had the opportunity to override anything the manager was able to do out there. And I don't think people were used to being a part of and having ownership of something. It was hard for people to understand that the farm didn't belong to one or two people; it belonged to all of us. It was hard for black people to buy into that concept. And finally, when we got better financing and some grants, the people who gave the money insisted that we put five people on our board of their choosing. And then the drought started. We had a drought in '76, drought in '77, and a drought in '78. It forced us to go to Farmers Home Administration to try to get an emergency loan and the county supervisor, who was white, said we would get one over his dead body. We finally got an FHA loan but to me that was the beginning of the end as well. That's just another layer on. You end up where you can't fully pay the notes, but you can't maneuver even though you have assets because FHA has control over it. So we lost it. It was sold in 1985.[52]

Oh, it was such a big loss. For fifteen years, I had spent just about every day out there on the farm. When I knew it was going to be over, I can remember walking out on the farm and thinking, "Well, this is probably my last time walking down this road" and so forth. And that was when I made a decision then that things have just got to change.

Alease Brickers was born in 1913 in Seaboard, North Carolina, a small, predominantly African American community near Roanoke Rapids. Her parents rented land on which they grew peanuts, cotton, and tobacco. As a young teenager, she moved to Norfolk where she attended junior high until money troubles forced her to go to work. Like her mother, Brickers did domestic work in private homes, an occupation she remained in for forty-five years. She lived in the South most of her life, but, as her interview suggests, she is a citizen of the world; Brickers became involved in a range of local, national, and international causes that she considered important—poverty, urban development, AIDS, and apartheid in South Africa. She addressed these concerns by working through a variety of organizations, including explicitly partisan associations and her church. Here she describes some of her activities and her more general approach to speaking up and exercising her rights and responsibilities as a citizen. Her no-nonsense commitment to "getting things done" typifies the approach of many black women.

I joined the NAACP in about 1975, something like that. I'm still in that. I belong to the City Democratic Club. I belong to the Black Women's Democratic Club. I was a senator with the Silver Hair Legislature, and that was to help the elderly get some of the funds that were due them. We had another organization that was all black, called Concerned Citizens. That, too, was to help people get funds that were due them, and anything else that we could do to help the community. Say, for instance, I would go down to the city council and speak up. We have two black men on our city council. I read in the paper this morning where they wanted to take a community and put some kind of business there. They are taking a lot of the black community and telling them, "When you move, we're going to build some nice houses for you." But that's a lie; they're not building houses. They put in houses there that are [priced] so high you can't buy them unless you've got the money. This is what we have got to stop, but our black people have got to go to these meetings, these city council meetings and all of that, and let them know. So I saw in this morning's paper that one of the black city councilors voted last night not to do this. He opened his mouth. Usually our black men on city council, they might say one or two things, but they really don't talk up like they should. So I called him this morning, and I told him that I wanted to congratulate him because he did open his mouth.

So he said, "Well, Mrs. Brickers, I thank you, and I want you to get some petitions for me."

I said, "Well, I'm sick, but I will go to church and take those petitions. If you get them to me, I will take them."

See, when I take things like that to the church, I get it done. Even here, there are 225 tenants in this building, and they all vote at my precinct. I've been a committee woman at that precinct for twenty-four years, and they vote at my precinct. I get things done. So if he gets me those petitions, I get things done. But, a lot of our black people, not all of them, but a lot of them, go to the polls, they vote for the black candidate, and that's all. They don't keep up with what they are doing. If there's bills that's coming up in the city council or the Congress, and you know that that bill is going to help your community, then you should write your legislator and tell him to vote for or against that bill.

People say, "They aren't going to do nothing after they get there." But you've got to let these people know what you want. You put them there, and the same way you put them there, you can take them down, because you don't have to vote for them the next time they run. I know what's happening. There's two channels, C-SPAN 1 and C-SPAN 2. I know what's going on in Congress.

Now, my black legislators in Congress from Virginia, I keep up with them. I go to Washington and tell them what I want them to do. If there's a bill coming up in Congress that I think would help the black people, I tell them I want them to vote for it or against it. And I love political work. Now, I love that. I love the church, and I do work in the church. My denomination, the United Church of Christ, they write me about the bills that are coming up in Congress, and they want me to write our legislators and ask them to vote for or against it, support it, and I do. I have the evidence that I do these things. And I love working.

When I got to Norfolk, I wasn't real young, but I was younger than I am now, and I met these people and they got me connected, just like this lady at our church. After she found out that I could sing, she right away put me in the choir, started me singing, and I've been doing it since. Well, same thing with politics. Mrs. Evelyn Butts[53] was the first black in Norfolk on the school board to get integration in the schools, back in the 1950s. They found out that I was interested in working with Mrs. Butts and others. There were other women that worked with her, along with me. We worked with her to do these things. She was an activist.

Now, when they had sanctions for South Africa, I went to Washington. I paid my own way. I went to Washington. I lobbied. I marched for sanctions in South Africa three times. When they had Solidarity Day in Washington, I went and I marched. I have marched here for the AIDS walk. We call it a walkathon for AIDS. I am interested in all of that. I did have a forum at our church on AIDS. I did. I sponsored it myself. I did very, very well. I had a good panel on there, a representative of the television, the paper, and the business. I just like the work. I just like the work. I like to get something done.

Afterword

Starting with memories of childhood and family, in some cases reaching back into slavery, the interviews in this book have passed through work and community life before ending with a discussion of activism. Not only do the narratives convey a sense of progress, but also the order of the collection advances a tone of optimism. Some of positivity builds in the book as a function of the interviewing process. From Dora Dennis and Blanche Davis, both born in 1900 to Shirley Sherrod who was born in 1947, the book's narrators told their stories to younger people who conducted the interviews. They passed on to the interviewers—black, white, and Latino students operating within an integrated educational system—hopes, dreams, and encouragements as much as the realities of their lives. Regardless of the questions they were asked, it was important to interviewees to tell uplifting stories of change, and perhaps they perceived that these were the stories they should tell. For the *Behind the Veil* interviewees are among last generation to have known enslaved persons, or to have received that history from people who had known slaves. Cora Flemming's (Chapter 5) approving assessment that "black people can stand up for themselves now," reveals one of the most significant changes that occurred during our narrator's lives: African Americans gained the right to fight for their own liberation, an aspiration they carried into freedom and across the color line.

It would be disrespectful for us to disagree with our interviewees.

Lest we view Jim Crow and race-based discrimination as relics of the past, defeated by African American efforts, and existing only in memories of old people, we are reminded that these interviews took place before the images of Hurricane Katrina splashed across television screens. And lest we give way to the easy retort that nothing has changed, we are also reminded of the election of Barack Hussein Obama in 2008. We suspect our narrators would not have been shocked by the local chaos, the state confusion, or the federal incompetence evidenced in the official response to the 2005 Gulf Coast hurricane. Many narrators had learned to mistrust the responses of law enforcement and government to emergencies by witnessing nonexistent or reluctant interventions and investigations of racial violence. We suspect they would have been pleased by the election of Obama. Most our interviewees were active voters who hoped for the day a black person might be elected to the highest office in the land. They would have seen his election as a direct outcome of the energies they put into obtaining the vote and in marshaling black electoral power. But they would not have been surprised by the racial hostilities expressed toward his campaign and toward his early initiatives in domestic policy,

And lest we be surprised at Obama's election, we would do well to recall that in 1993, when the interviews began, the first African American woman elected to the U.S. Senate, Carol Moseley Braun of Illinois, took office. By then several other black women were serving in the U.S. House of Representatives, including Eva Clayton from North Carolina, Cynthia McKinney of Georgia, and Maxine Waters of California. Black women's success in the electoral arena was an extension of our narrators' struggle to claim voting rights: Florenza Grant lived in Eva Clayton's district. Thus this book's narrators reflect a continued sense of the ability—and the necessity—of determined individuals to affect societal transformations.

Certainly, by the 1990s when these interviews were conducted, some of the worst expressions of race hatred and white supremacy had diminished or, at least, had been suppressed. It is in this historical context that the *Living with Jim Crow* narrators recalled their life experiences. They remember earlier events but filter their meaning through the changes brought by the mass activism of the 1950s and 1960s. In this way, their interviews provide evidence of the complicated relationship between history and memory. Notwithstanding the massive shifts in American social and political culture, this narrative of progress belies other more complicated understandings of change. It is important to note, for instance, that these women are the survivors, who lived into their seventies, eighties, nineties, and beyond. Most black women born in the Jim Crow years did not live to such an advanced age. The average life expectancy for African Americans in 1910 was only thirty-six years. Exhaustion and disease exacerbated by limited access to health care—the effects of persistent poverty—claimed the lives of African Americans earlier than whites. We are reminded in their stories about giving birth and rearing children that these were the most precarious years in a woman's life, ages fifteen to forty-five, when the death rate for African American women exceeded that for white women, black men, and white men. Although those born later in the century could expect to live longer, the longevity of women interviewed for this project was remarkable, making it important to consider how their lives differed from those of women who did not survive into the 1990s.[1]

Still, our narrators express a sense of discontent even as they bear witness to change. They wonder if the benefits of black community institutions and black role models that they experienced have declined with school desegregation, and worry that the affirming aspects have not returned with resegregation. African

American teachers who worked throughout the process of school desegregation, for example, voiced their opinions with the benefit of decades of hindsight
regarding the complicated outcomes of this process. For at the time of the *Brown
v. Board of Education* decision, African Americans felt hopefulness and vindica-
tion: as citizens of the United States, they were guaranteed the protections of the
law. "I thought the *Brown* ruling was a wonderful decision," Dorothy Fletcher
Steele (Chapter 3) exclaims, "I wanted it to happen when the sun came up the
next morning." *Brown* provided a moment of optimism, but the revolution is
not complete.

Other interviews hint at the concerns of elderly women for the opportunities that are available to younger generations. In their interviews, Harrieta
Jefferson and Lanetha Branch (Chapter 5) remark on the absence of young people at community commemorations and at activities where they had once been
inspired—to fight for citizenship for example—through the teaching of black
history. Similarly, energetic activist Alease Brickers (Chapter 5) criticizes the
failure of others in her community to pay attention to politics and to exercise
citizenship rights on a regular basis and not just on election day in November.
Narrators' disappointments and their sense of loss is evident: who, they worry
collectively, will take their places?

So, it is clear through these interviews that while the segregation signs have
come down, and the official color line has been eliminated, issues of race and
racism remain salient in the lives of our narrators and their children, grandchildren, and great-grandchildren. And for this reason, many of them retain their
activist tendencies, despairing at the perceived lack of political interests on the
part of younger generations. The positive trajectory of the interviews in this collection does not cancel out the frustrations, tragedies, and, sometimes, horrors
that these interviewees experienced. For, in some, bitterness practically jumps off
the page, even when mediated through the format of an edited interview. These
women, and many others in the larger *Behind the Veil* Collection—continued
to face racism in the early 1990s. Corporate pig farms polluted their drinking water; their children struggled financially; and their grandchildren attended
overcrowded, understaffed, under-resourced schools. Too many of the *Behind
the Veil* interviewees continued to live in poverty, some in ramshackle homes
without basic necessities, like indoor plumbing. Many suffered ill health or had
been disabled by work-related injuries, and survived on meager Social Security
incomes. A surprising number of them continued to work well beyond a reason-
able retirement age. But their resilience and sense of themselves as survivors
remained strong.

Georgia Bays, for example, whose interview in Chapter 2 talks about working long hours as a farmer and as housekeeper for white landowners, had "quit
work" only four months before she gave her interview, at the age of eighty-one.
Bays conveys this news without complaint; indeed, she defends her working

life against insinuations that domestic labor was demeaning or inappropriate, explaining, "This is my job, this is what I was raised to do—washing, cooking, scrubbing the walls, scrubbing the kitchen, cleaning the yard, and everything. This is what I learned to do." Yet, the physical cost of such labor must have been great. So, one wonders if Bays continued to work for reasons other than affection for her job or for the sake of work itself. But Georgia Bays viewed herself as a survivor, "not bragging, just facts," she said about her struggles. Within this framework, tragedies get reconfigured as opportunities and hardships as battles overcome.

Whatever the limitations and the biases of their memories, these accounts provide valuable documentation that fills gaps in historical evidence and adds vital information to our understanding of individual communities, of the South as a region, and of the United States as a whole. In this way, these voices counter tendencies among Americans to shy away from historical topics that explore less-than-glorious aspects of the nation's past or to depict those who talk about racism and discrimination as provocateurs, responsible for inflaming tensions by bringing such issues to light. Offering a reminder that Americans alive today still remember former slaves helps collapse time, making issues of racism more immediate and framing the fragile victories of the 1960s as part of a still very recent past. By reflecting on the tremendous changes, as well as the unfulfilled promises of equality, the narrators in *Living with Jim Crow* challenge generalizations about African American life in the Jim Crow South and, indeed, about the nature of history and memory.

List of Interviews

All interviews are from *Behind the Veil: Documenting African American Life in the Jim Crow South*, Center for Documentary Studies at Duke University, Rare Book, Manuscript, and Special Collections Library, Duke University, Durham, North Carolina. The interviews appear here arranged in alphabetical order by narrator's last name.

Aaron, Dolores T. Interviewed by Michele Mitchell. June 30, 1994. New Orleans, Louisiana.

Adams, Wilhelmenia R. Interviewed by Chris Stewart. June 8, 1993. Charlotte, North Carolina.

Alexander, Essie Mae. Interviewed by Paul Ortiz. August 10, 1995. Greenwood, Mississippi.

Bays, Georgia. Interviewed by Doris Dixon. August 1, 1995. Lyons, Mississippi.

Blue, Ila J. Interviewed by Blair Murphy and Kisha Turner. June 2, 1995. Durham, North Carolina.

Borders, Florence E. Interviewed by Michele Mitchell and Kate Ellis. June 20 and August 12, 1994. New Orleans, Louisiana.

Branch, Lanetha C. Interviewed by Doris Dixon. June 16, 1995. Memphis, Tennessee.

Branchcomb, Flossie R. Fuller. Interviewed by Mary Hebert. August 8, 1995. Portsmouth, Virginia.

Brickers, Alease Virginia. Interviewed by Blair Murphy. July 26, 1995. Norfolk, Virginia.

Browne, Corinne J. Interviewed by Tunga White. July 26, 1994. St. Helena Island, South Carolina.

Carter, Dorcas E. Interviewed by Karen Ferguson. August 5, 1993. New Bern, North Carolina.

Cherry, Olivia J. Interviewed by Blair Murphy. August 10, 1995. Chesapeake, Virginia.

Clarke, Juanita. Interviewed by Paul Ortiz. June 29, 1994. Birmingham, Alabama.

Davillier, Brenda Bozant. Interviewed by Michele Mitchell. July 15, 1994. New Orleans, Louisiana.

Davis, Blanche. Interviewed by Tywanna Whorley and Mausiki Scales. August 28, 1994. Birmingham, Alabama.

Dennis, Dora Strong. Interviewed by Paul Ortiz. July 19, 1995. Forrest City, Arkansas.

Ely, Vermelle Diamond. Interviewed by Leslie Brown and Anne Valk. June 17, 1993. Charlotte, North Carolina.

Flemming, Cora E. Interviewed by Paul Ortiz. August 7, 1995. Indianola, Mississippi.

Flowers, Aurie B. Interviewed by Sally S. Graham. July 1, 1994. Cairo, Georgia.

Fort, Marie. Interviewed by Doris Dixon. June 19, 1995. Memphis, Tennessee.

Gavin, Annie Joyner. Interviewed by Chris Stewart. August 3, 1993. New Bern, North Carolina.

Giles, Alice. Interviewed by Paul Ortiz. August 8, 1995. Indianola, Mississippi.

Grant, Florenza M. Interviewed by Sonya Ramsey. June 27, 1993. Tillery, North Carolina.

Howard, Helen. Interviewed by Doris Dixon. July 19, 1995. Cotton Plant, Arkansas.

Jackson, Ruthe Lee. Interviewed by Mausiki Stacey Scales. August 10, 1995. Itta Bena, Mississippi.

Jefferson, Harrieta. Interviewed by Tywanna Whorley and Mausiki Stacey Scales. August 8, 1994. Tallahassee, Florida.

Johnson, Mandie. Interviewed by Doris Dixon. August 4, 1994. Greenwood, Mississippi.

Lucas, Julia H. Interviewed by Leslie Brown. September 21, 1995. Durham, North Carolina.

Lucas, Willie Ann. Interviewed by Paul Ortiz. July 7, 1995. Brinkley, Arkansas.

Lyons, Theresa Cameron. Interviewed by Leslie Brown. August 16, 1995. Durham, North Carolina.

Mitchell, Cleaster. Interviewed by Paul Ortiz. July 16, 1995. Brinkley, Arkansas.

Monroe, Irene. Interviewed by Tywanna Whorley and Mausiki Scales. July 11, 1994. Bessemer, Alabama.

Pitts, Elizabeth. Interviewed by Mausiki Stacey Scales. July 24, 1995. Greenwood, Mississippi.

Pointer, A. Elizabeth Harris. Interviewed by Paul Ortiz. July 22, 1994. Tuskegee, Alabama.

Porter, Celestyne Diggs. Interviewed by Kisha Turner. August 2, 1995. Norfolk, Virginia.

Rogers, Margaret Sampson. Interviewed by Kara Miles. July 14, 1993. Wilmington, North Carolina.

Rolling, Susie M. Interviewed by Mausiki Scales. August 8, 1995. Yazoo City, Mississippi.

Russell, Sue K. Interviewed by Paul Ortiz. August 5, 1994. Tallahassee, Florida.

Sherrod, Shirley Miller. Interviewed by Charles H. Hamilton, Jr. June 30, 1994. Albany, Georgia.

Steele, Dorothy Fletcher. Interviewed by Leslie Brown. June 16, 1993. Charlotte, North Carolina.

Veazy, Rodie B. Interviewed by Paul Ortiz. June 16, 1995. Memphis, Tennessee.

Wade, Harriet V. Interviewed by Rhonda Mawhood. August 1, 1993. New Bern, North Carolina.

Wells, Julia. Interviewed by Blair Murphy and Kisha Turner. July 6, 1995. Sumter, South Carolina.

White, Bernice. Interviewed by Paul Ortiz. August 10, 1995. Indianola, Mississippi.

Williams, Hortense Spence. Interviewed by Kisha Turner. July 17, 1995. Norfolk, Virginia.

Wilson, Catherine M. Interviewed by Kara Miles. June 10, 1993. Charlotte, North Carolina.

Wilson, Emogene W. Interviewed by Mausiki Stacey Scales. July 5, 1995. Memphis, Tennessee.

Sample Edited Transcript, from Interview with Ila J. Blue

The following interview excerpt is provided to illustrate for readers the process involved in preparing transcripts for publication. The longer edited version of this interview with Ila Blue appears in Chapter 1 (starting on page 24). For comparison, a segment of the raw transcript is printed here. Words that are deleted from the original transcript are crossed through. Words that are moved from one place to another are underlined, appearing in brackets in their new location.

[Begin Tape 1, Side 2]

~~Blue:~~ ~~...our farm, and we'd go down there and fish. We ate, but we didn't have any money, that was our problem.~~

~~Q:~~ ~~Your family owned that land?~~

~~Blue:~~ ~~Oh, yes.~~

~~Q:~~ ~~How did they come to own that land?~~

Blue: My mama's daddy gave it to them. I'll tell you how. ~~You know, that's another story.~~ My two grandfathers were slaves, but both of them had no problem with growing up or anything. In the first place, my paternal grandfather was the old master's son, and that was one thing. So he was special. ~~All right.~~

But my maternal grandfather, he was ~~a youngster,~~ much younger than my paternal grandfather[.], ~~because I think w~~[W]hen ~~it~~ [the Civil War] was over, when the northerners rushed through there and swept it out, and the people were saying, "Burn up Georgia," he was in ~~the~~ [his] teens. He was lucky. ~~If you read about slavery and listen to the people who know about slavery, now and then you would find a contrary or mean [unclear], but for the most part, you know Harriet Tubman and the underground railroad. You know what her success was with the white women who helped her. They couldn't go in the daytime because the people would see them, all those people.~~

~~My paternal grandfather would tell all about this, you know, because he knew all about it. He didn't tell me much, because I didn't know him, but he told that the white ladies—of course, there were some white ladies that wouldn't do it, of course. You're~~

~~always going to get some good and mean. See, the white ladies would hide the slaves in the daytime down in their cellars. My grandfather told my family that. Of course, the law found it out, but they couldn't do anything about it, because you don't never say you doubt what the white man is saying. The white lady was in there.~~

~~He told about some that he knew about, that Harriet Tubman had this group. Of course, there was more than one group, but she was the big one, and had a sick child in it. The old Missus had them down in the cellar. Said somebody told the law, said the law came, heard they were there, and she told them, no, nobody was there. Said this sick child started crying, so Missus went over to that piano and she did some playing so they couldn't hear anything. Then after [unclear], she said, "I told you . . ." something like that, what the words were. So they left. You can't doubt the white lady's word, you know. So the law left. But they knew they were down there. At night, she bundled them up and sent them on their way.~~

~~Did you ever read *Uncle Tom's Cabin?*~~

Q: ~~Yes.~~

Blue: ~~That's the way. Said it was a white missus here. Not every one, but you'd get a good one.~~

~~To go back to my grandfather, my maternal grandfather, t~~[T]his is what he told my mama. ~~I think he was 16 or 18 when the war was over, and h~~[H]e said that sometimes you had a very cruel overseer on the farm~~, so he~~[who] was going to beat the boys for nothing. ~~He said b~~[B]ut ~~all you had to do,~~ the boys could outrun him. ~~All you've got to do, you go to that house to the missus, his missus—not everyone didn't do that, but~~ ~~h~~[H]e says that he'd run to the missus, and she would put a hand on that boy and she'd keep him around the house and say, "He's going to help me in the day, two or three," 'til all this wear out. Then she'd let him go back to the field. But he said he had run a many a day. ~~That man was [unclear], he said he'd beat it to that house.~~ But, see, he was lucky.

~~I don't know, maybe women are just more humane to men, I don't know, but he said you never would have made the underground railroad if it hadn't been for some of those white ladies. They would hide them in the daytime. My grandpapa told Mama about the one, said they had them there, and they knew they were there, so somebody told the law. She told them, no, they weren't there. Then when he heard the baby crying, said she started playing that piano. The white lady started playing the piano.~~

Q: ~~Did he run away from slavery?~~

Blue: ~~No! He wasn't doing any work. I told you the boss was his daddy.~~

Q: ~~That was your paternal grandfather?~~

Blue: ~~My paternal grandfather. My maternal grandfather was much younger. Let me tell you about him. Mama told us this. He told Mama, of course, because he was, I think, 17 when the war was over. You see, what you call now Wagram and Laurinburg and Raeford, Raeford wasn't in, but it was in that area down there, that's where we lived, and that was his land. He lived in Hoke County between Laurinburg and Raeford and Fayetteville and Ray Springs and Aberdeen and all that stuff.~~

He told Mama that he was 16 or 17 when the war was over. ~~Okay. He said that~~ ~~t~~[T]he Yankees came through and just swept anything they wanted to, because they had won. Said that ~~they~~[his white owners] called him and said, "Dave, I want you to keep the horses." It's a place we call Lumber River; it's not a river, but there's water and a bridge there and everything. [You wouldn't see the horses. It's sand all around.] [They] ~~S~~said, "I want you to keep them down here," and ~~all the white people in there,~~ the white men brought their best horses, because the Yankees~~, as you know,~~ were riding through, just taking them, and gave them to Dave. Said, "Dave, you keep them quiet now." ~~And had them down at Lumber River, this place you can go to~~ you wouldn't see the horses. It's sand all around. ~~It could have been a beach if you had somebody to do it, you know. Because we look at it now when we go to Laurinburg, say, "Dave was down there with the horses."~~ He had a gang of horses, all the best that these people had, because the Yankees would ride through and just take them.

~~Okay. Her daddy was listening.~~ He could hear them coming, hear the Yankees coming, because they ~~was~~ [were]making a lot of noise. They had won and they were taking things. He said he just waited. ~~Said he took off his shirt. He had on a white shirt. So he took it off and he was~~ down there with the horses~~, took his shirt off.~~ He heard them hit the bridge, a long bridge over Lumber River. He heard them hit the bridge. He took off~~, took~~ his white shirt, and he stopped them right there. He said, "Come over here and get all these horses."

They went down there, and every man took one, and he rode off with them. [He gave all the horses away. Then he jumped bareback, didn't even have a saddle, like a wild man, rode on off with them.] He knew he had to go or they would have killed him. He stayed off for years, ~~he said, he rode on,~~ and finally went to New York. ~~He left and went to a little place, I don't know whether it was Jamaica, somewhere.~~ He stayed off 'til he was grown. He came back, and I guess all the masters were dead when he came back.

Q: ~~So he went to New York?~~

Blue: ~~He didn't stay there. He went on with the Yankees, because he knew he had to go now.~~ [He gave all the horses away. [Laughter] Said he took off his shirt. "Come on!" Then he jumped bareback, didn't even have a saddle, like a wild man, rode on off with them.]

~~As I say, Mama had a job for everybody to do. [Laughter] "This is your week to do so and so, your week to do so and so." But I thought that was great, myself. My sisters and brothers told me, "You didn't have any better sense." [Laughter]~~

Q: ~~Your family got your land from your paternal grandfather?~~

Blue: ~~Maternal grandfather.~~

Q: ~~And he acquired the land how?~~

Blue: ~~Oh, well, after he left and went away, he stayed away a few years, you see. He was grown up when he left. I guess he was about 17 when he left.~~ When he came back, he had some money, but he ~~didn't buy it then. He came back and~~ worked. He was working on this farm. ~~If you remember a little of history, that they were selling land almost for nothing once upon a time.~~ He bought several, several acres. He had three children, ~~but he had~~ two girls and a boy, but the boy died, so he divided it between his two daughters, my mama half of it and my aunt half of it.

Q: ~~Did he have any problems with white people around, holding on to the land?~~

Blue: ~~No, no problems. I don't perhaps know all of the ins and outs of this, but I don't know what period it was, but they were just selling land almost dirt cheap. I don't know how much it was, but Mama was telling us. I never knew him. But she said he was always a go-getter, and she said people heard him talking, thinking maybe he degraded~~

something, you know. He'd say, "You see that black nigger over there?" And Mama said, "I guess nobody said anything, because he was black himself." [Laughter] He was very dark.

But, see, he was always enterprising. He gave all those horses away. He thought that up. "Now, Dave, I want you to keep them. Just keep them so when they come through here, they'll take all the horses." They were taking horses, anything they needed. They were the heroes then. They had won the war. He told them, yeah, he would. I think he was 17 then. But he knew he was going to leave there then, so he jumped on one of those horses, didn't even have a saddle on it, nothing.

Q: The white men thought he was going to keep the horses for them.

Blue: Well, not only one; it was those in that area, because they were taking horses. They'd ride one and go get them another one, go to that man's house and take his, take another, throw a saddle on that one, go on off. And Dave told them, yeah, he'd keep them. [Laughter]

Q: What church did you go to?

Notes

Introduction: We Did Well With What We Had: Remembering Black Life Behind the Veil

1. Jim Crow is a colloquial term for the system of racial repression deployed by southern whites as a means to control African Americans and sustain white supremacy. A web of laws, customs, and practices, Jim Crow took the form of racial segregation, discrimination, oppression, and violence sanctioned by the courts and the American legal structure.
2. Olivia Cherry interview. All interview citations appear in Appendix A.
3. *Behind the Veil Documenting African American Life in the Jim Crow South*, funded by the National Endowment for the Humanities, the Ford Foundation, and the Duke Endowment, was a multiyear teaching and research project that connected faculty, graduate students, and undergraduate students to research, learn, and write about black life during the period of legal segregation. The project was hosted at Duke University's Center for Documentary Studies, and included participants from college and universities across the region. See: William H. Chafe, Raymond Gavins, et al., *Remembering Jim Crow: African Americans Tell about Life in the Jim Crow South* (New York: New Press in association with Lyndhurst Books of the Center for Documentary Studies of Duke University: distributed by W.W. Norton & Co., 2001).
4. The Federal Writers' Project of the 1930s recorded more than 10,000 life stories of men and women from a variety of occupations and ethnic groups. As a part of this project, some 2,300 interviews were conducted with ex-slaves. The slave narratives were assembled as a multi-volume collection, *Slave Narratives: A Folk History of Slavery in the United States from Interviews with Former Slaves,* and later published. See also: George P. Rawick, ed., *The American Slave: A Composite Autobiography*, 25 vols. (Westport, CT: Greenwood Press, 1979) and "Born In Slavery: Slave Narratives from the Federal Writers Project, 1936–1938," http://memory.loc.gov/ammem/snhtml/.
5. A fuller description of the project, the interviews, and the archival collection can be found at the website of the Duke University Special Collections Library; see: http://library.duke.edu/digitalcollections/rbmscl/btv/inv/.
6. "What a woman ought to be and to do" comes from Zora Neale Hurston, *Their Eyes Were Watching God* (New York: J. P. Lippincott Publisher, 1937; reprint, New York: Harper & Row, New Perennial Library Edition, 1990), 15. Also see: Stephanie Shaw, *What a Woman Ought to Be and to Do: Black Professional Women Workers during the Jim Crow Era* (Chicago: University of Chicago Press, 1996).

7. On African American women's history, see Shaw, *What A Woman Ought to Be and to Do*; Paula Giddings, *When and Where I Enter: The Impact of Black Women on Race and Sex in America* (New York: William Morrow, 1984); Glenda Elizabeth Gilmore, *Gender and Jim Crow: Women and the Politics of White Supremacy in North Carolina, 1896–1920* (Chapel Hill: University of North Carolina Press, 1996); Tera W. Hunter, *To 'Joy My Freedom: Southern Women's Lives and Labors after the Civil War* (Cambridge: Harvard University Press, 1997); Victoria W. Wolcott, *Remaking Respectability: African American Women in Interwar Detroit* (Chapel Hill: University of North Carolina Press, 2001); Darlene Clark Hine, et al., *Black Women in United States History*, 16 vols. (Brooklyn: Carlson Publishing, 1990).

8. Elsa Barkley Brown, "Womanist Consciousness: Maggie Lena Walker and the Independent Order of St. Luke," *Signs* 14 (Spring 1989): 610–633. Also see: Evelyn Brooks Higginbotham, *Righteous Discontent: The Women's Movement in the Black Baptist Church, 1880–1920* (Cambridge: Harvard University Press, 1993); Deborah Gray White, *Too Heavy a Load: Black Women in Defense of Themselves, 1894–1994* (New York: W. W. Norton Press, 1999); Patricia Hill Collins, *Black Feminist Thought: Knowledge, Consciousness and the Politics of Empowerment* (New York: Routledge, 2000).

9. W. E. B. Du Bois, *The Souls of Black Folk: Essays and Sketches* (Chicago: A.C. McClurge & Co., 1903). Numerous scholars have documented black communities in the Jim Crow South. See, for example, Earl Lewis, *In Their Own Interests: Race, Class, and Power in Twentieth-Century Norfolk, Virginia* (Berkeley: University of California Press, 1991); Neil R. McMillen, *Dark Journey: Black Mississippians in the Age of Jim Crow* (Urbana: University of Illinois Press, 1990); Gilmore, *Gender and Jim Crow*; Allison Dorsey, *To Build Our Lives Together: Community Formation in Black Atlanta, 1875–1906* (Athens: University of Georgia Press, 2004).

10. Karen E. Fields, writing of the memoir she produced based on interviews with her grandmother, makes a similar point. "Matters of race and color are a permanent presence without being her principal subject. They are constituent to life, but they do not define life." From Karen E. Fields, "What One Cannot Remember Mistakenly," in Jaclyn Jeffrey and Glenace Edwall, eds. *Memory and History: Essays on Recalling and Interpreting Experience* (Lanham, MD: University Press of America, 1994), 98. See also: Mamie Garvin Fields with Karen Fields, *Lemon Swamp and Other Places: A Carolina Memoir* (New York: Free Press, 1985).

11. Evelyn Brooks Higginbotham, "African American Women's History and the Metalanguage of Race," *Signs* 17 (Winter 1992): 251–274.

12. Jacqueline Jones, *Labor of Love, Labor of Sorrow: Black Women, Work, and the Family, from Slavery to the Present* (New York: Basic Books, 1985); Sharon Harley and The Black Women and Work Collective, *Sister Circle: Black Women and Work* (New Brunswick, NJ: Rutgers University Press, 2002).

13. Charles S. Johnson, *Patterns of Negro Segregation* (New York: Harper & Brothers, 1943); Pauli Murray, *States' Laws on Race and Color* (Cincinnati: Women's Division of Christian Service, Board of Missions and Church Extension, Methodist Church, 1952).

14. Theresa Jan Cameron Lyons interview; Harriet Wade interview; Irene Monroe interview.

15. Ruthe Lee Jackson interview; Bernice White interview; Olivia Cherry interview.

16. City newspapers in Lexington, Kentucky, for example, refused to cover stories about civil rights protests. Catherine Fosl and Tracy E. K'Meyer, *Freedom on the Border: An Oral History of the Civil Rights Movement in Kentucky* (Lexington: University Press of Kentucky, 2009): 85–86.

17. Alessandro Portelli, *The Death of Luigi Trastulli and Other Stories: Form and Meaning in Oral History* (Albany: State University of New York Press, 1991), 50.

18. Deborah Gray White, *Too Heavy a Load* and *Ar'n't I a Woman: Female Slaves in the Plantation South* (New York: W. W. Norton Press, 1985).

19. On respectability, see Leslie Brown, *Upbuilding Black Durham: Gender, Class, and Black Community Development in the Jim Crow South* (Chapel Hill: University of North Carolina Press, 2008); Wolcott, *Remaking Respectability*; Gilmore, *Gender and Jim Crow*; Higginbotham, *Righteous Discontent*.

20. For an overview and discussion of the institutionalization of Jim Crow, see Leon Litwack, *Trouble in Mind: Black Southerners in the Age of Jim Crow* (New York: Vintage Books, 1998); C. Vann Woodward, *The Strange Career of Jim Crow* (New York: Oxford University Press, 1955); Joel Williamson, *The Crucible of Race: Black-White Relations in the American South since Emancipation* (New York: Oxford University Press, 1984).

21. Brown, *Upbuilding Black Durham*; Michele Mitchell, *Righteous Propagation: African Americans and the Politics of Racial Destiny after Reconstruction* (Chapel Hill: University of North Carolina Press, 2004).

22. We also narrowed our selection to interviews from the *Behind the Veil* Collection that already were transcribed. Interviews were selected for transcription on the basis of ratings assigned by the interviewers; thus the transcribed collection represents narratives that were considered of highest quality, containing accounts of historical significance and interest. Of the 1,200 interviews in the *Behind the Veil* Collection, approximately one-third are transcribed.

23. On editing, see Michael Frisch, *A Shared Authority: Essays on the Craft and Meaning of Oral and Public History* (Albany: State University of New York Press, 1989), 81–146.

24. The Oyez Project, *Plessy v. Ferguson*, 163 U.S. 537 (1896), available at http:// oyez.org/cases/1851–1900/1895/1895_210; The Oyez Project, *Brown v. Board of Education, Topeka, Kansas* (I), 347 U.S. 483 (1954), available at http://oyez.org/ cases/1950–1959/1952/1952_1.

25. See, for example, C. Vann Woodward, *Origins of the New South, 1877– 1913* (Baton Rouge: Louisiana State University Press, 1951); Edward Ayers, *Promise of the New South* (New York: Oxford University Press, 1992); Howard Rabinowitz, *Race Relations in the Urban South, 1865–1890* (New York: Oxford University Press, 1978); Jerrod M. Packard, *American Nightmare: The History of Jim Crow* (New York: St. Martin Press, 2002); Peter H. Irons, *Jim Crow's Children: The Broken Promise of the Brown Decision* (New York: Viking Press, 2002).

26. Jacquelyn Dowd Hall, "The Long Civil Rights Movement and the Political Uses of the Past," *Journal of American History* 91 (March 2005): 1233–1263.

27. For example, see Charles M. Payne, *I've Got the Light of Freedom: The Organizing Tradition and the Mississippi Freedom Struggle* (Berkeley: University of California Press, 1995); Robin D.G. Kelley, "We Are Not What We Seem: The Politics and Pleasures of Community," in *Race Rebels: Culture, Politics, and the Black Working Class* (New York: Free Press, 1994); John Dittmer, *Local People: The Struggle for Civil Rights in Mississippi* (Urbana: University of Illinois Press, 1994); Emilye Crosby, *A Little Taste of Freedom: The Black Freedom Struggle in Claiborne County, Mississippi* (Chapel Hill: University of North Carolina Press, 2005); J. Todd Moye, *Let the People Decide: Black Freedom and White Resistance Movements in Sunflower County, Mississippi, 1945–1980* (Chapel Hill: University of North Carolina Press, 2004); Hunter, *To 'Joy My Freedom*; Elsa Barkley Brown, "To Catch the Vision of Freedom: Reconstructing Southern Black Women's Political History, 1865–1890," in Henry Giroux, ed., *Border Crossings: Cultural Workers and the Politics of Education* (New York: Routledge, 1992); Jennifer Ritterhouse, *Growing Up Jim Crow: How Black and White Southern Children Learned Race* (Chapel Hill: University of North Carolina Press, 2006); Hasan Kwame Jeffries, *Bloody Lowndes: Civil Rights and Black Power in Alabama's Black Belt* (New York: New York University Press, 2009); Grace Elizabeth Hale, *Making Whiteness: The Culture of Segregation in the South, 1890–1940* (New York: Pantheon Books, 1998); David R. Roediger, *Wages of Whiteness: Race and the Making of the American Working Class* (London: Verso Press, 1991).

28. Dorothy Fletcher Steele interview.

1 The Foundation Was There: Growing up a Girl in the Jim Crow South

1. On childhood, see Jennifer Ritterhouse, *Growing Up Jim Crow: How Black and White Southern Children Learned Race* (Chapel Hill: University of North Carolina Press, 2006).

2. Sharecroppers farmed land owned by other families, typically according to arrangements laid out in a yearly contract. Sharecroppers provided the labor of their family and a share of the profits made from crops in exchange for housing and the use of land. Many landowners required sharecroppers to purchase farming and family supplies from a commissary, buying on credit with the understanding that monies plus interest spent on such purchases would be deducted from profits reaped over the agricultural season. Commissary prices could be steep and families had little control over book keeping. If annual commissary expenses exceeded a family's income from sale of crops they became indebted to landowners and were forced to work another year. Nan Woodruff describes life in the Delta in *American Congo: The African American Freedom Struggle in the Delta* (Cambridge: Harvard University Press, 2003).

3. A "bit" referred to 12.5 cents, so six bits would equal 75 cents.

4. Klondike Elementary School, which was built in 1902 at 1250 Vollintine, was the first public school in Memphis for black students.

5. LeMoyne Missionary School was founded in 1862 as a school for free people and contraband. In 1871 it became the LeMoyne Normal and Commercial School. Owen College began in 1947 as a junior college. Both institutions had roots in the Baptist tradition, and merged in 1968 into LeMoyne-Owen College.

6. Beale Street, part of Memphis' black business district, was renowned for its nightlife.

7. Fort is referring to skin lightening, or bleaching, cream.

8. Established in 1917, the Julius Rosenwald Fund provided monies for rural school buildings for African Americans. The project called for cooperation between black communities and county school officials, although African Americans put up most of the resources toward building construction. The Rosenwald Fund supported the building of almost 5,000 schools.

9. The school calendar in the South largely was determined by the agricultural seasons. In her interview, Blue describes lay-by time, usually in July and August, before the time to pick cotton. During this period when time in fields was minimal, children attended school. School typically stopped around Labor Day when it was time to gather crops.

10. Mary Potter School was a Presbyterian-run boarding school, founded in the 1880s, for black children. Located in Oxford, North Carolina, the school was about sixty miles from Blue's home.

11. Livingstone College, in Salisbury, North Carolina, was formed in the 1870s by the A.M.E. Zion Church to train ministers. Like many African American colleges at the time, it offered high school level courses in addition to a college curriculum.

12. The Penn Normal, Industrial, and Agricultural School served African American children from throughout the Sea Islands. Originally opened in 1862, its mission was to educate the children of freed people. Until it closed in 1948, the school trained teachers, farmers, and craftspeople. After the school closed, the campus operated as the Penn Community Services Center, offering social services and programs to enhance the livelihood and self-sufficiency of Sea Islanders. In the 1960s, it was an important civil rights movement site, used by the Southern Christian Leadership Conference, the Peace Corps, and other organizations. Since the 1980s, it has functioned primarily as a historic and cultural preservation center.

13. A pensioner received money from the federal government for having served in the military.

14. Now Hampton University, this historically black college [HBCU] was founded during the Civil War to provide education for freed people. Booker T. Washington was a graduate of Hampton, where he was encouraged to open his own school, Tuskegee Institute, now Tuskegee University, in Tuskegee, Alabama.

15. Southern states bucked the trend toward compulsory school attendance laws, specifically because such laws would have provided education for blacks. Even in those places where they existed, compulsory school laws were rarely enforced by white officials, although blacks used the law to demand educational options for their children. Child labor laws operated similarly, enforced or not at the whim of white authorities. Public schools facilities were few and far between. Many

schools that operated on or near plantations were established and supported by black communities, organizations, or individuals.

16. A furnish consisted of an amount of credit to be redeemed for use at a store operated or approved by the plantation owner. The plantation stores used suspect methods for keeping track of sharecroppers' debts and payments. As Mitchell describes, the system was set up to keep sharecroppers indebted to the plantation owner, thus owing another year's labor. The illiteracy that characterized most sharecropping families also contributed to this cycle of debt, making it impossible for many families to keep track of their income and expenses and thus unable to challenge the owner's records.

17. Some farming families that did not own land would hire out their labor on a daily basis, expecting to get paid at the end of the day. Sharecropping families, in contrast, worked under contract for a year, providing their labor and their crops in exchange for housing and a share of the profits from the sale of those crops.

18. Many employers hired workers for short-term jobs—cleaning or cooking, doing construction, or manual labor—in this manner, selecting from men and women who gathered on particular street corners to wait for day work.

19. Parker High School in Birmingham opened around 1900 and became an important part of Birmingham's black community.

20. Dr. Parker was the principal.

21. Barber Memorial Seminary in Anniston, Alabama, opened in 1898 for African American girls. In 1930, it merged with Scotia College in North Carolina, becoming Barber-Scotia College.

22. The Tremé neighborhood is one of New Orleans' oldest areas and was formerly a community for free people of color.

23. Shotgun houses are a typical southern architectural form. Small in size, they are generally a single story and one-room wide.

24. Construction of Independence Boulevard began in 1946 and continued for several years. An urban expressway, the Boulevard disrupted many settled communities and turned primarily residential neighborhoods into commercial districts, with stores lining the route. Such construction demonstrated the impact of post–World War II consumerism and Charlotte's transformation from a small city to a larger metropolis.

25. Stagville Plantation was owned by the Bennehan-Cameron family and was home to about 900 slaves at the start of the Civil War. It now operates as a historic site.

26. As U.S. factories shifted to war-related production, American consumers were required to cut back on their purchases of nonessential goods. With rationing, families received coupons that could be redeemed for restricted quantities of food, gas, or other goods.

27. Blind Boy Fuller was a blues guitarist and singer, originally from North Carolina. He performed in Durham, North Carolina, and made numerous recordings. His lyrics dealt explicitly with topics such as unemployment, poverty, imprisonment, love, and street culture.

28. Hayti was Durham's largest African American neighborhood and home of the city's largest black business district.

29. Children were required to stay in school until age sixteen, but these laws were not routinely enforced.

2 What Is Expected Of You: Gender and Sexuality

1. Elizabeth Pitts from Mississippi discusses "eye rape," the accusation that black men looked at white women with inappropriate lust.
2. On women's decisions about family size, see Darlene Clark Hine and Kathleen Thompson, *A Shining Thread of Hope: The History of Black Women in America* (New York: Broadway Books, 1998), 219–222.
3. Bays' father's "company" would have consisted of other men; the kind of drinking she describes would not have occurred in mixed-sex company.
4. Menstrual period.
5. Menopause.
6. Bays uses this expression to refer to the fact that she was still young, a child.
7. Bays and her husband farmed as sharecroppers.
8. Daily housework: cleaning, cooking, ironing, mending.
9. In the late twentieth century, misunderstanding and misinformation about HIV (human immunodeficiency virus) and AIDS (acquired immunodeficiency syndrome) led to victims' being socially ostracized if not isolated.
10. Midwifery was regulated at the state and county levels, although enforcement was inconsistent. Most women continued to use midwives even after passage of the 1946 Hospital Construction and Survey Act (also known as the Hill-Burton Act), which granted money to states to build or modernize hospitals and public health clinics. The Act stipulated that all services funded under the law must be provided without regard to race. These provisions were difficult to enforce but still expanded black southerners' access to hospital care. On black health care see, for example, David T. Beito and Linda Royster Beito, "'Let Down Your Buckets Where You Are' The Afro-American Hospital and Black Health Care in Mississippi, 1924–1966," *Social Science History* 30 (Winter 2006): 551–569.
11. Quinine was used to stop early labor.
12. Located in Salisbury, North Carolina, Livingstone College is a historically black school affiliated with the American Methodist Episcopal Zion Church.
13. Across the United States, Florence Crittenton homes offered rooms to pregnant and unwed women from the late nineteenth century into the present. The homes were locally run and financed, with support from the National Florence Crittenton Mission.
14. Corregidor and Bataan were sites of important military battles between the U.S., Philippines, and Japanese forces during World War II, and both marked locations of U.S. defeat early in the war.
15. A historically black college in Daytona Beach, Florida, founded by Mary McLeod Bethune. It began as the Daytona Educational and Industrial Training School for Negro Girls in 1904 and was renamed Bethune-Cookman College in 1929.
16. Starting in 1944, the GI Bill—officially known as the Servicemen's Readjustment Act—provided benefits to returning veterans, including payment to cover tuition

costs and low-interest rate mortgages. The GI Bill's tuition benefits helped millions of men to pursue higher education.

17. Mary McLeod Bethune served in President Roosevelt's "Black Cabinet" during the New Deal, as Director of Negro Affairs for the National Youth Administration and an advisor to the President. She served as president of Bethune-Cookman College until 1942. She also initiated the National Council for Negro Women, an umbrella organization to coordinate activities and consolidate the power of black women's organizations concerned with social and civic issues.

18. In addition to her work as an educator and reformer, Bethune served as president of the Central Life Insurance Company of Tampa, and as director of the Afro-American Life Insurance Company of Jacksonville.

19. Meharry Medical College is affiliated with Fisk University in Nashville, Tennessee. Meharry is one of the two medical schools attached to historically black colleges and, therefore, one of the main institutions preparing black doctors during the Jim Crow period.

20. Rogers attended Fayetteville State Teachers' College in North Carolina. Originally a historically black school, it is now part of North Carolina's public university system.

21. Fort Bragg, an army post located near Fayetteville, North Carolina, housed black and white soldiers in segregated quarters.

22. Names changed at narrator's request.

23. Shaw Air Force Base, located in Sumter, South Carolina, opened in 1947, two years before the Air Force began to gradually desegregate its forces.

24. Red bone refers to a light-skinned African American woman.

25. Morris College is a historically black school, operated by the Baptist Educational and Missionary Convention of South Carolina. It is located in Sumter.

26. Many black schools provided housing for women teachers. Because women typically were prohibited from teaching if they were married, the presence of single women teachers in communities often prompted the need for housing that would offer protection and allow unmarried women to maintain their respectability. Many communities considered teachers' cottages a solution to these problems.

27. Oral contraceptives were approved for sale in the United States in 1960 but their use was limited by legal restrictions in most states. In 1965, the Supreme Court ruled in *Griswold v. Connecticut* that laws that banned the use of contraceptives by married couples violated Americans' constitutional right to marital privacy. Still, access to birth control pills remained inconsistent across the country.

3 You Are All Under Bondage, Which Is True: Working Lives

1. On black women and work, see Jacqueline Jones, *Labor of Love, Labor of Sorrow: Black Women, Work, and the Family, from Slavery to the Present* (New York: Vintage Books, 1985); Tera Hunter, *To 'Joy My Freedom: Southern Black Women's Lives and Labors After the Civil War* (Cambridge: Harvard University Press, 1997).

2. On girls and household labor, see Elizabeth Clark Lewis, *Living In, Living Out: African American Domestics in Washington, D.C. 1910–1940* (Washington, DC: Smithsonian Institution Press, 1994); see also Sharon Harley, ed., *Sister Circle: Black Women and Work* (New Brunswick, NJ: Rutgers University Press, 2002).

3. Elizabeth Ross Haynes, "Negroes in Domestic Service in the United States," *Journal of Negro History* 8 (October 1923): 384–432; Elizabeth Clark Lewis, "This Work Had an End': African American Domestic Workers in Washington, D.C. 1910–1940," in Carol Groneman and Mary Beth Norton, eds., *To Toil the Livelong Day: American Women at Work.* (Ithaca: Cornell University Press, 1987), 196–212.

4. U.S. Department of Commerce, Bureau of the Census, *Negroes in the United States, 1920–1932* (Washington, DC: Government Printing Office, 1935), 307; Gerda Lerner, *Black Women in White America: A Documentary History* (New York: Vintage Books, 1973), 226.

5. Ira Katznelson, *When Affirmative Action Was White: An Untold History of Racial Inequality in Twentieth-Century America* (New York: W. W. Norton, 2005).

6. Stephanie Shaw, *What a Woman Ought to Be and to Do: Black Women Professional Workers During the Jim Crow Era* (Chicago: University of Chicago Press, 1996).

7. Public assistance from local, state, or federal government. Relief did not always take the form of money.

8. Gavin worked as a live-in maid, residing with the family that employed her.

9. Gavin's comments about Jewish families suggest that they occupied a distinct place in the South's social structure, separate from others who were defined as "white."

10. According to historian Jacqueline Jones, picking between 150 and 200 pounds of cotton in a day was considered respectable for the average worker. Jacqueline Jones, *Labor of Love, Labor of Sorrow*, 15–17.

11. Hampton Institute, now Hampton University, was founded during the Civil War as a school for freedpeople.

12. On the role of black teachers, see Adam Fairclough, *A Class of Their Own: Black Teachers in the Segregated South* (Cambridge: Harvard University Press, 2007); Sonya Y. Ramsey, *Reading, Writing, and Segregation: A Century of Black Women Teachers in Nashville* (Urbana: University of Illinois Press, 2008); Mamie Garvin Fields with Karen Fields, *Lemon Swamp and Other Places: A Carolina Memoir* (New York: The Free Press, 1983).

13. Normal schools offered two years of preparation for future teachers.

14. West Chester University began in 1871 as a teacher preparatory school.

15. This list refers to some of the most prominent historically black colleges, considered among the best schools to prepare African American students for entrée into the black middle class.

16. Many southern cities had segregated branches of the YWCA. The black YWCA branches were typically named for Harriet Tubman or Phillis Wheatley.

17. Probably a reference to Davis having light skin or "white" features.

18. North Carolina A&T College, in Greensboro.

19. Steele refers to three black fraternities: Alpha Phi Alpha, Kappa Alpha Psi, and Omega Psi Phi.

20. This term referred to someone active in community and professional organizations that raised money or developed programs to promote black accomplishments or political rights.

21. The Greenville section of Charlotte, where the parents of Steele's students worked, was home to many domestic and service workers employed in Myers Park, a wealthy white area.

22. In Charlotte, as in many communities, school integration plans were not implemented until the mid 1960s, many years after the 1954 *Brown v. Board of Education* ruling.

23. Steele attended Teachers' College at Columbia University in New York during summers, working toward her master's degree.

24. *Brown v. Board of Education*, the 1954 Supreme Court ruling declaring segregated schooling unconstitutional.

25. Duke University remained segregated into the 1960s.

26. Lyons and her husband lived in Mutual Heights, a community developed after WWII where many of Durham's black middle-class residents lived.

27. Lyons went to college because she believed her lack of an advanced degree kept her from promotions.

28. Lyons attended Shaw University in Raleigh, North Carolina.

29. An educational program for insurance and financial service professionals.

30. Viola Turner was treasurer at North Carolina Mutual and the first woman on the company's executive board.

31. In Lawrenceville, Virginia.

32. The 1964 Civil Rights Act outlawed race and sex-based discrimination in employment and segregated public accommodations.

33. The War on Poverty began in 1964 with passage of the Economic Opportunity Act. The Act created the Office of Economic Opportunity to distribute funds to communities to create jobs programs, Head Start programs, and legal services projects.

34. Bonding is a form of insurance for small businesses.

35. World War II.

36. The Tidewater Virginia Federal Employees Metal Trades Council, a labor organization representing workers at the Norfolk Naval Base.

37. On unions in Memphis, see Michael Honey, *Black Workers Remember: An Oral History of Segregation, Unionism, and the Freedom Struggle* (Berkeley: University of California Press, 2002); Laurie Green, *Battling the Plantation Mentality: Memphis and the Black Freedom Struggle* (Chapel Hill: University of North Carolina Press, 2007).

4 A Society Totally Our Own: Institutional and Cultural Life

1. The phrases "behind the veil" and "upbuilding" were originally coined by W. E. B. Du Bois, who wrote extensively about African American life during the period of segregation. An activist (he helped found the National Association for the Advancement of Colored People and edited its magazine) and a scholar,

Du Bois focused on the status of African Americans within the United States and on the often-conflicted identity that African Americans assumed, torn because of their status as Americans who felt white America's inability to extend full citizenship.

2. On the role of churches in black communities after Emancipation, see Elsa Barkley Brown, "Negotiating and Transforming the Public Sphere: African American Political Life in the Transition from Slavery to Freedom," *Public Culture*, 7 (1994): 107–146; Evelyn Brooks Higginbotham, *Righteous Discontent: The Women's Movement in the Black Baptist Church, 1880–1920* (Cambridge: Harvard University Press, 1993). On southern black community life after Emancipation, see Earl Lewis, *In Their Own Interests: Race, Class, and Power in Twentieth-Century Norfolk* (Berkeley: University of California Press, 1991); Leslie Brown, *Upbuilding Black Durham: Gender, Class and Black Community Development in the Jim Crow South* (Chapel Hill: University of North Carolina Press, 2008); Allison Dorsey, *To Build Our Lives Together: Community Formation in Black Atlanta, 1875–1906* (Athens: University of Georgia Press, 2004).

3. Numerous scholars have written about so-called race riots that destroyed African American communities. See Timothy B. Tyson and David S. Cecelski, eds., *Democracy Betrayed: The Wilmington Race Riot of 1898 and Its Legacy* (Chapel Hill: University of North Carolina Press, 1998); Scott Ellsworth, *Death in a Promised Land: The Tulsa Race Riot of 1921* (Baton Rouge: Louisiana State University Press, 1982); Alfred Brophy, *Reconstructing the Dreamland: The Tulsa Race Riot of 1921: Race, Reparations and Reconciliation* (New York: Oxford University Press, 2002); Gregory Mixon, *The Atlanta Riot: Race, Class, and Violence in a New South City* (Gainesville: University of Florida Press, 2005); Mark Bauerlein, *Negrophobia: A Race Riot in Atlanta, 1906* (San Francisco: Encounter Books, 2001).

4. A process for paving streets using crushed stones. The macadamized street was a sign of the community's prosperity and modernity, given that most streets in southern black communities were left unpaved.

5. A reference to the Ku Klux Klan, an organization that used terrorism and violence to assert white supremacy.

6. The National Recovery Administration and the Works Progress Administration were New Deal agencies established to create jobs for those unemployed during the Depression.

7. Vehicle used by police to transport prisoners.

8. Referring to baptism by submersion in water, usually a pond or stream or, sometimes, a pool installed inside the church for this purpose.

9. The Order of the Eastern Star is a nondenominational, mixed-sex fraternal organization associated with Freemasonry. Historically segregated by race, Eastern Star chapters undertake charitable work for their communities.

10. A reference to lay-by time, the period before cotton was ready to be picked.

11. WGRA began broadcasting in 1949 and is based in Cairo, Georgia.

12. Home demonstration agents were hired by states to teach economical or efficient means of cooking and household chores. The cooperative kitchen and mattress making projects that Howard describes likely were set up by the Works Progress Administration or the Agricultural Adjustment Agency.

13. A North Carolina beach not far from Wilmington, with limited access only across a bridge from the mainland.
14. Sea Breeze was one of several beaches on the Atlantic Coast reserved for, and controlled by, African Americans. Others included American Beach in Florida and Atlantic Beach, "The Black Pearl," in South Carolina. Bop City, also known as Freeman Beach, was named after a family of freed slaves who settled in the area in the 1850s.
15. Other recreation areas in eastern North Carolina.
16. Williston was the segregated high school in Wilmington.
17. The high school for white students.
18. Bob Mann, who played football for the University of Michigan in the 1940s, subsequently became one of the first black players on the NFL's Detroit Lions team.
19. Meharry Medical College in Nashville, Tennessee, was established in 1876 for African American students. At the time, it was one of the few institutions that provided medical training for African American students.
20. Jack and Jill of America began in 1938 to organize black mothers who would coordinate philanthropic activities and arrange recreational opportunities for children.
21. NCNW is an umbrella organization that unites black women's organizations. Formed in 1935 by Mary McLeod Bethune, NCNW was intended to extend the power of individual organizations through coordinated activity to address the concerns of black women and their communities.
22. Brawley was a black educator and author of books related to African American history and literature. He served as Dean at Morehouse College, a prominent black men's college in Atlanta.
23. Dr. Carter G. Woodson was a historian, author, and professor at Howard University. He started the Association for the Study of Afro-American Life and History and is generally considered the "Father of Black History" in the United States.
24. Cullen and Hughes were influential poets in the 1920s and 1930s, participants in the Harlem Renaissance, an artistic and political movement to establish the value of African American creative expression.
25. The Moles Club was chartered in Norfolk in 1950. A national organization with chapters in more than a dozen states, the Moles began as a group of friends who organized for fellowship and community service.
26. The Community Hospital was established in 1915 as Tidewater Colored Hospital. In 1932 it merged with the Maternity Ward run by the Tidewater Colored Graduate Nurses Association. The new hospital building opened shortly thereafter.
27. Drink house. Drink houses were privately owned locations that offered entertainment, alcohol, food, and sometimes prostitution. White customers could patronize black-owned cafes and houses, although white-owned establishments were generally closed to African American customers. And although black and white customers both patronized Monroe's cafe, it is not clear from her account how much they interacted across the color line.
28. Monroe may be referring to selling beer on Sunday in violation of laws prohibiting alcohol sales that day of the week.

29. The places Monroe refers to would have been on the chitlin' circuit, venues that were safe and hospitable to black performers during the segregation era.
30. The musicians that Monroe names were African American performers who played blues or R&B. Evelyn "the Whip" Young toured with B.B. King and played on some of his recordings.

5 I Like To Get Something Done: Fighting for Social and Political Change

1. Jacquelyn Dowd Hall, "The Long Civil Rights Movement and the Political Uses of the Past," *Journal of American History* 91 (March 2005): 1233–1263.
2. The Voting Rights Act outlawed discriminatory practices, including many of the prerequisites such as literacy tests that kept so many African Americans from registering to vote.
3. Numerous scholars have written about women's distinctive participation in political campaigns and other social change efforts. Charles Payne refutes the notion that women actually experienced fewer risks or faced less danger than men in *I've Got the Light of Freedom: The Organizing Tradition and the Mississippi Freedom Struggle* (Berkeley: University of California Press, 1997); Karen Sacks discusses the role of "center women" whose leadership was demonstrated through their ability to connect people in *Caring by the Hour: Women, Work and Organizing at Duke Medical Center* (Urbana: University of Illinois Press, 1997); see also Belinda Robnett, *How Long? How Long? African-American Women in the Struggle for Civil Rights* (New York: Oxford University Press, 2000).
4. Cora Flemming interview.
5. On May 20, 1865, the Emancipation Proclamation was publicly read by Union commanders in Florida. Although the Proclamation took effect earlier, the day when it was publicly announced in Florida has long been commemorated as "Emancipation Day."
6. This may be a reference to "The Negro in It," by Lena Mason. One verse in this poem states:
    White man, stop lynching and burning
    This black race, trying to thin it,
    For if you go to heaven or hell
    You will find some Negroes in it.
7. Now Florida A&M University.
8. Now Florida State University. At the time, the Florida State College was restricted to white students. Russell notes that Doak Campbell was president at the time of these protests but her chronology appears mistaken. Campbell presided over Florida State College for Women from 1941 to 1957; his predecessor, whose term in office would have coincided with Russell's years as a student, was Edward Conradi (president 1909–1941).
9. "Good" hair is loose-textured, straight or with loose curls.
10. Racial disturbances were frequent throughout the South. One of the most notorious incidents, the Rosewood Massacre, occurred in Florida in 1923, when whites

demolished a relatively prosperous African American community, destroying homes and businesses and causing most of the population to flee.

11. French Town was a predominantly black neighborhood in Tallahassee, home to many restaurants, cafes, and night clubs. Johnson's role as mayor would have been an honorary title extended to someone who the community considered a leader and intermediary with white politicians and economic leaders.

12. Black citizens in Tallahassee began a bus boycott in 1956, shortly after the similar boycott began in Montgomery. Tallahassee's boycott lasted seven months.

13. Martin Luther King did not start the Montgomery Bus Boycott. The boycott began when Mrs. Rosa Parks was arrested for refusing to move from her seat on a city bus, but it was planned and organized by the Women's Political Council, a group of women faculty and faculty wives at Alabama State College. After speaking at the rally following the first day of the boycott, King emerged to lead the Montgomery Improvement Association, the organization that coordinated the boycott and negotiated with local white leaders.

14. Reverend Ralph Abernathy pastored a Baptist church in Montgomery, Alabama, and was a close associate of King in the Southern Christian Leadership Conference.

15. Workers organized racially segregated chapters of the Tobacco Workers International Union in Durham in the 1930s.

16. Light-skinned.

17. The grandfather clause was one of a series of restrictions in place to keep white political power in the South. Enacted along with literacy tests, poll taxes, and other provisions to restrict African American voting, grandfather clauses exempted from the restrictions people able to vote before the Civil War and their descendants. In practice, grandfather clauses meant that white southerners could vote even if they might not meet other qualifications to register, while black southerners, assumed to be descendants of slaves, would not similarly benefit.

18. Halifax is the county seat and home to county offices.

19. A reference to an incident in 1892 when a white grocery store owner shot three black men who he considered competitors for his business. The incident made national headlines, thanks mainly to courageous coverage provided by Ida B. Wells, who urged African Americans to leave the South. For her statements, Wells was forced to leave Memphis; she went on to work as a journalist and a crusader against lynching. Although the incident occurred decades before Branch's birth, her statement suggests that the memory of this violent act remained a strong deterrent on African American activism.

20. Black Mondays began in 1969 and lasted a couple of months until participants won concessions from the city council that led to black representation on the board. According to one source, more than 600 teachers and 65,000 students stayed out of the schools. Wendi C. Thomas, "Black Mondays Signaled New Day," *Memphis Commercial Appeal*, 22 February 2009.

21. The strikes occurred in 1969, so Branch's chronology is wrong here.

22. In early 1968, Memphis sanitation workers launched a strike to protest wages and working conditions—sometimes deadly—and as part of an effort to organize a labor union. Nearly all of the sanitation workers were African American men and the assertion "I AM A MAN," seen frequently on workers' picket signs,

summed up their demand to be treated with dignity. Recognizing that the workers' demands constituted a civil rights issue, as well as a claim for economic justice, Martin Luther King, Jr. rallied to the Memphis workers' defense. A rally in support of their cause brought him to Memphis, where he was murdered on April 4, 1968.

23. Mason Temple, a Church of God in Christ facility, served as one of the main spots for mass meetings during the civil rights movement in Memphis. Clayborn Temple, home of an African Methodist Episcopal Church, served a similar role in the 1950s and 1960s. Both facilities hosted meetings during the sanitation workers strike.

24. The first march that King attended in support of the sanitation workers, on March 28, 1968, resulted in disruptions and violence, including hundreds of arrests and the death of one teenager. Distressed by the outbreak, King returned to Memphis on April 3, hoping to hold a peaceful demonstration.

25. In 1963, black parents in Tuskegee sued to desegregate the town's schools and won their case, opening the way for limited integration of its high school. The effort was blocked by Alabama's governor, George Wallace, who ordered state troopers to the town to prevent black students from entering the white high school. After a week's delay, Tuskegee High School opened to thirteen black students and nearly 300 white students. Shortly after, however, most of the white students transferred to area private schools, leading to more than a year of fights over accreditation, new placements for the black students, and violence.

26. National Committee on Household Employment, formed in 1965, organized and represented household workers. In 1971, NCHE held a national conference. NCHE pushed for minimum wage standards laid out in the Fair Labor Standards Act and to have employers sign on to model contracts that would specify hours, wages, and working conditions as well as provide a mechanism for workers to file grievances against employers.

27. Charlotte Area Fund is a social service agency that provides grants to support community and economic development initiatives.

28. In the 1950s, Archbishop Joseph Rummel ordered an end to segregation in the Archdiocese of New Orleans. As Davillier's interview reveals, it took several years for individual churches to act on this order.

29. Equal Employment Opportunities Commission is the federal agency responsible for protecting workers against race-based discrimination. The EEOC was created as part of the 1964 Civil Rights Act. That Act was bolstered by Title VII in the early 1970s, which prohibits all federally funded programs from discriminating on the basis of race or gender.

30. The Congress of Racial Equality and the Student Nonviolent Coordinating Committee, were active in Mississippi between 1961 and 1965. Both CORE and SNCC brought organizers into Mississippi communities where they worked to build a local movement by nurturing leaders among the residents and by helping local communities articulate and then fight to address their economic and political problems.

31. In 1965, Indianola adopted a school desegregation plan based on geographic zones. The zones were drawn such that virtually all children continued to attend

racially segregated schools. Black parents went to court to appeal the desegregation plan and eventually had it overturned.

32. The Mississippi Freedom Democratic Party was organized by civil rights activists in 1964. The MFDP mobilized African Americans across the state to register to vote and to protest their exclusion from the state's official—and all white—Democratic Party. MFDP representatives made national headlines when they traveled to the Democratic National Convention in August 1964 to challenge the national Party's seating of the all-white official delegation.

33. A note is a secured loan, such as an automobile loan or a house mortgage.

34. Several organizations set up relief efforts in Mississippi in the 1960s, collecting and distributing food and clothing to help residents who suffered repercussions after attempting to vote or joining other Movement activities. These organizations included SNCC; COFO (the Council of Federated Organizations, which included SNCC); and the American Friends Service Committee. Giles is probably referring to one of these organizations using her family's store as a center for distributing goods to local families.

35. In 1955, Till, a teenager from Chicago, was murdered while visiting relatives in Money, Mississippi, a town not far from Flemming's home in Indianola. The case made national headlines after Till's mother displayed her son's battered body in his coffin. His murderers were tried and acquitted by an all-white jury. They later confessed.

36. COFO, the Council of Federated Organizations, an umbrella group of civil rights organizations working in Mississippi, took the lead in organizing voter registration efforts across the state.

37. The Child Development Group of Mississippi was a statewide group of organizers, mostly African American women civil rights activists, who set up the first Head Start centers in the state in 1965. For more, see John Dittmer, *Local People: The Struggle for Civil Rights in Mississippi* (Urbana: University of Illinois Press, 1995).

38. Local organizers considered Sunflower County one of the hardest areas to organize, with extensive white resistance to civil rights struggles. African American residents lost jobs and suffered violent recriminations for activities including attempts to register to vote; such moves prompted some black churches to refuse activists space for meetings and programs lest they also suffer negative repercussions. Ibid., 254.

39. The Albany Movement was an umbrella organization formed in 1961 to coordinate civil rights efforts in the area, focusing on ending segregation and expanding the right to vote.

40. Baker County had a reputation among civil rights workers as one of the places that most exemplified rural poverty, economic inequalities, and racist violence. Stephen G.N. Tuck, *Beyond Atlanta: The Struggle for Racial Equality in Georgia, 1940–1980* (Athens: University of Georgia Press, 2001), 186–187.

41. Clark College was founded in 1869 by the Methodist Episcopal Church to educate former slaves. In the 1980s, it merged with Atlanta University. Upward Bound is a federally funded program to support the academic study of first-generation college students and low-income students.

42. SNCC had begun working in southwest Georgia in the fall of 1961, trying to organize a movement of local African American activists and white activists

from elsewhere to conduct a voter registration campaign. Charles Sherrod, a college student from Richmond, Virginia, was one of SNCC's lead organizers in southwest Georgia. SNCC began to work in rural Baker County in July 1965. On the Albany Movement and the campaign in Baker County, see Tuck, *Beyond Atlanta*; Clayborne Carson, *In Struggle: SNCC and the Black Awakening of the 1960s* (Cambridge, MA: Harvard University Press, 1981).

43. Attorney C.B. King from Albany, Georgia, supported the civil rights movement as a lead lawyer on many discrimination cases and as a participant in protests and political campaigns.

44. The Gator was the Baker County sheriff, Lee Warren (Gator) Johnson, Sr., who held that position from the late 1950s into the 1970s. Among African American residents of the county and civil rights activists in the area, Johnson was renowned for his use of violence. After Johnson retired, his son was elected to fill his position.

45. Charles Sherrod was on the staff of SNCC and helped build the mass protest movement in Albany and southwest Georgia. He and Shirley later married.

46. Fort Valley State was started as a segregated industrial high school in the 1890s. It merged with the State Teachers and Agricultural College to form Fort Valley State College in the 1930s.

47. Georgia Bureau of Investigation.

48. "Cracker" is a derogatory term used for white southerners.

49. The Office of Economic Opportunity was the primary administrator of the War on Poverty under President Lyndon B. Johnson, overseeing the work of VISTA (Volunteers in Service to America), Head Start, and other programs. It was dismantled in 1974 under the Nixon administration.

50. A collaborative meeting, usually to solve a design problem.

51. Lester Maddox served as Georgia's Governor from 1967 to 1971, winning office after running a pro-segregationist campaign. Barred by term limits from holding that office longer, in 1971 he ran for lieutenant governor, a post he held until 1974.

52. New Communities joined a suit brought by black farmers against the U.S. Department of Agriculture, charging the federal agency with racial discrimination. *Pigford v. Glickman* (later *Pigford v. Vilsack*) was settled in favor of the farmers, with cash awards paid to farmers for loss of their land and loss of income. Pete Daniel, "African American Farmers and Civil Rights," *Journal of Southern History* 73 (February 2007): 3–38.

53. Evelyn Butts, a seamstress and activist, successfully challenged the legality of the Virginia poll tax. Her case went to the Supreme Court and in 1966 the Court declared the poll tax unconstitutional if it was used as a requirement for voting in state or local elections.

Afterword

1. Leslie Brown, *Upbuilding Black Durham: Gender, Class, and Black Community Development in the Jim Crow South* (Chapel Hill: University of North Carolina Press, 2008), 148. For mortality information, see Department of Commerce,

Bureau of the Census, *Negro Population, 1790–1915* (Washington, DC: Government Printing Office, 1918), 331; *Negroes in the United States*, 1920–1932 (Washington, DC: Government Printing Office, 1935), 452; and *Mortality Among Negroes in the United States*, Public Health Bulletin No. 174 (Washington, DC: Government Printing Office, 1938), 30; Mary Grover, "Trend of Mortality Among Southern Negroes Since 1920," *Journal of Negro Education* 6 (Summer 1937): 276–288.

Index

LaVergne, TN USA
09 November 2010
204136LV00002B/10/P